ARTIFICIAL INTELLIGENCE AND ART HISTORY

Since 1905, the *Proceedings of the British Academy* series has provided a unique record of British scholarship in the humanities and social sciences. Each themed volume drives scholarship forward and is a landmark in its field. For more information about the series, please visit www.thebritishacademy.ac.uk/proceedings

PROCEEDINGS OF THE BRITISH ACADEMY • 285

ARTIFICIAL INTELLIGENCE AND ART HISTORY

LOOKING AT IMAGES IN AN ALGORITHMIC CULTURE

Edited by
KATHRYN BROWN

Published by THE BRITISH ACADEMY
Marketed and distributed by Liverpool University Press

Published by The British Academy
10–11 Carlton House Terrace, London SW1Y 5AH

Marketed and distributed by Liverpool University Press
4 Cambridge Street, Liverpool L69 7ZU

First edition published in 2026

British Library Cataloguing in Publication Data
Data available

Library of Congress Cataloguing in Publication Data
Data available

Typeset by Newgen Publishing UK
Printed in Great Britain by CMP, Poole, Dorset

ISBN 978-1-80-596660-9 (print)
ISBN 978-1-80-596661-6 (pdf)
ISBN 978-1-80-596662-3 (epub)

ISSN 0068-1202

The manufacturer's authorised representative in the EU for product safety is:
Easy Access System Europe, Mustamäe tee 50, 10621 Tallinn, Estonia
https://easproject.com (gpsr.requests@easproject.com)

Contents

List of Figures and Tables

Figures

Tables

Notes on Contributors

Kathryn Brown is Reader in Art Histories, Markets and Digital Heritage at Loughborough University. Her books include *Women Readers in French Painting 1870–1890* (2012), *Matisse's Poets* (2017), ed. *Digital Humanities and Art History* (2020), *Henri Matisse* (2021), *Dialogues with Degas* (2023) and *Art Auctions: Spectacle and Value in the 21st Century* (2024). She has held visiting fellowships at the Center for Advanced Studies in the Visual Arts (Washington DC), the Humanities Research Centre of the Australian National University, Tulane University, the Beinecke Library (Yale University), and the Getty Research Institute. Brown's research has been funded by the Arts and Humanities Research Council (UK), the British Academy, the Independent Social Research Foundation, and the Terra Foundation for American Art. She is the series editor of *Contextualizing Art Markets* for Bloomsbury Academic.

Eva Cetinić is Senior Researcher at the Institute of Art History, University of Zurich, where she leads the SNSF Ambizione-funded project 'The Canon of Latent Spaces: How Large AI Models Encode Art and Culture'. Prior to that, she was a postdoctoral fellow at the Centre for Digital Visual Studies, hosted by the University of Zurich and funded by the Max Planck Society. She also worked as a postdoctoral researcher in Digital Humanities and Machine Learning at the Department of Computer Science, Durham University, and as a postdoctoral researcher and professional associate at the Rudjer Boskovic Institute in Zagreb.

Amalia Foka is Associate Professor of Computer Science and Multimedia Applications in Art at the University of Peloponnese, Greece. Her research and artistic practice explore the intersections of artificial intelligence, data mining, and visual culture, with a focus on gender, emotion, and environmental narratives. She has published in *Leonardo*, *Artnodes*, and *ECCV*, and presented her work at ISEA, EVA London, and CVPR. Her AI-generated artworks have been exhibited internationally, receiving a Special Mention at the Festival Internacional de la Imagen and the Arte Laguna Special Prize. Foka's interdisciplinary approach combines critical theory and computational methods to examine how emerging technologies shape artistic and cultural production.

Leonardo Impett is Research Group Leader at the Bibliotheca Hertziana (Max Planck Institute for Art History) and Assistant Professor in Digital Humanities at the University of Cambridge. He has a background in machine learning and computer vision and was previously Assistant Professor of Computer Science at Durham University. His work looks at the intersections of artificial intelligence and the history of art. Alongside his research in digital art history, he frequently works with machine learning in arts and culture, including for the Liverpool Biennial, the Royal Opera House, and the Whitney Museum of American Art.

Jia Li is a Professor of Statistics and (by courtesy) Computer Science at The Pennsylvania State University. Her research interests include machine learning, artificial intelligence, probabilistic graph models, and image analysis. She received an M.Sc. in Electrical Engineering (1995), M.Sc. degree in Statistics (1998), and a Ph.D. in Electrical Engineering (1999), from Stanford University. She was Editor-in-Chief of Statistical Analysis and Data Mining: The ASA Data Science Journal from 2018 to 2020. She is a Fellow of the Institute of Electrical and Electronics Engineers and a Fellow of the American Statistical Association.

Elizabeth C. Mansfield is Professor of Art History at The Pennsylvania State University. A specialist in 18th- and 19th-century European art and art historiography, her publications include the books *The Perfect Foil: François-André Vincent and the Revolution in French Painting* (2011) and *Too Beautiful to Picture: Zeuxis, Myth, and Mimesis* (2007). The latter was awarded the Charles Rufus Morey book prize by the College Art Association in 2008. Past positions include academic appointments at New York University and at Sewanee: The University of the South.

Manas Mehta is a Ph.D. candidate in the College of Information Sciences and Technology at The Pennsylvania State University. They received their Bachelor's and Master's degrees in Computer Science from Worcester Polytechnic Institute in 2020 and 2022, respectively. Their primary research interests include vision and language, generative models, and efficient neural networks.

Nuria Rodríguez-Ortega is Professor of Art History and Director of the Department of Art History at the University of Malaga, where she directs iArtHis_Lab, a research, training and innovation laboratory focused on the study of artistic culture from digital, computational, and techno-critical perspectives. Her research addresses the convergence between computational languages, digital media and artistic culture, with special emphasis on the application of data analytics for the study of complex cultural systems, natural language processing for the analysis of artistic texts, the configuration of new visual-formal epistemologies in the field of computer vision and the exploration of alternative narratives associated with mixed reality technologies.

John Russell is Associate Professor and Digital Humanities Librarian at The Pennsylvania State University Libraries and Associate Director of the Center for Virtual/Material Studies. He holds a B.A. from the University of Vermont and an M.L.S. from Indiana University.

Tracy Stuber received her Ph.D. in Visual and Cultural Studies from the University of Rochester. She is currently the Digital Humanities postdoctoral fellow for the NEH-funded 'Mapping Color in History' project at Harvard University. Previously, she was Research Specialist for the Digital Art History department at the Getty Research Institute, where she focused on the use of emerging technologies such as computer vision and machine learning to discover new research possibilities within photographic archives. Her research and digital scholarship has been supported by the Andrew W. Mellon Foundation, the Kress Foundation, and Humanities New York.

James Z. Wang is a Distinguished Professor in the Data Sciences and Artificial Intelligence area of the College of Information Sciences and Technology at The Pennsylvania State University. He received a Bachelor's degree in mathematics, *summa cum laude*, from the University of Minnesota (1994) and an MS in mathematics (1997), an MS in computer science (1997), and a Ph.D. in medical information sciences (2000) from Stanford University. His research interests include image analysis, affective computing, image modelling, and image retrieval and their applications.

Amanda Wasielewski is Associate Senior Lecturer of Digital Humanities and Associate Professor of Art History in the Department of ALM (Archives, Libraries, Museums) at Uppsala University in Sweden. Her research focuses on the use of artificial intelligence tools to study and create art and images. Wasielewski is the author of three monographs including *Computational Formalism: Art History and Machine Learning* (2023). She is co-editor of the volume *Critical Digital Art History* (2024), and the author of 'Unnatural Images: On AI-Generated Photographs' (*Critical Inquiry*, Autumn 2024). Her fourth monograph, *Digital Photography after AI*, is forthcoming in 2026.

Shuhua Yang is a Ph.D. candidate in the College of Information Sciences and Technology at The Pennsylvania State University. She received her Bachelor's degree in Mathematics and Applied Mathematics from Zhejiang University and her Master's degree in Applied Statistics from the University of Science and Technology of China. Her primary research interests include machine learning, reinforcement learning, and computer vision.

Zhuomin Zhang is an Applied Scientist at Amazon in Seattle. She received her Ph.D. in Information Sciences and Technology from The Pennsylvania State University in 2022 under the joint supervision of Professors James Z. Wang and Jia Li. She received her Bachelor's in Computer Science from Nanjing University in 2016. Her primary research interests include computer vision, machine learning, and multimedia.

Introduction

KATHRYN BROWN

OVER THE PAST decade, artificial intelligence (AI) has transformed cultural landscapes and museum cultures around the world. From the advent of generative AI to the integration of chatbots into heritage settings, the use of computer technologies to monitor museum environments or assist curation, and the steady rise of exhibitions about AI, technology has been pushed to the forefront of heritage discourses and their associated public imaginaries.[1] If one adds to this the integration of AI into markets for art – including the sale of AI-generated art and the use of computer vision to assist with questions of attribution – the circle (artist–museum–market) seems to be complete.[2]

The present volume confronts both the possibilities and tensions that are arising in this fast-paced, cross-disciplinary field. Drawing on the approaches of scholars in art history, computer science, data science, and digital humanities, chapters are motivated by the following key questions: can computers encourage humans to see art differently? To what extent does the integration of AI into art historical research change the role of the art historian? What is the impact of computer vision analysis on the ontological status of the artwork? What new ethical dilemmas does the use of AI spur in the context of art historical research?

The first point to note for the purpose of this discussion is that the term 'artificial intelligence' is a catch-all for a variety of computational tasks and models

[1] Representative examples include 'AI: More than Human', Barbican Immersive, London (2019); the AI Gallery of the National Gallery, London; 'AI: Mind the Gap', MIT Museum, Cambridge MA (2024–5); the Guangzhou International Artificial Intelligence Exhibition (2024); La Maison de l'Intelligence Artificielle (Sophia Antipolis, Biot, France), 'Le Monde selon l'IA', Musée du Jeu de Paume, Paris (2025), 'Machine Love: Video Game, AI and Contemporary Art', Mori Art Museum, Tokyo (2025); and the creation of a museum of AI, Dataland, in Los Angeles (2025). On the role of museums in shaping ideas about AI see Alisa Maksimova, 'Negotiation of Dominant AI Narratives in Museum Exhibitions', *AI & Society*, 40 (2025), pp. 3813–26. https://doi.org/10.1007/s00146-024-02140-6

[2] For further discussion see Jo Lawson-Tancred, *AI and the Art Market* (London: Lund Humphries and Sotheby's Institute of Art, 2024).

including, for example, machine learning, deep learning, natural language processing, computer vision, and generative systems.[3] Rita Raley and Jennifer Rhee note, however, that the discursive weight of 'artificial intelligence' as a term allows it to function effectively as a 'shorthand in headlines, marketing copy, and popular representations' of technology.[4] Similarly, for Leonardo Impett, the 'sci-fi associations' of the term have made it appealing to the private sector and have prompted its subsequent integration into technical discourse.[5] In the following discussion, I use the term 'AI' as an umbrella concept to cover a wide range of computational approaches to the study of art. More specific operations and models will be explored and problematised by authors in the following chapters. Throughout this volume, attention will be given not just to the ways in which computational methods are being used in art historical research, but also to the impact of such technologies on the discourses and conceptual apparatus of art history.

Where does the art historian fit into this new technical landscape? In some cases, AI is opening new perspectives on provenance research, stylistic analysis, and the study of pose and gesture in artworks.[6] In the field of museum studies, a significant body of literature has developed on the aesthetic implications of using AI as a creative and curatorial tool, the harnessing of technology to attract and monitor audiences, and the integration of autonomous systems into the practical operation of heritage spaces.[7] The public policy implications of these developments are also being critically examined in various countries.[8] Paradoxically, however, the uptake of computational methodologies by art historians has been slow, and the emerging scholarly discourse has been dominated by researchers in computer science. The result is that questions and strategies often appear to be imposed on humanities research, and key theoretical ideas that have shaped the modern discipline of art

[3] See Leonardo Impett, 'Digital Art History as Critical AI', *The Art Bulletin*, 106:2 (2024), pp. 11–14, note 3, p. 14.

[4] See Rita Raley and Jennifer Rhee (eds), 'Critical AI: A Field in Formation', *American Literature* 95:2 (2023), pp. 185–204.

[5] Impett, 'Digital Art History as Critical AI', note 3, p. 14.

[6] Examples include Fabio Mariani, Lynn Ross, and Max Koss, 'Teaching Provenance to AI: An Annotation Scheme for Museum Data', in *AI in Museums: Reflections, Perspectives and Applications*, edited by Sonja Thiel and Johannes C. Bernhardt (Bielefeld: Transcript Verlag, 2024), pp. 163–72; James Z. Wang, Baris Kandemir, and Jia Li, 'Computerized Analysis of Paintings', in *The Routledge Companion to Digital Humanities and Art History*, edited by Kathryn Brown (New York: Routledge, 2020), pp. 299–312; Leonardo Impett, 'Analyzing Gesture in Digital Art History', in *The Routledge Companion to Digital Humanities and Art History*, edited by Kathryn Brown, pp. 386–407.

[7] Thiel and Bernhardt (eds), *AI in Museums*; Sofia Ceccarelli, Amedeo Cesta, Gabriella Cortellessa, Riccardo De Benedictis, Francesca Fracasso, Laura Leopardi *et al.*, 'Evaluating Visitors' Experience in Museum: Comparing Artificial Intelligence and Multi-partitioned Analysis', *Digital Applications in Archaeology and Cultural Heritage*, 33 (2024), pp. 1–14. https://doi.org/10.1016/j.daach.2024.e00340

[8] Council of Europe, *Guidelines given the latest technological developments, such as AI, complementing Council of Europe standards in the fields of culture, creativity and cultural heritage*, 13 December 2024 (CDC(2024)3); Sander Münster, Ferdinand Maiwald, Isabella di Lenardo, Juha Henriksson, Antoine Isaac, Manuela Milica Graf *et al.*, 'Artificial Intelligence for Digital Heritage Innovation: Setting up a R&D Agenda for Europe', *Heritage*, 7:2 (2024), pp. 794–816. https://doi.org/10.3390/heritage7020038

history are omitted from studies that position themselves at the intersection of AI and the arts. This has led some art historians to worry that the discipline has been 'hijacked' by AI and the so-called digital humanities more generally.[9] Looking at broader trends in humanities and social sciences research, Jonathan Roberge and Michael Castelle refer to AI as having provoked nothing less than an 'epistemic shock' that impacts ways of both knowing and being in the world.[10] Many researchers in computer science, meanwhile, feel that innovative work emanating from their discipline 'has often been accused – not always unreasonably – of being naïve, outdated, or straightforwardly problematic' by art historians.[11]

In 2011, a volume of conference proceedings edited by David G. Stork, Jim Coddington, and Anna Bentkowska-Kafel was co-published by the Information Sciences & Technology and Society of Photo-Optical Instrumentation Engineers.[12] Reporting on this interdisciplinary conference, the editors of the volume enthusiastically argued that the 'reading of artifacts can be enhanced, and new data discovered, through application of imaging techniques', but that this would depend on the willingness of researchers to 'step outside the inherited modes of operation and the comfort of one's own mind set'.[13] It was time, they argued, for art historians, heritage professionals, and computer scientists to embrace each others' languages and learn the terms of an unfamiliar discipline.

Over a decade later, and in the wake of intellectually and socially transformative developments in AI, this injunction is both more compelling and more vexed. In 2024, Elizabeth C. Mansfield drew together scholars in art history, information technology, and computer science to write a series of essays aimed at art historians that would 'capture a moment in the emerging historiography of art history after computer vision'.[14] While Mansfield also encouraged collaborative, cross-disciplinary research, she noted that the majority of projects applying computer vision to the history of art had, to date, involved very few art historians: 'This has led to a skewed historiography, with extant research conducted mostly by computer

[9] See Sonja Drimmer, 'How AI is hijacking art history', *The Conversation*, 1 November 2021. https://theconversation.com/how-ai-is-hijacking-art-history-170691; Claire Bishop, 'Against Digital Art History', *International Journal for Digital Art History*, no. 3 (July 2018). https://doi.org/10.11588/dah.2018.3.49915

[10] Jonathan Roberge and Michael Castelle, 'Toward an End-to-End Sociology of 21st-Century Machine Learning', in *The Cultural Life of Machine Learning*, edited by Jonathan Roberge and Michael Castelle (Palgrave Macmillan, 2020), pp. 1–29. https://doi.org/10.1007/978-3-030-56286-1_1

[11] Impett, 'Digital Art History as Critical AI', p. 11.

[12] *Computer Vision and Image Analysis of Art II*, edited by David G. Stork, Jim Coddington, and Anna Bentkowska-Kafel, *Proceedings of The Society for Imaging Science and Technology*, 7869 (20 April 2011). https://doi.org/10.1117/12.888808

[13] David G. Stork, Jim Coddington, and Anna Bentkowska-Kafel, 'Introduction', *Computer Vision and Image Analysis of Art II*, p. ix.

[14] Elizabeth C. Mansfield, 'Introduction: Art History after Computer Vision', *The Art Bulletin*, 106:2 (2024), pp. 6–10 (p. 8). DOI: 10.1080/00043079.2024.2296269. For other examples of this disciplinary nexus see: *The International Journal for Digital Art History* (founded in 2015) and *Digital Humanities and Art History*, edited by Kathryn Brown (New York: Routledge, 2020).

scientists whose interest in cultural heritage is often ancillary to their concern with a particular technical challenge, their access to a well-labeled dataset, or their pursuit of a commercial application or cultural cachet.'[15]

Mansfield's comments capture a key dilemma in this field, namely, how the study of art might simultaneously advance humanities and computer science methodologies. The transparency of research aims takes on new importance in this context because artworks become more than objects of study in their own right and, instead, serve as tools for advancing goals in another discipline. Glossing the terminology of philosopher Gilbert Simondon, the artwork becomes both an aesthetic and a technical object that motivates the creation of new discursive networks and research communities.[16]

Rather than viewing the relationship between art history and AI as either an easy partnership or an agonistic battle over cultural heritage discourses, chapters in this volume seek to make sense of the dialogues and intellectual partnerships that can ensue from this cross-disciplinary research trajectory. In many cases – and as Amanda Wasieliewski notes in her contribution to the present volume – this involves stepping back from some of the enthusiastic rhetoric that has developed about AI and its possibilities. Yet it also entails reflection on the ambitions of art history in the 21st century, and on the traditions and ideas that have shaped the discipline.

Technology is not new to art history. Indeed, scholars in the humanities have long been familiar with, and have advanced the development of, digital tools such as mapping, digital imaging projects, heritage games, and techniques for digitising collections.[17] In art history, as in literary studies, musicology, and education, AI now enables researchers to engage with data at scales that far exceed the analytical capacities of the individual.[18] Yet, AI also represents a significant change in direction because it prioritises the creation of models that enable machines to recognise

[15] Mansfield, 'Introduction', p. 8.

[16] Gilbert Simondon, *On the Mode of Existence of Technical Objects* [1958], translated by Cécile Malaspina and John Rogove (Minneapolis: University of Minnesota Press, 2017). Current debates about the social impact of AI have led to renewed interest in Simondon's work. See, for example, Mercedes Bunz, 'The Calculation of Meaning: On the Misunderstanding of New Artificial Intelligence as Culture', *Culture, Theory, and Critique*, 60:3–4 (2019), pp. 264–78; Susanna Lindberg, 'Being with Technique–Technique as Being-with: The Technological Communities of Gilbert Simondon', *Continental Philosophy Review*, 52 (2019), pp. 299–310.

[17] For an overview, see Kathryn Brown (ed.), *Digital Humanities and Art History* (New York: Routledge, 2020); Jorge Sebastián Lozano, 'Mapping Art History in the Digital Era', *The Art Bulletin* 103:3 (2021), pp. 6–16.

[18] Alexandra Belibou and Liviu Iftene, 'Artificial Intelligence and Music: A Literature Review', *Information and Communication Technologies in the Musical Field*, 14:2 (2024), pp. 53–60. DOI: 10.47809/ICTMF.2024.01.05; Will Slocombe and Genevieve Liveley (eds), *The Routledge Handbook of AI and Literature* (New York: Routledge, 2024); Bill Cope and Mary Kalantzis, 'On Cyber-Social Learning: A Critique of Artificial Intelligence in Education', in *Trust and Inclusion in AI-Mediated Education: Where Human Learning Meets Learning Machines*, edited by D. Kourkoulou, A.O. Tzirides, B. Cope, and M. Kalantzis (Cham: Springer, 2024), pp. 3–34. https://doi.org/10.1007/978-3-031-64487-0_1

patterns, provide quantitative solutions to certain kinds of problem, mathematically measure outcomes, and – crucially – behave autonomously once they have been trained. The resulting 'black box' elements of machine learning and deep learning raise important issues about trust, accountability, and methodological transparency that are challenging to the ethical relationship between researchers, their audiences, and the object of study.[19] The art historian now shares an interpretative space not just with computer scientists, but with imperfect interlocutors in the shape of machines and the datasets on which their models have been trained.

Having regard to recent advances in computer vision, David G. Stork has argued that 'algorithms have become powerful tools to aid art scholars in performing their analyses and crafting their interpretations'.[20] As simply another interpretative tool in the art historian's repertoire, AI seems, on this view, an anodyne extension of existing technologies used in image analysis (e.g., spectroscopy, thermal reflectography, speckle pattern interferometry) and should not, therefore, be contentious.[21] Yet, in art history, as in many other domains involving the use of AI, discussions often anticipate the advent of artificial *general* intelligence and, therefore, an enhanced or even independent visual literacy on the part of machines.[22] As Stork puts it:

> Algorithms have begun to perform simple 'interpretations' themselves and … in a few cases these lead to readings of certain aspects of works that are more accurate – more 'perceptive' – than those crafted by art scholars working without the benefit of such tools. What computer systems lack in human experience and knowledge can be, currently in a few limited areas, compensated by the fact that computer algorithms can 'see' more artworks than any human can in thousands of lifetimes.[23]

Numerous assumptions and some important caveats (evidenced by the use of scare quotes) are built into this statement, including the idea that the quantity of data examined by a machine can serve as a substitute for the epistemic, perceptual, and interpretative work undertaken by humans in their encounters with art.[24] Yet

[19] For a recent overview and the rise of explainable AI, see V. Hassija, V. Chamola, A. Mahapatra, A. Singal, K. Huang, S. Scardapane *et al.*, 'Interpreting Black-Box Models: A Review on Explainable Artificial Intelligence', *Cognitive Computation*, 16 (2024), pp. 45–74. https://doi.org/10.1007/s12559-023-10179-8.

[20] David G. Stork, 'Preface', in *Pixels & Paintings: Foundations of Computer-Assisted Connoisseurship* (Hoboken, NJ: Wiley Blackwell, 2024), p. i.

[21] For discussion of these and other conservation techniques, see Braeden Borg, Michelle Dunn, Andrew Ang, and Carl Villis, 'The Application of State-of-the-Art Technologies to Support Artwork Conservation: Literature Review', *Journal of Cultural Heritage*, 44 (2020), pp. 239–59.

[22] See, for example, Sam Altman's comments on the creation of superintelligent tools in John Koetsier, 'OpenAI CEO Sam Altman: We know how to build AGI', *Forbes* (6 January 2025), https://www.forbes.com/sites/johnkoetsier/2025/01/06/openai-ceo-sam-altman-we-know-how-to-build-agi/ [accessed 16 January 2025].

[23] Stork, *Pixels & Paintings*, p. i.

[24] Stork, *Pixels & Paintings,* p. liii. When Stork invites a comparison between the achievements of machine 'seeing' and developments in AI that enable a computer to outperform a human at chess or Go, he does not take into account the difference between the computational methods used to process combinations of patterns at high speed, and the range of perceptual, imaginative, and cultural factors necessary to make sense of an artwork.

the quantity of comparative data that a machine is capable of processing does not necessarily yield new explanatory factors in art history and, as Meredith Broussard notes in her discussion of the computer programme AlphaGo (created by what is now Google DeepMind), 'not everything in the world is a calculation'.[25] The idea that algorithms are, or ever will be, capable of offering readings of artworks that are 'more perceptive' than those by humans will likely be dismissed by a large number of art historians. Stork's comments do, however, raise the question of what 'meaning' implies in this context and who (or what) is capable of producing it.

Answers to questions about both the present and future capabilities of AI might divide some humanities and science researchers, but they also evoke different responses within scientific communities themselves.[26] In a call for the use of greater care in describing the potential of AI in the field of natural language processing, for example, Emily M. Bender and Alexander Koller contest claims that large language models (LLMs) can be described as 'understanding' human speech or 'capturing meaning'.[27] They argue, instead, that 'a system trained purely on form will not learn meaning'.[28] The authors go on to make a further important point, namely, that humans themselves are willing 'to attribute communicative intent to a linguistic signal or a language we speak, even if the originator of the signal is not an entity that could have communicative intent'.[29]

The same applies to the results of computer vision analyses of artworks where the 'interpretation' of an image by a machine can mean something as basic as object or feature recognition. In the extraction of so-called 'low-level' features of images (e.g., edges, contours, angles, and colours), human input is needed to integrate the results of computer vision analysis into a wider interpretative framework. The machine neither produces an answer to an art historical question (in contrast to a win/loss in chess or Go) nor offers a synthetic 'reading' of a work's content. Instead, computational analysis yields a new set of raw, visual data in the form of accretive images. These might be understood as 'technical metapictures' as discussed by Fabian Offert and Peter Bell in their extension of the term proposed by W.J.T. Mitchell.[30] For Bell and Offert, 'critical machine vision' opens a new kind of

[25] Meredith Broussard, *Artificial Unintelligence: How Computers Misunderstand the World* (Cambridge, MA: The MIT Press, 2019), p. 36.

[26] Broussard's *Artificial Unintelligence* is a good example of this more sceptical approach.

[27] Emily M. Bender and Alexander Koller, 'Climbing towards NLU: On Meaning, Form, and Understanding in the Age of Data', in *Proceedings of the 58th Annual Meeting of the Association for Computational Linguistics*, online (Association for Computational Linguistics, 2020), pp. 5185–98. https://doi.org/10.18653/v1/2020.acl-main.463

[28] Bender and Koller, 'Climbing towards NLU'.

[29] Bender and Koller, 'Climbing towards NLU'.

[30] Fabian Offert and Peter Bell, 'Perceptual Bias and Technical Metapictures: Critical Machine Vision as a Humanities Challenge', *AI & Society*, 36 (2021), pp. 1133–44. https://doi.org/10.1007/s00146-020-01058-z; W.J.T. Mitchell, *Picture Theory: Essays on Verbal and Visual Representation* (Chicago: University of Chicago Press, 1995).

transdisciplinary challenge that is situated 'at the interface of computer science and visual studies/Bildwissenschaft'.[31]

Just as humans need to make sense of the 'speech' of machines powered by LLMs, so too interpretative work is required to make sense of the output of machine 'seeing'. As Bell and Offert highlight, such outputs are neither obvious nor neutral and any approach to them requires heightened critical awareness on the part of the researcher. Such an approach to the use of computer vision in art history can, therefore, be located in the wider discourse of what has become known as 'critical AI'.[32] According to Lauren M.E. Goodlad, debates in this field acknowledge 'the significant need to question and counter boosterism: unaccountable, technodeterministic, and disempowering discourse and hype (including doomerist hype) that undermine informed public discussion, knowledgeable journalism, and democratic oversight'.[33] In the context of the present discussion, it also involves examining the underlying biases of AI, particularly in cases of its dependence on large-scale image databases and language models that conceal human biases and stereotypes pertaining to, for example, gender, race, and sexuality. While quantitative analyses based on large amounts of data seem to offer the promise of objectivity, Joy Buolamwini reminds us that 'the past dwells in our data' and that benchmarks or promises of numerical accuracy in training models are not 'composed of a structure representative of all of humanity'.[34] Developing Buolamwini's point, art historians now need to take into account biases that have shaped the history of their own discipline, while also being attentive to those that are impacting the development and use of new AI-driven tools. Amanda Wasielweski points out that while issues of decolonisation continue to be widely addressed in art history and museum studies, this very issue is arising afresh in the creation of art datasets that are based largely on Western art.[35] Illustrating this point, Mashinka Firunts Hakopian debates how canons and datasets operate to reinforce existing relations of power, and glosses Linda Nochlin by posing the question 'why have there been no great feminist datasets?'.[36] Here, as elsewhere in this emerging field, art historians are able to draw on feminist and decolonial methodologies and put them to use in a wider methodological context that impacts both the sciences and the humanities.

[31] Offert and Bell, 'Perceptual Bias and Technical Metapictures', p. 1134.

[32] See Raley and Rhee, 'Critical AI: A Field in Formation'.

[33] Lauren M.E. Goodlad, 'Editor's Introduction: Humanities in the Loop', *Critical AI* (2023), pp. 1–2. https://doi.org/10.1215/2834703X-10734016. See also Impett's call for a 'new critical understanding of computer vision' in 'Digital Art History as Critical AI', p. 13.

[34] Joy Buolamwini, *Unmasking AI* (New York: Random House, 2024), p. 81. See also Linda Kronman, 'Classifying Humans: The Indirect Reverse Operativity of Machine Vision', *Photographies*, 16 (2023), pp. 263–89. https://doi.org/10.1080/17540763.2023.2189160

[35] Amanda Wasielewski, 'Zombie Canon: Art Datasets, Generative AI, and the Reanimation of the Western Art Canon', in *Critical Digital Art History*, edited by Amanda Wasielewski and Anna Näslund (Bristol: Intellect, 2024), pp. 123–45.

[36] Mashinka Firunts Hakopian, 'Art Histories from Nowhere: Or the Coloniality of Experiments in Art History and Artificial Intelligence', *AI & Society*, 39 (2024), pp. 29–41 (p. 39). https://doi.org/10.1007/s00146-023-01768-0

The chapters in this volume can be understood as a contribution to the discourse of critical AI in so far as they seek to evaluate the potential of collaborative approaches to the integration of AI into art history without over-compensating for technology's limitations or dismissing anomalous results as outright failures. While artworks offer a rich source of material for analysis by computer scientists, so too the expertise of art historians in forging a discursive conduit between artworks, images of artworks, and computational data about artworks opens a new transdisciplinary role for the humanities.

An algorithmic art historian?

The subtitle to the present volume refers to acts of looking in an 'algorithmic culture'. This term was used by Alexander R. Galloway in 2006 to capture the impact of a then burgeoning video game industry.[37] In 2015, Ted Striphas extended the term's remit in his analysis of the semantic implications of inhabiting an increasingly data-driven world.[38] For Striphas, the 'semantic dimensions of algorithmic culture' (including phenomena such as big data, data mining, and analytics) are as important as the technical innovations to which they refer. Developing an idea proposed by Raymond Williams, Striphas sought to show how developments within language could open 'new existential territories that only later come to be populated by technical artifacts'.[39] If Striphas is right, heightened awareness of the terms used in both art history and technology is vitally important in the emergence of a new scholarly field.

As will become clear from the chapters in this volume, language plays a major role in current debates about, and uses of, AI in art history. Whether in the form of text prompts for generative AI, the emergence of conversational norms for engaging with chatbots, or the extension of data science vocabulary, the navigation of a computational art history requires researchers to rethink the conceptual and linguistic remits of their typical ways of describing and analysing artworks. The term that interests me for the purpose of this discussion, however, is more fundamental and impacts on the self-conception and public image of the researcher in this field: 'art historian'.

On the face of it, there is no reason why the flourishing of an AI culture should impact on the meaning of this descriptor. Yet one noticeable consequence of data-driven approaches to art historical analysis has been a conflation of the terms 'art historian' and 'connoisseur'. The reason for this is that computer vision technologies

[37] Alexander R. Galloway, *Gaming: Essays on Algorithmic Culture* (Minnesota: University of Minnesota Press, 2006).

[38] Ted Striphas, 'Algorithmic Culture', *European Journal of Cultural Studies*, 18:4–5 (2015), pp. 395–412. DOI: 10.1177/1367549415577392

[39] Striphas, 'Algorithmic Culture'. See also Raymond Williams, *Keywords: A Vocabulary of Culture and Society*, revised edition (New York: Oxford University Press, 1983).

have tended to focus on the extraction of 'features' from paintings (brushstrokes, edges, shapes, colours, etc.) in the hope of providing new insight into an artist's style, the classification and dating of works, and the correct attribution of authorship. In consequence, computer scientists have equated the work of the contemporary art historian to that of historical connoisseurship because the capabilities of the computer effectively map onto this role.

In this spirit, Saleh Babak and Ahmed Elgammal praised the capacity of the computer 'to mimic the art historian's ability to categorize paintings based on their style, genre, and the artist who made it'.[40] A few years later, Bell and Offert argued not just that a new kind of observer had come into being (the machine), but that it was possible to model its ways of seeing that 'seem to stay close to the human connoisseur'.[41] Finally, the subtitle of David G. Stork's book – *Foundations of Computer-assisted Connoisseurship* – posits a relationship between human and machine and, in consequence, a particular conception of the role of art historian.[42]

The notion of the 'connoisseur' has a vexed history because it is a role that is typically associated with privileges of class, race, methodological conservatism, and the workings of European art markets.[43] As Elizabeth C. Mansfield points out: 'Connoisseurship is now rarely viewed as an art historical end in and of itself but rather as subsidiary to historical interpretation and analysis.'[44] Indeed, to connect the undertaking of contemporary art history to the recognition and description of patterns and, hence, feature categorisation, is to posit an extremely limited role for the researcher. It is also an idea that likely encourages art historians to reject cross-disciplinary dialogue. Contributions to the present volume contribute to a redefinition of the kinds of role that both art historian and computer scientist can play at this disciplinary nexus by offering new perspectives on the kinds of exchange that are unfolding (or are capable of unfolding) in this emerging field.

If the role of the art historian has been challenged by the advent of AI, so too has that of the object of analysis itself – the artwork. I noted above the conflation of aesthetic and technical properties of artefacts in the context of data-driven analyses, but this point extends to more fundamental questions about the ontology

[40] Babak Saleh and Ahmed Elgammal, 'Large-Scale Classification of Fine Art Paintings: Leaning the Right Metric on the Right Feature, *International Journal for Digital Art History*, 2 (2016), pp. 71–93. https://doi.org/10.11588/dah.2016.2.23376

[41] Peter Bell and Fabian Offert, 'Reflections on Connoisseurship and Computer Vision', *Journal of Art Historiography*, 24 (2021), pp. 1–10.

[42] Stork, *Paintings to Pixels*.

[43] Some of these familiar tropes associated with connoisseurship are challenged by David Carrier in 'In Praise of Connoisseurship', *Journal of Aesthetics and Art Criticism*, 61:2 (2003), pp. 159–69. https://doi.org/10.1111/1540-6245.00103

[44] Elizabeth C. Mansfield with Zhuomin Zhang, Jia Li, John Russell, George S. Young, and James Z. Wang, 'Techniques of the Art Historical Observer', *Nineteenth-Century Art Worldwide*, 21:1 (2022), pp. 125–36. See also Kathryn Brown, 'Humanist-in-the-Loop: Machine Learning and the Analysis of Style', in *Modeling Visual Aesthetics, Emotion, and Artistic Style*, edited by James Z. Wang and Reginald B. Adams (Cham: Springer, 2023), pp. 219–27 (p. 225).

of the artwork. Computer vision studies of visual artworks, for example, use digital images as objects of study and thereby deflect attention from both physical artefacts and the cultural and epistemic contexts in which they originated and circulated. Although studies speak, for example, of 'brushstroke analysis', the machine is calculating statistical patterns of pixels. Nuria Rodríguez-Ortega has argued further that a reliance on digital information creates an ontological shift in the art historian's practice: cultural artefacts are transformed into numerical values that are computed and segmented into units of information.[45] While the transition from analogue to digital artefact creates a new range of mobile cultural objects, it also opens ethical questions about the ownership of artworks and their associated data. Furthermore, if computational research methods do not train their focus on physical art objects, but on datasets derived from images of those objects, what kinds of art historical writing might ensue from this development?

A tension that runs through discussions in this field derives from the fact that computer vision models are trained on the visible features of artworks (typically paintings) and the resulting scholarship prioritises and provides insight into the formal qualities of the object (via its digital surrogate). For Amanda Wasielewski, this ushers in a 'computational formalism' that forces art history backwards by shifting focus away from the theoretical and analytical insights and approaches that have developed in the field over the last 70 years.[46] One of the fundamental challenges is how to preserve the insights of contemporary art historical methods and approaches while harnessing new epistemic resources offered by AI. By exploring the new dialogues that are developing – including the points at which the analytical ambitions of researchers diverge or compete with each other – the following chapters examine the new roles that humanists can play, and the ethical challenges they must now navigate, in writing histories derived from quantitative data pertaining to visual artefacts.

Structure

The subtitle of this volume refers to 'images' rather than artworks. This is not to suggest that the uses of AI in art historical research are limited to two-dimensional works. Indeed, interesting studies have been undertaken on the use of computational technologies in the analysis of sculpture, textiles, the reconstruction of ancient mosaics, the processing of archival collections, conservation studies, and

[45] Nuria Rodríguez-Ortega, 'Image Processing and Computer Vision in the Field of Art History', in *The Routledge Companion to Digital Humanities and Art History*, edited by Kathryn Brown (New York: Routledge, 2020), p. 341.

[46] Amanda Wasielewski, *Computational Formalism: Art History and Machine Learning* (Cambridge, MA: MIT Press, 2023), p. 32. See also, Benjamin Zweig, 'Hyperformalism: Notes on Machine Vision and Art Historical Method', in *Critical Digital Art History*, edited by A. Wasielewski and A. Näslund (Bristol: Intellect, 2024), pp. 146–66.

of course human creativity itself.[47] The focus on images (broadly conceived) in the following chapters is, in part, practical (an attempt to draw boundaries around the scope of the discussion) and, in part, a reflection of influential intersections between AI and art history: computer vision for the study of paintings; the transformation of artworks into digital images for analysis by machines; and the creation of images by text-to-image models. Many parts of the following discussions do, however, have implications that extend to art created in a wider range of media.

The first two chapters explore fundamental challenges involved in cross-disciplinary work and the mediation of AI to humanities scholars. Opening the discussion through the lens of an historical model, Amanda Wasielewski examines Joseph Beuys's performance *How to Explain Pictures to a Dead Hare* (1965) and uses this as a metaphor for the black box aspects of artificial neural networks and generative AI. Wasielewski shows that the theoretical stakes of Beuys's philosophy and theories on art, creativity, and art's reception continue to resonate in the development of contemporary digital art history. While she suggests an analogy between the explanatory limitations of both Beuys's enterprise and the contemporary uses of AI, she also posits a positive connection between the two. This consists in the productive role of nonsense as a poetics and, therefore, a means of gaining insight beyond conventional linguistic norms. While accepting many of the problems associated with the use and mediation of AI in the field of art history, Wasielewski does, therefore, demonstrate how the underlying premises of a particular piece of performance art can suggest a positive route towards contemporary cross-disciplinary dialogue.

Eva Cetinić approaches these issues from a practical perspective by exploring some of the stumbling blocks that impede collaboration between art historians and computer scientists. Reviewing developments in this field that have taken place over the past decade, Cetinić debates the role of formalism in art history as discussed above and the kinds of insight that might or might not ensue from the use of computational methods. Having regard to changes wrought by Open AI's CLIP model in 2021 that facilitated the comparison of text–image representations at significantly higher levels of performance than in the past, she highlights the need to understand foundational models not simply as tools for analysis, but as objects that

[47] Chao Liu and Shengneng Guo, '3D Reconstruction of Chinese Traditional Sculpture Based on Artificial Intelligence Drawing', *Computer Aided Design & Applications*, 20:5 (2023), pp. 1–10; F. Pereira, V. Carvalho, R. Vasconcelos, and F. Soares, 'A Review in the Use of Artificial Intelligence in Textile Industry', in J. Machado, F. Soares, J. Trojanowska, and S. Yildirim (eds), *Innovations in Mechatronics Engineering*. icieng 2021. Lecture Notes in Mechanical Engineering (Cham: Springer, 2022) https://doi.org/10.1007/978-3-030-79168-1_34; Fernando Moral-Andrés, Elena Merino-Gómez, Redro Reviriego, and Fabrizio Lombardi, 'Can Artificial Intelligence Reconstruct Ancient Mosaics?', *Studies in Conservation*, 69:5 (2024), pp. 313–26; Emily Pugh, 'Computer Vision in the Archives', *The Art Bulletin*, 106:2 (2024), pp. 15–18; Katherine Mintie, Paul Meisser, and Damon Crockett, 'Closer Looking: Computer Vision in Material Studies of Art', *The Art Bulletin*, 106:2 (2024), pp. 29–32; Andreia Machado Oliveira, 'Future Imaginings in Art and Artificial Intelligence', *Journal of Aesthetics and Phenomenology*, 9:2 (2022), pp. 209–25. https://doi.org/10.1080/20539320.2022.2150467

demand study in their own right. As in Wasielewski's discussion, this raises issues about so-called 'explainable AI' and debates concerning how and to whom AI can be practically communicated. Cetinić discusses the distinctive contributions that humanities researchers can make to this enterprise and concludes that the demystification of, and critical reflection on, AI is one of the most compelling challenges of the present moment.

In my own contribution to this issue, I examine Michael Baxandall's notion of a 'period eye' proposed in his book *Painting & Experience in Fifteenth-Century Italy* and ask whether computer vision might constitute a new 'period eye' for the 21st century.[48] This consists in debating whether AI is capable of introducing a new set of shared interpretative precepts that reshape not just art history, but art worlds themselves. I examine relationships between visual perception, interpretation, and machine 'seeing' and question some of the claims that have been made about the potential of AI to bring about changes in the ways audiences perceive artworks. I then consider whether the integration of AI into art history opens a new set of social conditions that have the potential to shape not just ways of seeing, but also ways of talking and writing about art. This leads me to consider whether – like Baxandall's period eye – computer vision ushers in a new set of exclusive social relationships that shape the interpretation of art.

Leonardo Impett's contribution to this volume takes the theme of vision in a different direction by enquiring into the act of training data from which AI models learn to 'see'. According to Impett this is something that creates a new kind of visual culture, but one that poses a particular set of problems. Specifically, how do humans access and 'read' large data sets? Answering this question opens a new set of possibilities for visual analysis (and hence for practitioners of digital art history), namely, the articulation of an iconology of AI. Here, as elsewhere in the discussions of this volume, the art historian enjoys new contexts in which to practise visual analysis and to reflect critically on the development of associated research methods. Rather than a foreclosing of art history, AI – as both dependent on, and generative of, new visual data – encourages heightened critical visuality on the part of the researcher.

Nuria Rodríguez-Ortega's chapter proposes a theoretical framework for understanding cross-medial relations in text-to-image models. She begins by examining the concept of ekphrasis and goes on to consider the extent to which linguistic descriptions of visual images make sense in AI-mediated environments. The latter, she argues, pose a specific problem for analysing traditionally contrasting media (i.e. words and images) because they rely on the conversion of cultural objects into vectors in so-called 'latent spaces'. What kind of cultural value is supported in this 'post-semiotic' environment and what new conceptual categories are required to understand its remit and content?

[48] Michael Baxandall, *Painting & Experience in Fifteenth-Century Italy: A Primer in the Social History of Pictorial Style*, 2nd edn (Oxford: Oxford University Press, 1988).

While the majority of the chapters in this volume open debates about AI and its role in art history, I felt it was important to include work that actively uses AI and demonstrates its associated research results. Amalia Foka's contribution on text-to-image generation develops issues discussed in the chapters by Impett and Rodríguez-Ortega by showing how text-to-image models 'interpret' and generate images based on prompts derived from art historical analysis. Through a series of experiments with DALL·E, Midjourney, and Stable Diffusion, Foka investigates each model's distinctive 'understanding' of formal and iconographic elements in artworks spanning different periods and styles. Her analysis reveals both the potential of these models to offer new perspectives on art and their limitations in capturing nuanced symbolism and cultural context. Developing a point discussed in the previous section, Foka also draws attention to biases in the data on which these models are trained and shows how they default to racial and gender stereotypes in the imagery they produce from text prompts.

The final two chapters in this volume interface in different ways with photography. Manas Mehta, Elizabeth C. Mansfield, Shuhua Yang, Zhuomin Zhang, Jia Li, John Russell, and James Z. Wang explore issues of style in relation to paintings by the British landscape artist, John Constable. Specifically, they enquire into the notion of Realism communicated by Constable's works. In addition to debating the meanings attaching to both 'style' and 'Realism' in art, the authors explore whether computer vision can shed new light on the extent to which Constable conveyed 'visual truthfulness' in his paintings in a distinct, measurable way. Their study entailed training a model on photographs of clouds to determine whether – or to what extent – depictions of clouds by Constable and his peers could be quantified as 'realistic'. In this case, computer vision is used not just to provide insight into the artworks themselves, but also to reflect critically on the concept of Realism as is has been used in art history.

Tracy Stuber turns to a different engagement with photography in her chapter by asking whether the advent of AI-generated, photorealistic images challenges the ontology of photography itself. Whereas Mehta and his co-authors used photography as the basis for calculating the realism of Constable's paintings, Stuber suggests that the 'evidentiary value' of photography has been undermined by AI. Stuber relates her discussion to wider debates in photography, demonstrating how computer vision technologies both challenge and extend concepts that have helped to define the field. This leads her to consider how computers 'see' photographs and what kind of classification problems they encounter when recognising both the object qualities and the content of photographic images. Here, as elsewhere in this volume, AI becomes a means of rethinking familiar categories and opening new discussions within and across disciplines.

In its investigation of how AI technologies are working – or might work – in partnership with art historical methods, this volume hopes to open new research trajectories and to interrogate urgent ethical questions that are arising in this interdisciplinary field. By debating the results yielded by the application of computational methods in art history and the practices that are shaping this line of experimentation, traditional approaches to the study of cultural artefacts are re-evaluated and new fields of enquiry are opened in both the humanities and the sciences. For these reasons alone, the critical analysis of our current and potential algorithmic culture is a cross-disciplinary imperative.

1

How to Explain Pictures to a Dead Hare: Computer Vision, AI, and the Art Theory of Joseph Beuys

AMANDA WASIELEWSKI

On 26 November 1965, the German artist Joseph Beuys opened his first solo commercial exhibition at Schmela Gallery in Düsseldorf. The event began with a performance titled *How to Explain Pictures to a Dead Hare* (*Wie man dem toten Hasen die Bilder erklärt*). Inside the gallery space, which was closed to the public during the two-to-three-hour-long performance, Beuys gently cradled a dead hare in his arms. His head was covered in honey and pasted with gold leaf and gold dust. The gallery visitors standing outside could only view the performance from a doorway and the window on the street, where the curtains had been pulled back to show Beuys inside. He began the performance sitting in a chair with a radio at his feet, tied to an animal bone. He wore a sheet of iron on the sole of one foot and felt on the other. Rising from a chair at the beginning of the performance, he slowly moved around the exhibition space, 'showing' the hare each work in a deliberate manner and speaking softly to the dead animal. At times, he even lifted the hare's paw to touch some of the works.[1]

In this chapter, I use Beuys's piece as a metaphor for thinking through the implications of contemporary visual artificial intelligence (AI), especially the training of artificial neural networks (ANNs) in the context of computer vision and generative AI.[2] The locked gallery can be seen as a simplified stand-in for the black box model in which the audience (the users) can only partially see the processes taking place, neither fully entering nor apprehending them. Training the neural network

[1] Maja Naef, *Zeichnung und Stimme: Studien Zu Joseph Beuys* (Munich: Wilhelm Fink Verlag, 2011), pp. 99–101.

[2] This chapter deals with common aspects of ANNs that will be shared across a wide variety of deep learning instantiations and pipelines. These could be applied in a variety of circumstances, purposefully left open here, particularly classification or generation.

Proceedings of the British Academy, **285**, 15–35, © Authors 2025.

(equivalent to Beuys's role in the performance) is a form of 'explanation', creating an understanding of the training data (the works on display) for the eventual trained model (the dead hare) through feature extraction. In an interview from 1972, Beuys said of *How to Explain Pictures*: 'This was a complex tableau about the problem of language, and about the problem of thought.'[3] I contend that the training of ANNs to 'see' presents similar problems regarding the relationship between language, communication, and pictures.

Beyond the resonances between visual AI and this particular piece, my main motivation for framing AI in the context of Beuys's work is that his broader artistic philosophy on meaning-making and creativity informs and touches on theoretical and philosophical questions relevant to the field of visual AI at present. Both raise big, foundational questions: what is meaning and understanding? What constitutes learning and cognition? What is creativity? What is (artificial) life (and death)? This chapter tackles these questions only partially, in the specific context of Beuys's work and the extensively documented philosophy around it. In doing so, the aim is not to explain or theorise the totality of the vast and fast-moving field of visual AI, but rather to open up new avenues for thinking about these tools and what they do, using metaphor as a method. Both Beuys's work and the field of visual AI are complex and nuanced. A chapter such as this, which combines such separate domains of enquiry and scholarship, therefore risks treating both superficially and reductively. I nevertheless argue that productive insights can be gleaned from the comparison. Metaphor is a powerful tool for bridging understanding and bringing disparate discourses into useful dialogue.[4] The greater methodological aim is, therefore, for metaphor to perform an alchemy not dissimilar from that created by Beuys through his performances.

Explaining pictures

Beuys stated that *How to Explain Pictures* was conceived as a response to what he saw as the overly rational and intellectual art writing and criticism of the time.[5] This does not mean that he was against intellectualising art per se, as the multitude of

[3] Caroline Tisdall and Joseph Beuys, *Joseph Beuys* (New York: Solomon R. Guggenheim Museum, 1979), p. 101.

[4] A full rehearsal of the Western philosophical discourse on metaphor as method or poetic form, beginning with Aristotle, is outside the scope of this chapter. However, I would point briefly to Derrida who writes: 'Now, if metaphor … aims at an effect of cognition, it cannot be treated without being placed in relation to a knowledge that bears on *definitions*' [emphasis original]. Like a thought experiment, an extended metaphor allows one to match parts between disparate phenomena and thereby produce a kind of definitional knowledge or understanding. See Jacques Derrida, *Margins of Philosophy*, translated by Alan Bass (Chicago: University of Chicago Press, 1982), p. 247.

[5] Götz Adriani, Winifried Konnertz, and Karin Thomas, *Joseph Beuys: Life and Works*, translated by Patricia Lech (Woodbury, NY: Barron's Educational Series, 1979), pp. 130–1.

lectures, speeches, and interviews he gave on his work attest.[6] Beuys was, instead, interested in the interpretation of art only insofar as that interpretation was a symbolic and transcendental one rather than a rational, positivist, or materialist one.

Mari Dumett contextualises Beuys's stance in its historical moment, explaining that in the post-war period, 'the project of many West German critics had been to develop a theoretical foundation for the inferiority and in-authenticity of Eastern [i.e., East German] styles of cultural production'.[7] According to Yule F. Heibel, they did so through the equation of Romanticism, which they associated with East Germany, with the 'irrational, potentially barbaric, primitive, and hence crypto-Nazi'.[8] In this climate, 'pro-Western attitudes are equated with pro-reason ones'.[9] Beuys was thus situated in a particular socio-political context, where key elements of German philosophy were treated as taboo and undesirable, linked to the two ideological enemies of Nazism and Communism. However, in a broader sense, Beuys's stance against a rationalist critical discourse in art raises questions as to whether pictures – and art in general – defy reason-based explanation, and challenge the dominant mid-century formalist models of art criticism that sought to define art, particularly abstract art, by its autonomy rather than its integration into life.[10]

The old cliché that a picture is worth a thousand words expresses something similar, namely, the inability to explain or delineate exactly what we understand when we see an image. In other words, describing an image does not convey the same understanding as that provided by sensory experience. In the field of computer vision research, therefore, one must question whether one can define the 'understanding' of pictures through such rational and simplistic procedures as, for example, object or gesture recognition. Is this the essence of seeing and understanding an image or a scene? Are there other factors that defy rational parcellation? What is missing from this rationalised dissection of the visual sensory experience? Beuys comments precisely on the effect of visuality in isolation, saying: 'If one leaves the eye as it is, it will … tend rather to cool down and differentiate things, divide and analyse them, like a camera, separating things out from each in a crystalline way.'[11] Beuys's dissatisfaction with this purely visual and analytical understanding of the image is apparent in his work which challenges the retinal experience of art/image.

Beuys described himself as a shaman and invented a legend for his transformation into artist and mystic. He credited his mystical awakening to Tartars who

[6] Joseph Beuys and Volker Harlan, *What Is Art?: Conversation with Joseph Beuys* (La Vergne: Rudolf Steiner Press, 2012), p. 1.

[7] Mari Dumett, 'Throwing Fat in the Fire: Joseph Beuys in the Heat of Revolt, West Germany 1967–69' (University of British Columbia, 1998), p. 16.

[8] Yule F. Heibel, *Reconstructing the Subject: Modernist Painting in Western Germany, 1945–1950* (Princeton: Princeton University Press, 1995), qtd. Dumett, 'Throwing Fat in the Fire', p. 17.

[9] Heibel, *Reconstructing the Subject*, p. 72. qtd.

[10] Beuys and Harlan, *What Is Art?*, p. 14.

[11] Beuys and Harlan, *What Is Art?*, p. 18.

saved him after a plane crash and healed him with their (it is implied, 'primitive') knowledge of natural materials. Given that he was a member of the Hitler Youth, an aircraft radio operator, and a combat pilot for the Nazi regime, critics subsequently framed Beuys's romantic philosophising and self-mythologising as a cynical and politically suspect position, a delusion or cathartic activity meant to soothe a guilty conscience, and, thus, redeem himself and the German people in the process.[12] Benjamin Buchloh argues that 'the very negation of Beuys' origin in a historic period of German fascism affirms every aspect of his work as being totally dependent on, and deriving from, that period'.[13] It was as if his mysticism, myth, and ritual could somehow exorcise the high-tech horrors of the war, which were justified by rationalist pseudo-science though they were rooted in age-old bigotries and irrational fears. Meanwhile, this explicit urge to 'resurrect' the spirit of the German people has been framed as nothing more than crypto-fascism, i.e., another chauvinistic celebration of Germanness akin to that of the Nazi regime.[14]

There are, as this brief summary suggests, complicated and nuanced social and historical (and, even, psychological) circumstances that inform Beuys's work. In using *How to Explain Pictures* as a metaphor, however, I want to consider its larger philosophical implications, which expand beyond the convincing, yet restrictive reading of the work presented by Buchloh. In other words, Beuys's particular form of meditation on perception and knowledge have wider applicability beyond the specific context of post-war Germany. These concepts cannot, of course, escape the influence of German philosophy after Kant, especially the Romantic period of Fichte, Schiller, Goethe, Novalis, and others. However, this philosophical inheritance is, for Beuys, seamlessly merged with the use of modern technology.

Eric Michaud critiques Beuys for what he argues is his instrumentality, writing that it embodies an 'entirely classical conception of art in which the "form" is nothing but the unbetrayed vehicle of the "idea"'.[15] This criticism would seem to suggest that Beuys's work is a closed circuit between form and idea, rather than an open field where both form and idea expressed through language, action, and objects fall under the umbrella of artistic practice. The ideas expressed in his work derive from a close reading of theosophical texts, heavily influenced by the writing of Rudolf Steiner, which uncomfortably unite the spheres of spirituality and modern

[12] Tisdall and Beuys, *Joseph Beuys*; Benjamin H.D. Buchloh, 'Beuys: The Twilight of the Idol', January 1980, https://www.artforum.com/print/198001/beuys-the-twilight-of-the-idol-35846; Eric Michaud, 'The Ends of Art According to Beuys', translated by Rosalind Krauss, *October*, 45 (1988), pp. 37–46; Donald B. Kuspit, 'Beuys: Fat, Felt, and Alchemy', *Art in America* (May 1980); Joseph Beuys, *Sprechen über Deutschland: Rede vom 20. November 1985 in den Münchner Kammerspielen* (Wangen: FIU-Verlag, 2002); Gene Ray, *Terror and the Sublime in Art and Critical Theory: From Auschwitz to Hiroshima to September 11* (New York: Palgrave Macmillan, 2005).

[13] Buchloh, 'Beuys'.

[14] Michaud, 'The Ends of Art According to Beuys', p. 42.

[15] Michaud, 'The Ends of Art According to Beuys', p. 38.

science and attempt to forge a unity or coherence between seemingly unresolvable epistemologies.[16] Steiner's philosophy strips rationality from the sciences, rendering them (and the natural world) mystical once again. Beuys's work, then, is not the deployment of an instrumentalised idea but is, rather, a kind of technology-enabled séance that toes the line between prank/miracle and provocation/holy mission. There is a tension between text-as-thought, the image-form and the performance activity, which is positioned as the process and formation of meaning itself. This defies the rational reading of art – of pictures.

Like *How to Explain Pictures*, the training of contemporary ANNs is a *performance* of learning, a setup designed to mimic the acquisition of knowledge, or the steps taken toward understanding. In Beuys's work, this could be interpreted as an inauthentic – or, even, disingenuous – exercise insofar as neither the hare nor the audience actually receives an explanation. In this interpretation, the process of explaining pictures in Beuys's work and the training of ANNs is characterised by an absurdist failure in the cognitive power/potential of the recipient of the explanation. The network learns, essentially, to parrot rather than comprehend, as computational linguist Emily M. Bender and collaborators have steadfastly argued: there is no understanding happening within the trained model, only a semblance or appearance of it.[17] However, looking at the situation from a Beuysian perspective, the empirical fact that the dead hare is inanimate is faulty insofar as it is granted agency (and, thus, a kind of life) in the magic circle of the performance.[18] Likewise, it may not matter how 'dead' or non-conscious an ANN is on a structural level, as its agential and transformative power – its alchemy – is productive (or, in Beuys's terms, creative). In the following section, I expand my thinking on this assertion in more depth, using the performance and its actors as guides.

[16] Barbara Lange, *Joseph Beuys: Richtkräfte einer neuen Gesellschaft: der Mythos vom Künstler als Gesellschaftsreformer* (Berlin: Reimer, 1999), pp. 180–1.

[17] Emily M. Bender, 'Human-like Programs Abuse Our Empathy – Even Google Engineers Aren't Immune', *The Guardian*, 14 June 2022, sec. Opinion, https://www.theguardian.com/commentisfree/2022/jun/14/human-like-programs-abuse-our-empathy-even-google-engineers-arent-immune; Emily, M. Bender, Timnit Gebru, Angelina McMillan-Major, and Shmargaret Shmitchell, 'On the Dangers of Stochastic Parrots: Can Language Models Be Too Big?', *Proceedings of the 2021 ACM Conference on Fairness, Accountability, and Transparency* (2021), pp. 610–23, https://doi.org/10.1145/3442188.3445922; Emily M. Bender and Alexander Koller, 'Climbing towards NLU: On Meaning, Form, and Understanding in the Age of Data', in *Proceedings of the 58th Annual Meeting of the Association for Computational Linguistics*, online (Association for Computational Linguistics, 2020), pp. 5185–98. https://doi.org/10.18653/v1/2020.acl-main.463

[18] For discussions of such agency, see literature on new materialism, including, for example, Jane Bennett, *Vibrant Matter: A Political Ecology of Things* (Durham: Duke University Press, 2010). See also, Johan Huizinga, *Homo Ludens: A Study of the Play-Element in Culture* (Kettering, OH: Angelico Press, 2016).

The exhibition: an image dataset

ANNs are computational assemblages composed of multiple layers of processing units or nodes known as neurons, which are modelled on the neurons of biological brains.[19] Calling them 'neural networks' or 'neurons' is a metaphor rather than a true correspondence, given the vast differences between biomaterial structures and computational hardware. Nevertheless, the artificial neural layers found in the ANN can automatically retain and apply specific information by being fed training data. This training, like the ANN itself, is limited by the particular kind of sensory-equivalent input data it processes. The animal brain, on the other hand, operates based on highly intertwined sensory-based processes.[20] There is thus no real correspondence between the workings of ANNs and the operations of an animal brain, materially speaking. However, it is impossible to avoid describing the ANN in terms borrowed from the biological neural network, even if the method and outcome of its training diverge.

Training neural networks involves introducing a large amount of training data that stands in for a human sense (in this case, vision) and thus has a single functional goal (to see). In order to imitate visual recognition, therefore, AI models need to be trained on a type of visual data that *stands in* for the workings of the biological eye. Most commonly this means training based on two-dimensional images or video captured with photographic camera equipment. In order to achieve some semblance of what we know as vision, a rudimentary 'understanding' of pictures must be created. The foundation of this understanding is the visual material itself, the training data that the neural network must 'look' at to learn its form in a manner of speaking and, typically, connect that in some way with concepts via language.

In *How to Explain Pictures*, the 'training data' consists of the works being exhibited in the gallery space. As is true with any exhibition, curatorial decisions have to be made as to what to include. The limits of a physical exhibition space mean that no selection can be truly comprehensive, though this was the historical ideal for Western Modernism. The encyclopedic format of major Western art museums (e.g., the Louvre, Paris; the Metropolitan Museum of Art, New York; the National Gallery, London; Alte Nationalgalerie, Berlin) had comprehensiveness as its goal and embodied a desire to cover the wide range of human creation, albeit from the perspective of Western superiority.[21] In computer vision, large training datasets such as ImageNet, COCO (Common Objects in Context), Google Open Images, and others have naively taken up this ideal of creating supposedly

[19] Frank Rosenblatt, *Principles of Neurodynamics: Perceptrons and the Theory of Brain Mechanisms* (Washington, DC: Spartan Books, 1962).

[20] Diane Rogers-Ramachandran and Vilayanur S. Ramachandran, 'Right Side Up', *Scientific American*, 1 May 2008. https://www.scientificamerican.com/article/right-side-up-2008-05/

[21] Carol Duncan and Alan Wallach, 'The Universal Survey Museum', *Art History*, 3:4 (1980), pp. 448–69.

universal image repositories and therefore 'comprehensive' representations of the world. For both, the ostensible aim of creating such a repository is *learning*, in the one case for humans and the other for machines.

Researchers compiling image datasets for computer vision regularly assume that the material gathered or scraped from the internet is not only representative but universal.[22] Klaus Scheuerman *et al.* argue that computer vision datasets value 'universality over contextuality' and operate on the assumption that larger datasets equate to 'better approximations of the real world'.[23] For example, the makers of a dataset designed to estimate a person's age claimed: 'The derived human age estimator is universal owing to the diversity and richness of Internet images and thus has good generalisation capability.'[24] Even as data are gathered in non-systematic ways from unchecked sources online, assumptions such as this remain because the focus of research and development is typically on the process or tool, not the data behind it.

The text used as categories or labels for the images scraped online is also subject to assumptions within computer vision research. It is assumed to be neutral.[25] As Nanne Bonde Thylstrup points out, the utopian ideal of the universal archive or library has been a driving factor in mass digitisation efforts.[26] The internet and its networked precursors have been described, since the 1990s, as the manifestation of such utopian ideals.[27] Boris Jardine and Matthew Drage argue, however, 'The *scale* of Big Data, it transpires, is much less impressive than the ways in which scale is mobilised within a rhetoric of completeness'.[28] Since the 2010s, the view of the internet as a utopian repository of knowledge has been largely supplanted by a view of it as a poisoned well of fake news and misinformation fuelled by the activities of social media propagandists and the effects of filter bubbles.[29] What is the real

[22] Amanda Wasielewski, *Computational Formalism: Art History and Machine Learning* (Cambridge, MA: MIT Press, 2023), p. 100.

[23] Morgan Klaus Scheuerman, Alex Hanna, and Emily Denton, 'Do Datasets Have Politics? Disciplinary Values in Computer Vision Dataset Development', *Proceedings of the ACM on Human-Computer Interaction*, 18 October 2021, p. 26.

[24] Qtd. Klaus Scheuerman *et al.*, 'Do Datasets Have Politics?', p. 22.

[25] Wasielewski, *Computational Formalism*, pp. 63–4.

[26] Nanna Bonde Thylstrup, *The Politics of Mass Digitization* (Cambridge, MA: MIT Press, 2019), p. 106.

[27] Miroslav Kruk, 'The Internet and the Revival of the Myth of the Universal Library', *The Australian Library Journal*, 48:2 (1 January 1999), pp. 137–47; Fred Turner, *From Counterculture to Cyberculture: Stewart Brand, the Whole Earth Network, and the Rise of Digital Utopianism* (Chicago, IL: University of Chicago Press, 2006).

[28] Boris Jardine and Matthew Drage, 'The Total Archive: Data, Subjectivity, Universality', *History of the Human Sciences*, 31:5 (1 December 2018), p. 4.

[29] Eli Pariser, *The Filter Bubble: How the New Personalized Web Is Changing What We Read and How We Think*, reprint edn (Penguin Books, 2012); Nicola Righetti, 'Four Years of Fake News: A Quantitative Analysis of the Scientific Literature', *First Monday*, 20 May 2021, https://firstmonday.org/ojs/index.php/fm/article/view/11645; Melissa Zimdars and Kembrew McLeod (eds), *Fake News: Understanding Media and Misinformation in the Digital Age* (Cambridge, MA: The MIT Press, 2020).

relationship between text and image collected through large-scale webscraping, such as the process of data collection utilised for the CLIP model?[30]

Computer vision research continually defers to text as a descriptor – and thus an explanation – of images. The implication is that text is either an objectively true or false description of an image, and that text and image have a one-to-one, rational correspondence.[31] When the CLIP model, which drives visual tools to produce images based on text prompts, was released, the researchers responsible noted the advantage of scale in creating a web-sourced supervised model for computer vision, highlighting its advantages when compared to human-labelled datasets.[32] However, training text and image into a multimodal model has positioned text as something other than description and explanation in relation to images. Text and image are associated or statistically proximate rather than linked hierarchically as forms that explain or describe one another.[33] As media theorist Marshall McLuhan writes, 'the image of a unified ratio among the senses was long held to be the mark of our *ratio*nality, and may in the computer age become so again. For it is now possible to program ratios among the senses that approach the condition of consciousness. Yet such a condition would necessarily be an extension of our own consciousness'.[34] The products of text-to-image models illustrate this, subverting the assumed correspondence between text and image: text prompts are not merely a form of retrieval, but produce a highly associative correspondence and complex ratios that welcome subjective interpretation.

It is useful, then, to think of image datasets in the way we think of exhibitions: as curated arrangements that embody particular ideologies. Even automated webscraping activities have choices built into them, including the types of images or type of text gathered. For example, the open-source LAION dataset faced a scandal in December 2023 when researchers discovered that links to images of child sexual abuse material were included in the dataset.[35] The subsequent response from LAION stated: 'We developed and published our own rigorous filters to detect and remove illegal content from LAION datasets before releasing them.'[36] Within massive datasets of billions of images, therefore, moral and ideological choices are

[30] Alec Radford, Jong Wook Kim, Chris Hallacy, Aditya Ramesh, Gabriel Goh, Sandhini Agarwal *et al.*, 'Learning Transferable Visual Models from Natural Language Supervision', arXiv, 26 February 2021. https://doi.org/10.48550/arXiv.2103.00020

[31] Wasielewski, *Computational Formalism*.

[32] Radford *et al.*, 'Learning Transferable Visual Models from Natural Language Supervision', pp. 1, 3.

[33] For further discussion on this, see Eva Cetinić, Chapter 2, and Nuria Rodríguez-Ortega, Chapter 6 of the present volume.

[34] Emphasis original. Marshall McLuhan, *Understanding Media: The Extensions of Man* (Cambridge, MA: MIT Press, 2013), p. 60.

[35] LAION is not technically a dataset of images but a repository of URLs that a user must reconstitute with a tool like img2dataset, which protects the makers of the repository from copyright infringement. David Thiel and Jeffrey Hancock, 'Identifying and Eliminating CSAM in Generative ML Training Data and Models', 2023. https://purl.stanford.edu/kh752sm9123

[36] 'Safety Review for LAION 5B', 19 December 2023. https://laion.ai/notes/laion-maintenance

made. These may not be limited to illegal images, but may also filter other types of imagery that represent grey areas of what is objectionable or liable to censorship.

Beyond these filters and 'safety measures', however, a curatorial decision is made merely in the selection of the number of websites crawled and thus the web-based data included. Although claims have been made as to the comprehensiveness of AI training sets – and they certainly are large – they actually only represent a small portion of the data that can be found on the internet and so cannot claim to represent a universal beyond that. A report sponsored by the Mozilla Foundation details how Common Crawl, an open-source web archive and dataset provided by a nonprofit organisation, has served as the foundation of nearly every major generative AI application released since 2022. In the report, an engineer at the organisation states: 'Often it is claimed that Common Crawl contains the entire web, but that's absolutely not true. Based on what I know about how many URLs exist, it's very, very small.'[37] In essence, we can think of training datasets as a curatorial collection, even when the curatorial perspective has not been explicitly outlined or may even be unknown to the creators of the dataset. This lack of knowledge regarding the precise contents of the dataset does not mean that there are not subjectivities or choices inherent in it. Datasets contain within them a certain way of seeing.[38] The explanations that follow, therefore, will be coloured by the biases, omissions, and occlusions of these known and unknown curatorial choices in the data.

Beuys in the white cube, algorithms in a black box

The audience of *How to Explain Pictures*, standing outside the gallery, could see Beuys speaking/whispering to the hare, gesturing at the works, puppeting the animal. They could even, it is reported, vaguely hear his mumbled sounds filtering through the open window and doorway. However, the audience was not privy to exactly *how* Beuys explained the pictures to the dead hare. In other words, what exactly were the processes and methods of explanation taking place inside the locked gallery? The idea of explanation implies both a sender and a recipient, but does not guarantee that the latter understands, merely that they have received the explanation. The explanation itself is only partially hidden, however. The process is glimpsed, but is never fully revealed. Contained within this piece, therefore, is a sense of the unknowable in relation to the processes of learning about and explaining images.

[37] Stefan Baack and Mozilla Insights, 'Training Data for the Price of a Sandwich', Mozilla Foundation, 6 February 2024, p. 5. https://foundation.mozilla.org/en/research/library/generative-ai-training-data/common-crawl/

[38] Mitra Azar, Geoff Cox, and Leonardo Impett, 'Introduction: Ways of Machine Seeing', *AI & SOCIETY*, 20 February 2021; John Berger, *Ways of Seeing* (London: Penguin, 2008).

How, then, does Beuys explain pictures to the hare? There is a transformation within the 'machine' of Beuys's performance as he attempts to elucidate pictures for the animal. The inscrutability built into the performance implies that pictures defy explanations. There is no one-to-one correspondence between word and image, neatly packaged in rational description. In providing an explanation, choices must be made and, ultimately, a particular point of view has to be expressed. Explainability is multiple. What is lost in translation, so to speak, is thus difficult to determine. What is lost is the lack of unifying patterns, i.e., the individuality of pictures. By evoking explanation – rather than description or representation – Beuys points to the impossibility of the action.

The analogue to this in visual AI is the training of the neural network and its attendant opacity arising from the automation of the process. The great leap forward and huge advantage of the transition to using deep learning methods in computer vision was that it allowed automatic feature extraction rather than the use of hand-crafted (i.e., manually chosen and tested) features. The side effect of this automation, however, is that deep neural networks are black boxes where the processing layers are hidden from 'view'. The rapidly expanding field of explainable AI (XAI), has taken up the mandate of opening the black box and providing these tools with their own explanation(s). The hidden processual layers of ANNs used for deep learning are so complex, however, that it is impossible to document a step-by-step procedure. Instead, one can catch glimpses of the processes within the network through the application of external techniques (often additional neural networks) to produce, for example, text or visual explanations.[39]

There are two main rationales for XAI. One rationale is concerned with ethics and responsibility. Developers want to build transparency into highly automated systems and uncover the pathway taken to reach the result so that their use can be justified in a variety of applications.[40] Essentially, researchers want to find out whether the means justify the ends or whether the system itself contains fatal flaws or biases. The other rationale aligns with epistemological questions and the desire

[39] Researchers also seek to build explainability into the model itself without external recourse. See the taxonomies presented in A. Barredo Arrieta, N. Díaz-Rodríguez, J. Del Ser, A. Bennetot, S. Tabik, A. Barbado *et al.*, 'Explainable Artificial Intelligence (XAI): Concepts, Taxonomies, Opportunities and Challenges toward Responsible AI,' *Information Fusion*, 58 (2020), pp. 82–115, https://doi.org/10.1016/j.inffus.2019.12.012. Fabian Offert eloquently described the mediation of neural networks by other neural networks in a talk titled 'Machine Visual Culture' given at the 'AI and Visual Heritage' workshop at the Stockholm City Museum on 11 June 2023. See also, Fabian Offert and Peter Bell, 'Perceptual Bias and Technical Metapictures: Critical Machine Vision as a Humanities Challenge', *AI & Society*, 36 (12 October 2020), pp. 1133–44; Fabian Offert, 'Images of Image Machines: Visual Interpretability in Computer Vision for Art', ECCV Workshops, 2018.

[40] Barredo Arrieta *et al.*, 'Explainable Artificial Intelligence (XAI)'; Ning Xie, Gabrielle Ras, Marcel van Gerven, and Derek Doran, 'Explainable Deep Learning: A Field Guide for the Uninitiated', 30 April 2020, http://arxiv.org/abs/2004.14545v1; Amina Adadi and Mohammed Berrada, 'Peeking Inside the Black-Box: A Survey on Explainable Artificial Intelligence (XAI)', *IEEE ACCESS* 6 (2018), pp. 52138–60, https://doi.org/10.1109/ACCESS.2018.2870052.

to understand whether the basis of an outcome is logically sound or aligns with a human-based explanation.[41] This can mean, for example, that there are correlations beyond human perceptual knowledge that models use, i.e., artefacts in the data within which the model detects patterns but that humans would never process as meaningful information. It is this facet that most readily relates to *How to Explain Pictures*.

Computer vision proceeds from the assumption that pictures are data. As such, they can be ordered, categorised, dissected, analysed, arranged, sorted, and ranked. In other words, they have stable or objective meaning in relation to one another that can be automatically uncovered through pattern recognition. In Johanna Drucker's reframing of data in the context of visualisations, she writes: 'Data pass themselves off as mere descriptions of a priori conditions. … Nothing in intellectual life is self-evident or self-identical, nothing in cultural life is mere fact, and nothing in the phenomenal world gives rise to a record or representation except through constructed expressions.'[42] Human-labelled image datasets proceed from a logic where text can still be understood as descriptor or explanation for pictures. Multimodal text and image models, which train web-scraped text and image into a unified model, challenge the notion that text describes or explains pictures. Indeed, the way they relate text and image also, in turn, raises questions as to whether those human-created labels in older image datasets *do* actually explain pictures, not least when introduced to an ANN.[43]

This resistance of images to explanation can be understood through W.J.T. Mitchell's classic reframing of 'what pictures mean and what they do' to the question 'what do pictures want?'[44] Mitchell prefaces his argument with a meditation on what it means to imbue images with animism, agency and liveliness, even personhood, in the manner of 'traditional societies'. He debates whether it is the job of cultural critics to 'demystify' images, which he claims remains potent even in 'modern societies'.[45] Ultimately, he argues that pictures want the power they lack, comparing – not unproblematically – their lowly status to that of historically discriminated groups of people. He argues that some (commercial) pictures wear this desire for power overtly, some (fine art) pictures pretend to not want anything, and that some (abstract) pictures want to not be pictures at all. Mitchell concludes, 'Pictures want equal rights with language, not to be turned into language'.[46] Likewise, it could be

[41] M. Beatrice Fazi, 'Beyond Human: Deep Learning, Explainability and Representation', *Theory, Culture & Society*, 38:7–8 (1 December 2021), pp. 55–77. https://doi.org/10.1177/0263276420966386

[42] Johanna Drucker, 'Humanities Approaches to Graphical Display', *Digital Humanities Quarterly*, 5:1 (10 March 2011). http://www.digitalhumanities.org/dhq/vol/5/1/000091/000091.html

[43] This is already apparent in the absurdity of ImageNet labels explored by Kate Crawford and Trevor Paglen, 'Excavating AI: The Politics of Images in Machine Learning Training Sets', 2019, https://www.excavating.ai/.

[44] W.J.T. Mitchell, *What Do Pictures Want?: The Lives and Loves of Images* (Chicago, IL: University of Chicago Press, 2005), p. 28.

[45] Mitchell, *What Do Pictures Want?*, p. 32.

[46] Mitchell, *What Do Pictures Want?*, p. 47.

said that pictures do not want to be turned into data, turned into patterns, or have claims made as to their meaningfulness. As per Mitchell, they want 'to be seen as complex individuals occupying multiple subject positions and identities'.[47] Beuys treats the animism and subjectivity of pictures in his exhibition in just the ways that Mitchell describes.

Like Mitchell, Beuys turns the question in the title of his performance on itself. The title seems to ask, 'How does one explain pictures to a dead hare?' Yet the real question is, 'How does the dead hare explain pictures?' The immediate answer seems to be that it does not, but, as I show below, this scenario is not as clear-cut as it initially seems.

From language: the hare and the trained model

The hare was a recurring motif in Beuys's work, and the artist's performances have often been analysed for the ritualistic use of animals and animal bodies.[48] Beuys associated the hare with that which is 'low', the earth/the ground, blood and, through a gendered stereotype, the maternal.[49] The hare is thus the opposite of the head/the mind and the opposite of logic and rationality. As such, it counters the overly intellectualised sphere of criticism that Beuys was reacting against in this work. The hare also has deep-rooted spiritual and symbolic associations for Mediterranean and European, particularly German, cultures.[50] It is thus positioned in Beuys's work as a conduit to a spiritual realm, imbued with power and potency as an animistic symbol. Like the bone connected to the radio in *How to Explain Pictures*, the hare is not a dead animal, but rather a living medium, a conduit of information, and an ancient antenna of sorts.

In framing this discussion of AI around the metaphor of an artist explaining something to a lifeless animal, it might be assumed that I am making a critical argument against the ability of ANNs to process explanations of pictures. I am, however, only presenting this analogy as an initial reading, drawing as it does from Bender's work to dispel the hype around the cognitive function of AI.

[47] Mitchell, *What Do Pictures Want?*, p. 47.

[48] Martin Müller, *Wie man dem toten Hasen die Bilder erklärt: Schamanismus und Erkenntnis im Werk von Joseph Beuys* (Cologne: VDG, 1993); Annie Suquet, 'Archaic Thought and Ritual in the Work of Joseph Beuys', *RES: Anthropology and Aesthetics*, 28 (1995), pp. 148–62; Matthew Gandy, 'Contradictory Modernities: Conceptions of Nature in the Art of Joseph Beuys and Gerhard Richter', *Annals of the Association of American Geographers*, 87:4 (1997), pp. 636–59; Claudia Mesch, *Critical Lives: Joseph Beuys* (London: Reaktion Books, 2017), pp. 73–92; Victoria Walters, 'The Artist as Shaman: The Work of Joseph Beuys and Marcus Coates', in *Between Art and Anthropology* (Routledge, 2010); Timo Skrandies and Bettina Paust (eds), *Joseph Beuys-Handbuch: Leben-Werk-Wirkung* (Stuttgart: J. B. Metzler, 2021), p. 14.

[49] Tisdall and Beuys, *Joseph Beuys*, p. 101.

[50] Simon Carnell, *Hare* (London: Reaktion Books, 2010), p. 135.

The critique of AI hype contains a host of political dimensions, many of which have been carefully investigated and delineated by scholars and activists including Bender, Timnit Gebru and collaborators in the Distributed AI Research Institute (DAIR).[51] Gebru and Émile Torres coined the term TESCREAL ('transhumanism, Extropianism, Singularitarianism, (modern) Cosmism, Rationalism, Effective Altruism, and Longtermism') to describe a 'bundle' of current ideologies in the tech industry, many of which are busy building hype around AI and promoting the concept of AGI (artificial generative intelligence).[52] AGI is the science fiction version of artificial intelligence that would have cognitive super-abilities and be able to exercise autonomy across a spectrum of tasks in contrast to the limited functionality of AI at the moment. The cult-like philosophies that make up the TESCREAL acronym, which Gebru, Torres, and others have been so vociferously fighting against, believe that a powerful AGI may either save or annihilate humanity.[53] I agree with these critiques of TESCREAL and the dangers that they pose. I also believe that explaining pictures to a dead hare is as absurd as expecting a neural network to understand pictures. However, I would posit that critiques such as these, which aim to debunk the pseudo-science in the field in the strictest terms possible, may actually foreclose the possibility of productive and meaningful interpretations of the philosophical dimensions of contemporary AI. It is these dimensions of AI that desperately need assessment rather than wholesale dismissal.

It is with this in mind that I want to consider the animism of AI from the perspective of Beuys's work. Given that Beuys did not see the hare as a dead and inanimate object, I believe it might be useful to think through the mystical element of the metaphor and entertain, for a moment, the idea that both the animal and the ANN *do* receive and process the explanation directed toward it. Relegating both the dead hare and the neural network to the logic above precludes the fact that each 'object' is not a random inanimate thing, but a specific one imbued with the power associated with its particular form. They are both, thus, media that represent the hope of accessing an intelligence and knowledge beyond the confines of everyday experience. Exploring this perspective on AI models can, perhaps, inform the AI-related ideologies that currently exist in both the tech sector and the public imagination.

In Emily M. Bender and Alexander Koller's influential 2020 critique of cognitive theories about large language models (LLMs), the authors illustrate their

[51] Emily, M. Bender, Timnit Gebru, Angelina McMillan-Major, and Shmargaret Shmitchell, 'On the Dangers of Stochastic Parrots', Mystery AI Hype Theater 3000, https://www.dair-institute.org/maiht3k/ [accessed 21 June 2024]; Emily M. Bender and Alex Hanna, *The AI Con: How to Fight Big Tech's Hype and Create the Future We Want* (New York: Harper, 2025).

[52] Timnit Gebru and Émile P. Torres, 'The TESCREAL Bundle: Eugenics and the Promise of Utopia through Artificial General Intelligence', *First Monday*, 14 April 2024. https://doi.org/10.5210/fm.v29i4.13636

[53] Gebru and Torres, 'The TESCREAL Bundle'; Marc Andreessen, 'Why AI Will Save the World', *Andreessen Horowitz* (blog), 6 June 2023, https://a16z.com/ai-will-save-the-world/; 'Pause Giant AI Experiments: An Open Letter', Future of Life Institute, 22 March 2023, https://futureoflife.org/open-letter/pause-giant-ai-experiments/.

argument with a thought experiment.[54] In brief, this envisions two people, separate on their own islands, who communicate via an underwater cable. An octopus decides to listen to their conversations and, eventually, becomes very good at recognising and repeating the patterns of their speech. The octopus then decides to sever the cable and communicate with only one of the people, who does not suspect that they are talking to an octopus, but, rather, their friend on the other island. However, when the person is faced with a novel crisis and needs advice which only experience of land-based life would inform, the octopus cannot carry on the conversation effectively. It thus fails to demonstrate a true ability to learn and communicate based on understanding. Bender and Koller write: 'We do not talk for the joy of moving our articulators, but in order to achieve some communicative intent.'[55] They argue, thus, that this communicative intent is absent in the output of LLMs. Seen from the perspective of Bender and Koller's octopus metaphor, the hare as trained model that I have presented in this chapter is nothing more than a puppet for the artist to play with. The generative output does not demonstrate learning or understanding, but rather simply parroting or ventriloquism.

As noted, the discussion could end here with the absurdity of explaining pictures to a hare equated to the absurdity of explaining pictures to a neural network. However, I would like to nuance this comparison in light of Beuys's thinking on language and image.[56] Bender and Koller's pronouncement that meaningful articulations are defined by intentional communication could be construed as a stance against the idea of language as productive rather than descriptive, against *poiesis* itself.

Debates about language and representation were central to German Romanticism and the dual role that many of its protagonists played as poet and philosopher.[57] For both Beuys/the hare and the island dweller/octopus (i.e., human/LLM), the use of language is poetic. The hare has a poetics as a symbol in service of ritual, based on its liminal positioning in the work as a conduit or channel and the way Beuys breathes life into it through language. Beuys said, 'My path, strange as it is, took me by way of language; it did not originate from so-called artistic talent'.[58] His work thus begins with language and is generated from there. There is no special talent but, rather, merely the generative potential of language itself. The octopus/LLM has a poetics that is much like the poetics of *How to Explain Pictures.* It occupies a liminal position as an interpreter of sorts between data and a specific, individual

[54] Bender and Koller, 'Climbing towards NLU'.

[55] Bender and Koller, 'Climbing towards NLU', p. 5187.

[56] For broader discussion of the discourse around text and image in art history, see Nuria Rodríquez-Ortega in Chapter 6 of this volume.

[57] Hans Robert Jauss, 'Poiesis', translated by Michael Shaw, *Critical Inquiry*, 8:3 (1982), p. 600; Azade Seyhan, *Representation and Its Discontents: The Critical Legacy of German Romanticism* (University of California Press, 2023), pp. 7–9.

[58] Joseph Beuys, 'Talking About One's Own Country: Germany', in *Starting from Language: Joseph Beuys at 100*, edited by Nina Schallenberg and Max Rauschenbach (Berlin: Hatje Cantz, 2021), p. 20.

instantiation of that data (something that is generated). Even though – or perhaps *because* – it is not intentional, it serves as a conduit or a channel. Language that is generated without understanding still has the potential to *become* meaningful through its productive (creative) use.

Both the 'conversations' between Beuys and the hare or the human and LLM are, in a conservative reading of consciousness and material agency, complete nonsense. It is nonsense to explain pictures to a dead hare and nonsense to ask a statistical model for advice or to expect understanding. However, in this nonsense, there is the potential for poetics. Gilles Deleuze discusses the concept of nonsense in *The Logic of Sense*: 'When we assume that nonsense says its own sense, we wish to indicate ... that sense and nonsense have a specific relation which can not copy that of the true and false, that is, which can not be conceived simply on the basis of a relation of exclusion.'[59] Nonsense can be generative or creative (i.e., productive). Beginning from language, as Beuys does, highlights its open-endedness and thus its productive capacity beyond intention.

During the early nineteenth century, with the rise of Romanticism, Winfried Menninghaus argues that nonsense was created as a category in literature to complement the criterion of producing meaning. Menninghaus writes:

> For more than two thousand years poetics, buttressed by rhetoric, has inquired into whether or not literature is beautiful, sublime .... With the end of the rhetorical paradigm and the emergence of the hermeneutical paradigm, however, *one* claim above all is made upon literature: *to be infinitely meaningful*. Only with this claim does the correlative concept of nonsense become a relevant category of poetics.[60]

One might pinpoint a similar moment in fine art in the early 20th century, when art practice was increasingly measured by the criterion of meaning or coherence. Marcel Duchamp's readymades were the paradigmatic example of a nonsense art that countered this move.

As noted, Beuys explicitly describes *How to Explain Pictures* as about 'the problem of language, and about the problem of thought'.[61] He held that the greater understanding afforded through communing with a spiritual or animistic realm had been lost in modern life and that his work (and art and creativity in general) should fill it again.[62] His interest in language and communicative form owes much to his interpretation and application of spiritualist Rudolf Steiner's writing, particularly in his characterisation of the German language as sculptural.[63] Many of the artists

[59] Gilles Deleuze, *The Logic of Sense*, edited by Constantin V. Boundas, translated by Mark Lester and Charles Stivale (London: The Athlone Press, 1990), p. 68.

[60] Winfried Menninghaus, *In Praise of Nonsense: Kant and Bluebeard*, translated by Henry Pickford (Stanford: Stanford University Press, 1999), p. 6.

[61] Tisdall and Beuys, *Joseph Beuys*, p. 101.

[62] Tisdall and Beuys, *Joseph Beuys*, p. 23.

[63] Nina Schallenberg, 'On the Sculptural Power of Language and Its Limits', in *Starting from Language: Joseph Beuys at 100*, edited by Nina Schallenberg and Max Rauschenbach (Berlin: Hatje Cantz, 2021), pp. 8–10.

of the early 20th century, including Hilma af Klint, Piet Mondrian, and Wassily Kandinsky were influenced by Steiner and other theosophists. Though Steiner's writing was never accepted in mainstream academic discourse, it nevertheless left a considerable mark on Western art.[64] Beuys's use and positioning of language in his work is largely indebted to German Romantic thinkers as distilled through Steiner.[65]

Beuys saw himself and, by extension, his use of language as a medium, saying: 'I am a transmitter. I broadcast.'[66] In the Beuys literature on *How to Explain Pictures*, it is often mentioned that there is an electronic device (the radio) present in the performance, but this is rarely discussed at length.[67] The trappings of Beuys's military service – his military plane, the radio – become equally potent means of communing with a spiritual plane alongside bones, dead animals, felt, and other more basic materials and matter. Claudia Mesch argues that the presence of the radio implied 'that his whispered exegesis was being broadcast on an unknown frequency. … The artwork validates instinct as another possible form of knowledge'.[68] It is essentially about closing distance for Beuys. If language is locked in, we do not have the possibility to reach out and connect with the animistic, ancient forces that modern thinking typically dismisses.

The suggestion that language is a message in itself – pointing to a media theory of language – is demonstrated in a number of Beuys's works including *How to Explain Pictures*.[69] The connections that language allows, however, can only be achieved if language is not frozen through limited functionality. Indeed, Barbara Gronau argues that Beuys's work can be understood in the context of modern 'crises' of language, as he responded with either 'incessant talking or complex silence'.[70] Beuys was, it seems, trying to capture language as a material force, like a spell, incantation, or radio signal. As such, it was productive or generative even when it was nonsense. Beuys said, 'When one realizes that communication between people, generally, only occurs through the artwork of thinking and speech …

[64] Lange, *Joseph Beuys*, pp. 180–1.

[65] Schallenberg, 'On the Sculptural Power of Language and Its Limits'; Max Reithmann, 'Beuys und die Sprache', in *Joseph Beuys-Tagung, Basel 1.-4. Mai 1991*, edited by Volker Harlan, Dieter Koepplin, and Rudolf Velhagen (Basel: Wiese, 1991), pp. 39–48.

[66] '*Ich bin Sender, ich strahle aus*.' Often, this is translated in English as 'I am a transmitter. I radiate.' Or 'I am a sender. I radiate.' Given that the way Beuys used these words was as they are used in reference to a radio, 'transmitter' and 'broadcast' fit the context best. Nina Schulze, 'Kommunikation Als Kunstform', in *Joseph Beuys-Handbuch: Leben-Werk-Wirkung*, edited by Timo Skrandies and Bettina Paust (Stuttgart: J. B. Metzler, 2021), p. 117.

[67] Naef, *Zeichnung und Stimme*, p. 100.

[68] Mesch, *Critical Lives*, p. 82.

[69] Ludwig Jäger, 'Sprache Als Medium: Über Die Sprache Als Audio-Visuelles Dispositiv Des Medialen', in *Audiovisualität Vor Und Nach Gutenberg: Zur Kulturgeschichte Der Medialen Umbrüche*, edited by Horst Wenzel, Wilfried Seipel, and Gotthart Wunberg (Vienna: Kunsthistorisches Museum, 2001); John Guillory, 'Genesis of the Media Concept', *Critical Inquiry*, 36:2 (January 2010), pp. 321–62, https://doi.org/10.1086/648528; Edmund Snow Carpenter and Marshall McLuhan, *Explorations in Communication: An Anthology* (Boston, MA: Beacon Press, 1960); McLuhan, *Understanding Media*.

[70] Barbara Gronau, 'The Silence of Beuys', in *Starting from Language: Joseph Beuys at 100*, edited by Nina Schallenberg and Max Rauschenbach (Berlin: Hatje Cantz, 2021), p. 50.

where thinking is already a creation and an artwork'.[71] Beuys's work, therefore, demonstrates a concept of meaningful speech or conversation that goes against the idea that there are limited appropriate representational responses to any given utterance that depend on intentional description or explanation. Meaningful language is not only about sensical or coherent conversations between persons. For Beuys, an arguably even greater meaning can be found in opening new channels for communication. As he states, thinking and speech are generative – they are works of art.

This means that, drawing from Beuys, we may indeed 'talk for the joy of moving our articulators' insofar as language is used in a generative way. For example, Beuys's work *Ö Ö Programm*, which was performed at the matriculation ceremony of the Düsseldorf Art Academy in 1967, was based on an idea of language that could be stripped of communicative intent but remain meaningful as an act rather than for the contents its carried. After speeches by other officials at the school, Beuys stepped up to the microphone in front of the audience assembled and uttered a roaring ö sound into the microphone for 'minutes on end'.[72] Beuys explained that the work was 'simply language without content. Just the carrier wave. Language without the conceptual implantation of a concept, in the same way that animals make their sounds'.[73] Notably Beuys did not refer to this as 'sound' but as 'language', implying that language as a medium could be emptied into pure signal. The medium as the message.

In *How to Explain Pictures*, Beuys's generative idea of language is expressed in a different way. In both works, the audience is locked out of linguistic explanation. For *Ö Ö Programm*, they can hear a speech (that Beuys terms language) that does not 'explain' anything. For *How to Explain Pictures* they can vaguely hear that some sort of speech is being uttered but similarly receive no explanation from the artist. Nina Schulze writes:

> Instead of using a language geared towards verifiability and objectivity, Beuys assumes that, in his communicative relationship with others, it is neither important that the recipients of his messages have an exact knowledge of his conceptual definitions, nor that there is an inherent logic to his descriptions that his addressee(s) can follow.[74]

In other words, *How to Explain Pictures* is not a failure in communication but, rather, an affirmation of the special role that linguistic form itself can create. It is

[71] Beuys and Harlan, *What Is Art?*, p. 70.

[72] Holger Schulze, 'Uncomfortable Situations: The Materialism of Sound in the Work of Joseph Beuys', in *Starting from Language: Joseph Beuys at 100*, edited by Nina Schallenberg and Max Rauschenbach (Berlin: Hatje Cantz, 2021), pp. 72–3.

[73] Qtd. Schulze, 'Uncomfortable Situations', pp. 73–4.

[74] '*Statt eine auf Überprüfbarkeit und Objektivierbarkeit ausgerichtete Sprache zu nutzen, setzt Beuys voraus, dass es in seinem Kommunikationsverhältnis zu anderen weder darauf ankommt, dass die Empfänger seiner Botschaften eine exakte Kenntnis seiner begrifflichen Definitionen haben, noch, dass es auf eine seiner Beschreibungen innewohnende Logik ankommt, die seine Adresse/n nachvollziehen könnten.*' Schulze, 'Kommunikation Als Kunstform', p. 119.

an exchange of symbols, some of which remain (forever) cryptic, which releases language from the ho-hum one-to-oneness its more functional definition suggests. It is a reminder of its role as *poiesis*.

Having established Beuys's thinking, I would like to return to the case of AI and argue that the 'nonsense' of LLMs and their application in image creation is also a poetics. LLMs lack exact knowledge of the representative definitions of the symbols they exchange, but that does not mean that they are without poetry. How do we explain pictures to a neural network? The short answer is we do not introduce verifiable or objective definitions.

In John Searle's famous Chinese Room thought experiment, Searle posits that a person or machine can exchange symbols (in the case of the thought experiment Chinese ones for English ones) without actually understanding what they mean.[75] Likewise, a translating computer would not need to have any semblance of linguistic understanding to exchange symbols adequately. But what about non-linguistic symbols? What if Searle's Chinese Room is made into a picture room instead? What would it mean to exchange a picture for text?

For humans, it is more likely for meaning to come unbidden when faced with unfamiliar imagery as opposite to unfamiliar text, particular photographic imagery. Even for *unfamiliar* abstract imagery, the presupposition of any given symbol as a *picture* means that associations can arise unexpectedly, like interpretations of a Rorschach test. So, the person sitting in the picture room (knowing it is a picture) would see, say, a tree and see the word 'tree' and *learn*. They could not obliviously exchange symbols, but would be acquiring some understanding of both text and picture in the process.

This is, in fact, how most humans first learn to read a language. Children's picture books often have images of animals, cars, and all manner of things accompanied by words (usually single words or short phrases) in order to teach children to read and the basic things they might find in the world. So, the exchanger of symbols is, in fact, learning and understanding. However, this still implies that there is one text, one description, or one explanation for pictures. This is, of course, not the case, and the child would not find their knowledge of pictures or language satisfactory if they were to begin and end their learning process with the picture book. As a child continues to nuance simple picture–word associations, they build on what they have initially learned with more language and more explanation (they read other, progressively more complex texts), more pictures (they see more things), and, of course, they have more experiences that can elucidate and unlock the multivalent associations they might draw between the two.

In training image models with text, therefore, we can see that the concepts of learning and understanding are placed on a spectrum of which the LLM is restricted

[75] John R. Searle, 'Minds, Brains, and Programs', *Behavioral and Brain Sciences*, 3:3 (September 1980), pp. 417–24.

to, perhaps, only a very narrow slice. How, therefore, does one explain pictures to a neural network? Through the cognitive and conceptual limitations of language.

Conclusion: everyone is an artist

One of the most well-known statements from Beuys was that 'everyone is an artist'.[76] This is not, as it seems to suggest, an argument for extending the modern concept of the artist, with its special status and professional class, to everyone in society. Instead, it concerns dissolving the very concept of the artist as we know it. Thierry De Duve argues:

> Like labor power, but unlike talent—a notion on which classical aesthetics is based—creativity is the potential of each and every one, and it precedes the division of labor: being the capacity to produce, in general. From this it follows that everyone is an artist and that art is not a profession. All productive activity, whether of goods or of services, can be called art.[77]

In other words, creativity is not some special gift or power of a special class of people, but is something that everyone possesses and can readily access. Seen from this perspective, everyone and no one is an artist. It is about the autonomy of production. As De Duve writes, it means 'power to imagination'.[78]

Eric Michaud writes: 'Beuys's objects or performances should not, then, be taken for works having their ends in themselves. They are conceived to be read as so many repetitions of the message: you who are looking, you, also, are an artist.'[79] Is it Beuys who is the artist or is it the viewer who participates in the act of creation? This activity and active participation of the audience is what Beuys terms the 'social sculpture' which he sees as the overarching project of this oeuvre.[80] Beuys understood social sculpture as being 'from the people, by the people, for the people – as in the Gettysburg Address, but with a new emphasis on from/by/for as a creative process'.[81] It is precisely this funhouse mirror world of reflections and flows of creativity and agency that plays out in the current debates on generative AI.

The release of consumer-focused visual generative AI tools such as DALL·E, Midjourney, and Stable Diffusion in 2022 promised, for the first time, that anyone could actualise what they could imagine or see in their mind's eye. Those optimistic about the technology saw it as a force for democratising generative AI and creative technology. People with very few technical skills can now, essentially, play the role as creative producer (be an artist, in Beuys's conception). This is a sentiment

[76] Tisdall and Beuys, *Joseph Beuys*, p. 7.
[77] Thierry de Duve, 'Joseph Beuys, or The Last of the Proletarians', *October*, 45 (1 July 1988), p. 57.
[78] de Duve, 'Joseph Beuys, or The Last of the Proletarians', p. 55.
[79] Michaud, 'The Ends of Art According to Beuys', p. 38.
[80] Tisdall and Beuys, *Joseph Beuys*, p. 7.
[81] Tisdall and Beuys, *Joseph Beuys*, p. 207.

I saw over and over again in the fora devoted to these tools in the months after their release. An anonymous post on the official Midjourney Facebook group from 30 November 2022 encapsulated this:

> it really sucks that no matter where I go (personal fb to share with friends or twt/social media) I'm always seeing rants about how 'dead or unrealistic' it looks compared to 'real art' and that if I want to create things then I should be a 'real artist'. Like what if I can't draw or am not artistic at all? Or don't have the time/money to invest into years of study? Does that mean I don't deserve the chance to express myself through another medium? AI generated images are the only way I am able to bring to life the ideas in my head that I want to share.[82]

This post not only points to the speed with which criticism of generative AI arose, but the greater debates generative AI raised over what defines the role of the artist and creativity in general.

An open letter written by Molly Crabapple and published by CAIR (Center for Artistic Inquiry and Reporting) in May 2023 takes a staunch position against the use of generative AI. Signed by a number of high-profile intellectuals and artists, the letter states:

> AI purports to have the capability to create art, but it will never be able to do so satisfactorily because its algorithms can only create variations of art that already exists. … Over time, this will impoverish our visual culture. Consumers will be trained to accept this art-looking art, but the ingenuity, the personal vision, the individual sensibility, the humanity will be missing.[83]

In other words, many people in the creative industries fear that alienation from creativity and imagination may widen even further through the use of visual generative AI tools. The view expressed here is that true invention will fall by the wayside (the 'ingenuity' that only humans possess).

This open letter (and much of the debate around generative AI for creative practitioners) ignores or under-emphasises what I would argue are the salient social and political issues for generative AI: corporate control of foundation models, data privacy, and environmental impact. These areas present justifiable reasons against the use of visual generative AI.[84] However, these are not the arguments that the open letter presents. Instead, the letter argues that visual generative AI is not original, creative, or inventive. In so doing, however, it reinforces a highly conservative

[82] Anonymous participant, 'Group Appreciation Post', *Midjourney Official – Facebook*, 30 November 2022. https://www.facebook.com/groups/officialmidjourney/permalink/457609983197238/

[83] Molly Crabapple, 'Restrict AI Illustration from Publishing: An Open Letter', 2 May 2023. https://artisticinquiry.org/AI-Open-Letter

[84] See for example: Amanda Wasielewski, 'Appropriation or Theft? AI, Intellectual Property, and Deskilling in Art History' (in review); Meg Young, Upol Ehsan, Ranjit Singh, Emnet Tafesse, Michele Gilman, Christina Harrington, and Jacob Metcalf, 'Participation versus Scale: Tensions in the Practical Demands on Participatory AI', *First Monday*, 14 April 2024, https://doi.org/10.5210/fm.v29i4.13642; Sebastián Lehuedé, 'An Elemental Ethics for Artificial Intelligence: Water as Resistance within AI's Value Chain', *AI & SOCIETY*, 26 April 2024, https://doi.org/10.1007/s00146-024-01922-2.

position that the artist is a very special kind of professional and that only some people are worthy of this vocation.

This was, in other words, the very idea of art and creativity that Beuys was trying to dispel through his work: the modern myth of the singular, artistic genius as the font of creativity and imagination. It is possible, therefore, that the debate around generative AI can once again lead back to Beuys and his utopian mission to unleash the creative potential latent in every person and every vocation. To borrow Michaud's phrasing, I would say: you who are looking at AI-generated images, you who are prompting and producing AI-generated images, you who are fighting against the use of generative AI – you, also, are an artist. I contend, therefore, that the generative model is the beginning point, not the end, of the Beuysian creative process. Generative AI models are, in other words, what Beuys might term a social sculpture: 'how we mould and shape the world in which we live'.[85]

[85] Tisdall and Beuys, *Joseph Beuys*, p. 7.

2

A Decade of Bridging Computer Science and Art History

EVA CETINIĆ

MRS. HENDY: Oh! I never knew Schopenhauer was a philosopher!
MR. HENDY: Oh, yeah! He's the one that begins with an 'S'.
MRS. HENDY: Oh.
MR. HENDY: Umm, like, uh, 'Nietzsche'.
MRS. HENDY: Does 'Nietzsche' begin with an 'S'?
MR. HENDY: Uh, there's an 's' in 'Nietzsche'.
MRS. HENDY: Oh, wow. Yes, there is. Do all philosophers have an 's' in them?
MR. HENDY: Uh, yeah! I think most of 'em do.

Monty Python's *The Meaning of Life*, 1983.

Introduction

As a computer scientist working in the field of digital art history in the last decade, every now and then one finds oneself presenting the art historical equivalent of 'there is an "s" in Nietzsche' at some interdisciplinary conference. Usually organised precisely with the aim to 'bridge the gap' between disciplines so distinct in their nature as computer science and art history, such events often end up painfully highlighting the differences that they try to overcome. After years of trying to find meaningful ways of applying computational methods in the domain of art history that do not necessarily solve some practical problem but are more focused on quantifying complex concepts and providing novel representations of knowledge, I found it necessary to consider whether this field does not resemble in its essence some kind of Monty Python sketch. In this sketch, the computer scientist plays a role that requires perpetual justification for even daring to meddle with data coming from the arts. Furthermore, the computer scientist is constantly reminded that art history does not only consist of canonical works, or for that matter fine art paintings in general. While most computer scientists try to avoid this subject, every now and then a researcher happens to be naive enough to still think that

Proceedings of the British Academy, **285**, 36–50, © Authors 2025.

emotions have something to do with art. They then discover Plutchik's wheel[1] of emotions, collect universal truths from low-paid workers performing micro-tasks on crowdsourcing platforms, train and validate and test (and train and validate and test again) their deep neural network model, only to conclude that the *Mona Lisa* evokes amusement. Sometimes, more ambitious computer scientists try to become better acquainted with the field with which they mess around, so they discover Aby Warburg or Heinrich Wöllflin. They develop methods that numerically confirm theories grounded in cherry-picked 'empirical evidence' and proudly think they will finally present something that is interdisciplinarily relevant, only to discover that they are around 100 years too late because these theories are no longer of interest to a large part of today's art history research community.

This scenario serves as a fitting summary of my decade-long research at the intersection of computer science and art history. I initially became interested in exploring computational methods for artwork analysis precisely because it seemed so absurd to 'measure' anything related to art. Working with pixel-based statistical properties of images, how could we possibly address any meaningful research question in art history? Yet the idea of coming even remotely close to quantifying something as complex as, for example, the notion of style, even in its most simplified form, seemed truly intriguing back then. Although such tasks often posed significant methodological and computational challenges within computer science, the outcomes frequently appeared overly simplistic or banal from an art historical perspective. Haunted by the quest to attain a point of mutual and truly interdisciplinary research interest, over the years I repeatedly encountered similar challenges and points of divergence between disciplines. In this chapter, I will discuss these recurring discrepancies in relation to the most prominent research challenges and technological developments. Meanwhile, technology has advanced to the point where it is not only possible computationally to 'measure' style, but to mimic it so convincingly that it becomes a threat to the livelihood and working practices of contemporary artists. Therefore, in addition to providing an overview of the most common challenges of the past decade, this chapter will also address the impact of more recent technological advances in generative and multimodal artificial intelligence on digital art history.

Digital art history recapitulates art history?

Coined in 1866, Ernst Haeckel's famous statement 'ontogeny recapitulates phylogeny' formulated the idea that the development stages of an animal embryo represent a chronological replay of that species' past evolutionary forms.[2] Although debunked

[1] Robert Plutchik, *Emotion: A Psychoevolutionary Synthesis* (New York: Harper and Row, 1980).

[2] Ernst Haeckel, *Generelle Morphologie der Organismen. Allgemeine Grundzüge der organischen Formen-Wissenschaft, mechanisch begründet durch die von Charles Darwin reformirte Descendenz-Theorie* (Berlin: G. Reimer, 1866).

by experimental embryologists in the 20th century, the recapitulation theory, understood as a general principle in which the development of an instance of 'something' corresponds to the history of the 'something', became widely known and often served as an analogy in other fields.

One of the major sources of discrepancy at the intersection of computer science and art history over the last decade has been that the research focus and capacities of computational methods, although based on state-of-the-art technologies, often seem too rudimentary and outdated for the contemporary research interests of art history. This is particularly apparent in the context of computer vision, where methods usually operate solely on images, without establishing a proper contextual integration of the results. This lack of alignment between what 'computer science' can do and what contemporary 'art history' wants to do, often represented a source of criticism and an obstacle for collaboration. However, if we assume that digital art history, as the 'digital instance' of art history, must go through the same developmental stages as art history (within a condensed time frame), perhaps the digital art history of the last decade was just 'not yet a fully developed organism'?

In the last decade, research in the domain of computational art analysis has often been focused on tasks that utilise a high-school level knowledge of art history, but hold little value for research production in contemporary art history. However, this factual and elementary level of knowledge was not only necessary in order to build more complex analytical frameworks, but has been in itself very challenging to master from a computational point of view. The structure of my own Ph.D. research was conceptually inspired by the way exams were performed in my high-school art history class: we would randomly pick an item from a set of printed artwork reproductions and write an analytical essay which first indicated familiarity with the work (who, when, what), then described the various visual and structural elements of the work to demonstrate our understanding of formal analysis, and concluded with a subjective review of the work. My own research over the last decade – as well as the general dynamics of the intersection of computer vision and art history – reflect attempts computationally to address those aspects of analysis.

In the context of computer vision, the most basic 'who, when, and what' translates into the quest for automated classification, a topic on which papers have been continuously published for 20 years. These range from early attempts to classify small datasets of paintings according to artist, periods, or genres using low-level image features to the use of deep convolutional neural networks and scraping of large digitised artwork datasets available online, such as WikiArt.[3] Datasets and the taxonomy of labels within this field usually focus on popular artists from the Western canon, mostly embracing simplistic categorisations and anachronistic

[3] L. Shamir, T. Macura, N. Orlov, D.M. Eckley, and I.G. Goldberg, 'Impressionism, Expressionism, Surrealism: Automated Recognition of Painters and Schools of Art', *ACM Transactions on Applied Perception*, 7:2 (2010); *WikiArt.org - Visual Art Encyclopedia*, https://www.wikiart.org/ [accessed 10 December 2024].

interpretations of art historical concepts such as style.[4] The use of such datasets was often criticised by art historians mainly because they do not represent an institutionally curated and controlled selection of artworks and their corresponding metadata. For computer scientists, however, one of the main criteria for relying on popular online datasets of digitised artworks is the availability of a large number of images. My own first attempt to perform a classification experiment was based on a dataset of 200 digitised artwork images, manually assembled using Google image search.[5] Only a few years later, datasets such as WikiArt enabled computer scientists to work with more than 100,000 artwork images.[6]

It is important to note that in those few years, a major transformation happened within the field of computer vision which required the use of large datasets in order to keep up with state-of-the-art methodologies related to image classification and similar tasks. This transformation was triggered by the introduction of deep convolutional neural networks (CNNs) trained on the large-scale object dataset ImageNet.[7] The whole field of computer vision, regardless of the domain of application (artwork images, medical images, traffic images, etc.), gradually shifted from using so-called low-level image features, which describe basic characteristics such as edges, corners, colour, and texture, to more complex features extracted from ImageNet pretrained CNNs or to training or fine-tuning CNNs on large domain-specific datasets. Although this new approach usually resulted in significantly improved results, the question of automated artwork classification remained confined mainly to the interest of computer scientists. Most studies related to this topic focused on increasing the classification accuracy of specific tasks. Yet the fact that a new computational method can, for example, improve the state-of-the-art from a 68 per cent to a 77 per cent accuracy on the task of artist classification holds little significance for art historians.

Does automated classification offer any value for digital art history? Training neural network models to classify artworks provides little potential for new knowledge production, as it basically teaches computers to do something that art historians already know well enough. However, the inherent value of deep neural network models trained on specific datasets is that they numerically capture complex relationships and properties which exist in those datasets. To 'manually' construct and define metrics which would measure such properties is too difficult, if not impossible. Therefore, the value of models trained to classify artworks does not lie so much in the final predicted label or the overall performance accuracy, but in the fact that

[4] Amanda Wasielewski, *Computational Formalism* (Cambridge, MA: MIT Press, 2023).

[5] E. Cetinić and S. Grgic, 'Automated Painter Recognition Based on Image Feature Extraction', *Proceedings ELMAR-2013*, edited by J. Božek, M. Grgić, and B. Zovko-Cihlar (IEEE, 2013), pp. 19–22.

[6] E. Cetinić, T. Lipic, and S. Grgic, 'Fine-tuning Convolutional Neural Networks for Fine Art Classification', *Expert Systems with Applications*, 114 (2018).

[7] J. Deng, W. Dong, R. Socher, L.-J. Li, K. Li, and L. Fei-Fei, 'ImageNet: A Large-Scale Hierarchical Image Database', *Proceedings of the IEEE Conference on Computer Vision and Pattern Recognition* (Miami, FL, 2009), pp. 248–55.

they provide a mechanism for transforming complex data inputs into structured and meaningful numerical representations. In other words, they enable us to measure concepts that were previously considered impossible to describe numerically.

Of course, these measurements represent rough approximations. Many factors influence the formation of these numerical descriptors, including the choice of neural network architecture, the dataset, the definition of the task, and the parameters related to the training process. Often the impact of the interplay between these factors is not fully understood because of the overall complexity and the well-known 'black box' nature of neural network models. In the context of classifying artworks, the underlying starting point of categorisation is already a strong source of ambiguity. This is especially obvious with concepts such as 'style', where the usual categorisation is often a very fuzzy 'ground truth'. However, in order to start from somewhere, computer vision has had to accept the conventionalised typification and rough approximations of concepts such as style, form, abstraction, or figuration as Manas Mehta and his colleagues note in their discussion of Realism in Chapter 7 or the present volume.

Consequently, the concept of 'neural network embedding' has become the fundamental principle in resolving challenges in computer vision, machine learning, data analysis, and visualisation. The term embedding refers to the output of a specific layer in a neural network, often from the final layers, where the network generates a dense vector representation of the input data. In the context of computer vision, neural network-based image representations typically have relied on models trained on the ImageNet dataset, as this was the largest and most widely used dataset in the field throughout the 2010s. Because ImageNet is a dataset designed to categorise photographs of various objects and scenes (e.g., dogs, cats, aeroplanes, cars, etc.), using models trained on this dataset to extract embeddings implied that such data representations are focused primarily on capturing object-related information in images. This object-centred representation of images became apparent in various image-search frameworks or embedding-based visualisations, which became a particularly popular approach for showcasing digitised art and museum collections a few years ago.[8] In such frameworks, the notion of similarity is often accepted without going deeper into discussions about the implications of using models trained on object-related datasets. However, similarity of images is an ambiguous concept, and this becomes particularly obvious when working with artwork images. In this context, the value of models trained on different datasets and tasks (e.g., a model trained to classify images of artworks according to style categorisations) emerges from the fact that the models learn to quantify other relations between images, thereby enabling an exploration of different types of similarity.

[8] Google Arts & Culture, 't-SNE Map: Exploring Art Through Machine Learning', *Google Arts Experiments*, https://artsexperiments.withgoogle.com/tsnemap/ [accessed 1 December 2024]; Statens Museum for Kunst, 'PixPlot: Visualizing the Collection', *SMK*, https://pixplot.smk.dk/ [accessed 1 December 2024]; MetaLab at Harvard, 'Surprise Machines', *MLML*, https://mlml.io/p/surprise-machines/ [accessed 1 December 2024].

The potential value of models trained to classify artworks lies, therefore, in the fact that embeddings extracted from such models can serve as an alternative to the dominant object-based similarity relation integrated into the image search or visualisation frameworks of digitised and digital art collections.

The automated classification of artworks according to some well-known predefined categories such as genre or style has been a starting point of computational analysis of artworks in computer vision and traditionally one of the most commonly explored tasks. However, the use of neural network models to obtain complex numerical descriptors of data inputs is not limited to the tasks of style or genre classification. With enough labelled data, any kind of concept or relation can be quantified using neural network models. With the goals of making the computational analysis of artworks more interdisciplinarily relevant and of exploring the potential and limits of neural networks models, quantifying properties related to more subtle and detailed visual and stylistic qualities of artworks emerged as a new research challenge. In this context, concepts related to formalist theories of style analysis in art history increasingly became a source of inspiration for computer vision scientists. For example, in their study 'The Shape of Art History in the Eyes of the Machine', authors showed that neural network models trained to classify paintings according to different styles implicitly learned features related to stylistic concepts defined by Wölfflin in his book the *Principles of Art History* (1915).[9] Inspired by this work and the available labelled dataset, I further explored how neural network models can be trained to quantify and predict the values of those five contrasting principles in artwork images.[10] Although the resulting study indicated meaningful results and showed the potential of implementing such metrics for advanced image search, my experience of discussing this topic with art historians revealed a general lack of interest in this type of research.

As a computer scientist, it took me a while to understand why it was difficult to find collaborators in art history. Formalism represents a foundational approach for understanding the development of art history. However, contemporary research trends in art history have shifted towards the social and political dimensions of art. From the perspective of computer vision, the technological capabilities of the last decade were such that a formalist approach represented a goal that is difficult to achieve. From the perspective of art history, it represented a relapse into archaic ways of performing art historical research. Because computer vision deals with images and the analysis of artwork images, it is mostly performed without integrating any contextual information beyond basic metadata or categorisation labels. In the dominant discourse of this branch of research, the term 'art' has also mostly been associated with paintings, which together with the fact that these images are

[9] A. Elgammal, B. Liu, D. Kim, M. Elhoseiny, and M. Mazzone, 'The Shape of Art History in the Eyes of the Machine', *Proceedings of the AAAI Conference on Artificial Intelligence*, 32:1 (2018); H. Wölfflin, *Principles of Art History* (New York, NY: Dover Publications Inc., 1950).

[10] E. Cetinić, T. Lipic, and S. Grgic, 'Learning the Principles of Art History with Convolutional Neural Networks', *Pattern Recognition Letters*, 129 (2020).

studied out of context, often attracted dismissive criticism from art historians. This type of criticism was mainly based on the perspective of the needs and interests of contemporary art history, without a broader interest in, or awareness of, the technological possibilities and limitations of deep learning and computer vision. Recently, Amanda Wasielewski provided a more thorough critique of the field in her book *Computational Formalism*, presenting the idea that computer vision and deep learning have reintroduced formalism into digital art history.[11] This observation corresponds with the previously mentioned analogy of the recapitulation theory, where an emphasis on formalism marks a phase in the evolution of digital art history.

What, then, is the next phase in the development of digital art history? It is important to note here that the topics and issues that I have discussed in relation to the computational analysis of art mainly focus on the period between 2011 and 2021. The year 2021 marked a revolutionary milestone in the development of AI technologies with the introduction of multimodal foundation models and their tremendous impact on generative AI. The emergence of these technologies influences the development of digital art history in several ways. In the context of the recapitulation theory analogy, it could be argued that these new technologies have raised questions more closely related to the research paradigms and interests of contemporary art history.

The transformative impact of multimodal foundation models on digital art history

In early 2021, a fundamental paradigm shift happened within the AI research field. The previous decade was mainly marked by advancements in deep learning that were primarily achieved in the context of monomodal approaches. The term 'monomodal' implies that the data that are processed and analysed are usually of one modality (e.g., image, text, or audio). The modality of the data influenced not only the data preprocessing approaches, the design of deep neural network architectures, and training and optimisation methods, but also defined the specific research subfield. 'Natural language processing' comprises a wide area of research which is focused on the computational analysis of text. Similarly, the term 'computer vision' unites a variety of research topics where the analysis of images plays the central role.

On a conceptual level, using deep learning approaches to process and analyse data is quite similar regardless of the latter's modality. Deep neural network models transform data inputs into semantically relevant numerical descriptors. The aforementioned concept of 'neural network embedding' is a basic principle of deep learning. Specific types of neural networks were used when processing

[11] Wasielewski, *Computational Formalism.*

text and enabled the transformation of the textual input into word or sentence embeddings. Those embeddings can be understood as numerical representations of data encoded within a specific hyperdimensional feature space (i.e., latent space). Within that space, a certain notion of semantic similarity is preserved so the transformed data inputs can be compared in relation to their mutual similarity. In other words, deep neural networks trained for various text-related tasks enable the creation of a latent space in which similar words are grouped closer together. In the same way, neural network models trained on image-related tasks, transform images into a numerical feature space where they can be compared according to some notion of similarity.

With the advances in deep learning in the last decade, it became possible to compare texts or to compare images in relation to increasingly refined and complex notions of similarity in the context of the specific modality. However, it was still challenging to assess cross-modal similarity, e.g., the similarity between texts and images. Data representations of different modalities existed in different and mutually incomparable latent spaces.

The big revolution of 2021 was the introduction of the CLIP model by OpenAI.[12] With this model it became possible to compare visual and textual representation in the same hyperdimensional feature space and therefore to measure similarities between words and images. Of course, the subfield of multimodal deep learning existed long before 2021, and various methods of merging and combining data representations of different modalities had been developed. However, none of them was as successful and impactful as CLIP. The reason for its success lies in the fact that CLIP was trained on an immensely large dataset of image–text pairs, primarily compiled from data available on the internet. Training the model on such a large dataset using a contrastive learning mechanism which maximises the similarity between matching image–text pairs and minimises it between nonmatching pairs, permitted data points of different modalities to be mapped into the same high-dimensional feature space, preserving semantic similarity at a performance level that was previously not possible. The dataset used for training CLIP has not been made publicly available and little is known about the data-collection process. The lack of data transparency motivated researchers to develop alternative versions such as the OpenCLIP model, trained on the publicly available LAION dataset.[13]

[12] A. Radford, J.W. Kim, C. Hallacy, A. Ramesh, G. Goh, S. Agarwal, G. *et al.*, 'Learning Transferable Visual Models from Natural Language Supervision', *Proceedings of the International Conference on Machine Learning* (PMLR, 2021), pp. 8748–63.

[13] M. Wortsman, G. Ilharco, J.W. Kim, M. Li, S. Kornblith, R. Roelofs *et al.*, 'Robust Fine-Tuning of Zero-Shot Models', *Proceedings of the IEEE/CVF Conference on Computer Vision and Pattern Recognition* (2022), pp. 7959–71; C. Schuhmann, R. Beaumont, R. Vencu, C. Gordon, R. Wightman, M. Cherti *et al.*, 'LAION-5B: An Open Large-Scale Dataset for Training Next Generation Image-Text Models', *Advances in Neural Information Processing Systems*, 35 (2022), pp. 25278–94.

The CLIP model exemplifies what has come to be known as a 'foundation model'.[14] The concept of the 'foundation model' refers to models trained on a vast amount of data using extensive computational resources. These models, once trained, serve as a foundational layer from which they can be fine-tuned or adapted to perform a wide range of specific tasks in different domains. In parallel with the introduction of CLIP, OpenAI presented a 12-billion parameter network called DALL·E, which relied on CLIP and was trained to generate images from textual descriptions. DALL·E marked a milestone in the field of text-to-image synthesis and generative AI.[15] After the introduction of the CLIP and DALL·E models, the concept of multimodality began to attract considerable attention among AI researchers.[16] Consequently, the development and improvement of models capable of converting textual inputs to images, as well as text to other modalities such as video, music, or 3D objects, emerged as one of the field's most frequently explored research subjects.

This change has also had a strong impact on the intersection of deep learning and art, particularly on computer vision-based approaches to art analysis and generation. Many of the challenges related to tasks such as art classification or style transfer became obsolete with the emergence of multimodal foundation and text-to-image models. Since their initial introduction, text-to-image models were very much focused on improving the realistic appearance and aesthetic quality of generated images. Therefore, from a technical point of view, multimodal generative AI models outperformed earlier versions of image-based generation techniques such as generative adversarial networks which, a few years previously, represented the main technological protagonists of the AI Art movement.[17]

Besides the obvious improvement of the visual quality of generated images, a more important advancement is the possibility to address a seemingly unlimited set of potential tags and labels. Prior to the introduction of foundation models, methods employed in tasks related to art analysis or for generative purposes mostly relied on datasets with a predefined and limited set of labels, usually including names of popular artists or styles, such as the aforementioned WikiArt dataset. As stated, such datasets were criticised by art historians because they do not represent an institutionally curated and controlled selection of artworks and their corresponding metadata. However, in comparison to the vast amount of unlabelled and online-scraped data that became the standard input of contemporary foundation models, the datasets of digitised artworks previously dominating

[14] The Stanford Institute for Human-Centered Artificial Intelligence's (HAI) Center for Research on Foundation Models (CRFM) introduced the term 'foundation model' in August 2021, https://hai.stanford.edu/news/introducing-center-research-foundation-models-crfm [accessed 11 December 2024].

[15] OpenAI, *DALL·E: Creating Images from Text* (2021) https://openai.com/dall-e [accessed 11 December 2024].

[16] For further discussion, see Nuria Rodríguez-Ortega, Chapter 5 in the present volume.

[17] I. Goodfellow, J. Pouget-Abadie, M. Mirza, B. Xu, D. Warde-Farley, S. Ozair *et al.*, 'Generative Adversarial Networks', *Communications of the ACM*, 63/11 (2020).

computer vision tasks still represented a somewhat labelled, organised, and controlled selection and categorisation of artworks. Another frequent critique of early computer vision-based art analysis was that computational categorisation efforts mostly concentrated on a limited selection of well-known artists or style categories. This also significantly changed with the introduction of foundation models. Instead of resolving the previously criticised aspects, however, this shift brought about a new set of challenges.

In the early days of text-to-image models in 2021, a trend emerged to generate images that mimic stylistic features of specific artists. Soon everyone following the newly established scene of 'promptism' had seen examples of images generated in 'the style of', followed by the name of a specific artist. Initially, the focus was on some of the most popular artists from the Western canon, but it quickly became evident that these models could also imitate the styles of lesser-known artists. Because these models were trained on a large subset of internet data and not on a predefined dataset with a limited set of labels and artists' names, it became a challenge to explore which artists are 'known' by these models. Soon documents and websites dedicated to the exploration of this topic emerged, such as Remi Durant's artist studies dedicated to the exploration of the early CLIP+VQGAN implementation or the 'Disco Diffusion artists studies' focused on another open-source implementation of text-to-image methods popular at the time.[18] The concept behind artist studies was to create a list of artists' names, generate an image from a prompt that includes the name of each of these artists and check if the generated image bears any similarity with the known distinctive stylistic properties of that artist. The emergence of artist studies represented a sort of ironic twist on how neural networks had previously been used for art analysis. Prior to the development of text-to-image techniques, neural network models were mostly applied on datasets of artworks to automate the categorisation or generation process. On the other hand, text-to-image-based artist studies required the manual effort of compiling lists of names and testing the images in order to study the models. This example illustrates an important shift that arose with the introduction of large-scale models, where AI models were no longer perceived merely as tools, but as objects of study in their own right.

With the introduction and development of diffusion-based approaches to text-to-image generation, models became more advanced in generating realistic looking images where nuances of different styles became more obvious. In the span of just a few months, a plethora of diffusion-based text-to-image models emerged in 2022 such

[18] Remi Durant, *Artist Studies*, https://remidurant.com/artists/# [accessed 11 December 2024]; K. Crowson, S. Biderman, D. Kornis, D. Stander, E. Hallahan, L. Castricato, and E. Raff, 'VQGAN-CLIP: Open Domain Image Generation and Editing with Natural Language Guidance', *Proceedings of the European Conference on Computer Vision* (Cham: Springer Nature Switzerland, 2022), pp. 88–105; Weird Wonderful AI Art, *Disco Diffusion 70+ Artist Studies*, https://weirdwonderfulai.art/resources/disco-diffusion-70-plus-artist-studies/ [accessed 11 December 2024]; Alembics, *Disco Diffusion*, https://github.com/alembics/disco-diffusion [accessed 11 December 2024].

as DALL·E 2,[19] GLIDE,[20] Midjourney,[21] and Stable Diffusion.[22] New and improved versions of these models are continuously being released, followed by a constantly changing landscape of available frameworks, user platforms, and access rights. The initial artist studies are further explored in the form of style dedicated platforms, including the Midlibrary platform which explores various artists and styles featured in different versions of the Midjourney model.[23]

The significant interest these technologies garnered in 2022, coupled with the heightened commercialisation of the text-to-image sector in 2023, played a major role in expanding and altering the user base of these technologies. The practice of prompting also evolved from using simple and straightforward descriptions, to integrating complex, often model-specific, detailed descriptions and incorporating stylistic nuances, and specific references to art or culture. Communities formed around these models and started to develop a shared knowledge based on effective prompting. Consequently, the process of interacting with these models also became an object of study.

Recent studies have started to explore existing datasets of generated images and prompts such as DiffusionDB or JourneyDB.[24] These datasets extend the question of which artists' styles can be imitated by the models, to the exploration of which artists' styles users of these models are interested in emulating. Many recent studies have focused on exploring the corpus of existing prompts and investigating the most common topics and words utilised by users of text-to-image models. For example, a study focused on topic modelling performed on the 1.8 million unique user prompts from the DiffusionDB dataset showed that artist names are the main type of prompt specifier used after the main subject, while another study revealed the most common individual artists' names in different prompt datasets.[25]

After initial fascination with the capability of text-to-image models to mimic stylistic features of artists, followed by the questions of who is known or not known by these models and which names are most commonly prompted, another more

[19] OpenAI, *DALL·E 2: A Generative AI Model for Image Synthesis*, https://openai.com/dall-e-2 [accessed 11 December 2024].

[20] A. Nichol, P. Dhariwal, A. Ramesh, P. Shyam, P. Mishkin, B. McGrew *et al.*, 'Glide: Towards Photorealistic Image Generation and Editing with Text-Guided Diffusion Models', arXiv preprint, arXiv:2112.10741 (2021).

[21] Midjourney, https://www.midjourney.com/ [accessed 11 December 2024].

[22] R. Rombach, A. Blattmann, D. Lorenz, P. Esser, and B. Ommer, 'High-Resolution Image Synthesis with Latent Diffusion Models', *Proceedings of the IEEE/CVF Conference on Computer Vision and Pattern Recognition* (2022), pp. 10684–95.

[23] A. Kovalev, '*Midlibrary*', https://midlibrary.io/ [accessed 11 December 2024].

[24] Z.J. Wang, E. Montoya, D. Munechika, H. Yang, B. Hoover, and D.H. Chau, 'DiffusionDB: A Large-Scale Prompt Gallery Dataset for Text-to-Image Generative Models', arXiv preprint, arXiv:2210.14896 (2022); K. Sun, J. Pan, Y. Ge, H. Li, H. Duan, X. Wu *et al.*, 'JourneyDB: A Benchmark for Generative Image Understanding', *Advances in Neural Information Processing Systems*, 36 (2024).

[25] T. Sanchez, 'Examining the Text-to-Image Community of Practice: Why and How Do People Prompt Generative AIs?', *Proceedings of the 15th Conference on Creativity and Cognition* (2023), pp. 43–61; J. McCormack, M.T. Llano, S.J. Krol, and N. Rajcic, 'No Longer Trending on Artstation: Prompt Analysis of Generative AI Art', *International Conference on Computational Intelligence in Music, Sound, Art and Design (Part of EvoStar)* (Cham: Springer Nature Switzerland, 2024), pp. 279–95.

important issue emerged. The question of 'who is known?' soon transformed into the ethically more relevant question of 'who wants to be known?' In the early days of text-to-image models, professional contemporary artists whose work could be imitated by these models raised concerns about the use of their artworks as a data source for training AI models. With the subsequent technological advancements and increased commercialisation of platforms that provide access to these models, this question became increasingly relevant. In early 2023, a group of three artists filed a lawsuit against Stability.AI and Midjourney in what might be considered the first copyright infringement lawsuit of this kind in the US.[26] While the case is still in progress at the time of writing, it highlights important issues regarding the use of art as training data, and its resolution may set a precedent for similar legal challenges in the future.

Recent studies exploring artists' opinions about these technologies revealed that artists think model creators should be required to disclose in detail what art and images they use to train their AI models.[27] The artists also state they will reduce their online presence in order to avoid the use of their data without consent.[28] Regardless of the final judicial verdict, the lawsuit has attracted attention not only within the community of artists concerned about the impact of AI on their work, but also within the AI research community and among the creators of platforms that facilitate the use of such models.

The issue of style mimicry in generative AI became emblematic of the broader social, political, and ethical concerns surrounding the development and use of such models. The fact that these models have been trained on extremely large and uncurated datasets, mostly scraped from the internet, triggered debates about issues related to privacy violations, copyright infringement, and intellectual property.[29] Besides those issues, other problematic aspects of these models also became increasingly explored and discussed. One of the most commonly addressed topics in the critique of foundation models concerns the social biases and demographic stereotypes that emerge and are propagated by AI-generated images. The problem of bias, particularly in relation to gender and racial representations of persons in AI-generated images, started as a commonly observed characteristic of these models, mostly shared and discussed on social media in the early days of text-to-image models. Recently, the problem of bias has become a more systematically studied

[26] J. Vincent, 'AI art tools Stable Diffusion and Midjourney targeted with copyright lawsuit', *The Verge*, 16 January 2023. https://www.theverge.com/2023/1/16/23557098/generative-ai-art-copyright-legal-lawsuit-stable-diffusion-midjourney-deviantart [accessed 11 December 2024].

[27] J. Lovato, J.W. Zimmerman, I. Smith, P. Dodds, and J.L. Karson, 'Foregrounding Artist Opinions: A Survey Study on Transparency, Ownership, and Fairness in AI Generative Art', *Proceedings of the AAAI/ACM Conference on AI, Ethics, and Society*, 7 (2024), pp. 905–16.

[28] S. Shan, J. Cryan, E. Wenger, H. Zheng, R. Hanocka, and B.Y. Zhao, 'Glaze: Protecting Artists from Style Mimicry by Text-to-Image Models', *32nd USENIX Security Symposium (USENIX Security 23)* (2023), pp. 2187–204.

[29] Z. Epstein, A. Hertzmann, Investigators of Human Creativity, M. Akten, H. Farid, J. Fjeld *et al.*, 'Art and the Science of Generative AI', *Science*, 380:6650 (2023).

research field, mainly focused on the possibilities of quantifying and evaluating representational biases in large multimodal generative models. Most of the studies are focused on exploring gender biases in occupations, while fewer have examined factors such as power dynamics and geo-cultural characteristics.[30] There are many other socio-cultural patterns and biases that are encoded and propagated through those models which are more subtle and difficult to detect and which are currently underexplored. Although much research is dedicated to questions related to bias, the solution for this issue remains a complex interdisciplinary research problem. A broader discussion of the concept of bias is provided by Leonardo Impett in Chapter 4 of the present volume.

These issues highlight the previously mentioned methodological shift in how we approach deep neural network models, especially within research areas including digital humanities, digital art history, and cultural analytics. Specifically, these models are no longer viewed simply as tools, but as objects that need to be studied on various levels. There is an increased need to deconstruct and better understand the inner workings of such models. Within the AI discourse, the term 'explainability' typically refers to methods and techniques that enhance the understanding of a model's behaviour. A common scenario in contemporary AI is that a model is developed and then introduced. Over time, as the model gains popularity and a wider user base, the AI research community begins to conduct studies to investigate and explain its functionality. Essentially, the dynamics of model production involves creating something first and then trying to decipher its inner mechanisms.

This counterintuitive approach has become particularly prominent with complex foundation models that are trained on large datasets and perform well on specific tasks, yet the exact reasons for their overall success or specific failures often remains unclear. The lack of clarity about how foundation models function is an open research quest for AI researchers and an even more challenging topic for AI non-specialists. However, this should not imply that scholars from the humanities cannot contribute to the topic of explainability in relation to AI models. One important aspect of explainable AI revolves around determining 'to whom' the explanations should be directed, as various stakeholders involved in the development, deployment, and use of these models possess different levels of background knowledge about AI. Following the breakthroughs achieved with recent generative models, the hype around the notion of AI became even more intensified.

The general public and majority of people outside of the AI field heavily rely on media reports about AI, which often oversimplify AI capabilities or mislead readers about how AI systems actually work. The common tendency to anthropomorphise AI also influences the public perception and understanding of AI technologies. Attributing human-like characteristics to AI systems has not only been a dominant way of reporting about AI technologies in the media, but also an integral

[30] Y. Wan, A. Subramonian, A. Ovalle, Z. Lin, A. Suvarna, C. Chance *et al.*, 'Survey of Bias in Text-to-Image Generation: Definition, Evaluation, and Mitigation', arXiv preprint, arXiv:2404.01030 (2024).

part of designing interaction frameworks, e.g., the conversational tone and chat-like interfaces that serve as gateways to generative language or text-to-image models. Additionally, the narrative of AI entrepreneurship often exploits the hyped and anthropomorphised language in order to capitalise on the commonly perceived complexity and general lack of understanding of AI technologies. Therefore, the necessity to demystify, critically reflect, and explain the basic principles of AI technologies emerges as one of today's major goals and challenges.

This growing need for explainability could be compared with the concept of self-reflexivity. According to the recapitulation theory analogy, we could argue that with the emergence of foundation and generative AI models, digital art history is shifting from relying on traditional art history towards aligning more with the perspectives of postmodernity. With the goal to better understand, explain, and communicate the functional mechanisms, as well as to study the broader ethical, social, political, and economic implications of AI technologies, the divergence of interests that characterised the intersection of computer science and art history over the past decade, might be diminishing.

Conclusion

At the intersection of AI and art history, the past decade has been characterised mainly by the attempt to measure general concepts which were historically used for the categorisation and description of artworks. This quest for 'quantifying universalities', which manifested itself mainly in the form of 'computational formalism', served to explore the possibility of imposing a numerical framework to essentially nonnumerical concepts.[31] The reason for pursuing this research direction was not necessarily grounded in the naive assumption that everything can be measured, as the critique of such approaches commonly suggested. On the contrary, it could be considered an attempt to explore the limitations of the quantification and datafication of art – a way of better understanding the immeasurable.

I would argue that researchers in computer vision and deep learning, as well as those in digital art history, have underestimated the potential of deep learning-based quantification. With the emergence of foundation models, it suddenly became possible numerically to 'capture' (in the form of neural network embeddings) many concepts that were previously considered too complex and too subtle to be quantified. In the context of art, the application of AI technologies in the process of analysis or content generation was, for a long time, considered an 'exotic' and playful endeavour rather than a serious knowledge extraction method or a real threat to creativity.

The emergence of multimodal foundation models and the subsequent fast development of advanced generative AI models brought about a performance level

[31] Wasielewski, *Computational Formalism.*

that was surprising, not only to those outside of the field, but to many AI researchers as well. The rise of these technologies shifted the interests of scholars involved in the field of digital art history and triggered the engagement of many scholars who were previously not interested in exploring digital approaches to research in the arts and humanities. Prior to the introduction of the currently popular and powerful generative AI models, the most common critique was that AI-based methods are not good enough for any truly meaningful integration into humanities scholarship. Now these technologies have become almost too good, and the critique has shifted from discussing the drawbacks of the models themselves towards focusing on the socio-economic impact, potential risks, and ethical aspects of the development and use of AI models.

Of course, these models are not perfect, and many performance issues still remain, including the problem of hallucinations when models generate inaccurate or nonsensical content. Nevertheless, they have become good enough to be analysed and studied through critical theoretical and socio-political lenses. Therefore, we can observe an increased convergence of interest between critical AI studies and contemporary art history. It remains challenging, however, to consolidate perspectives from computer science and art history into new research methodologies. This continues to be an open question and ambitious goal of our future interdisciplinary research path with all of the intellectual and ethical risks that this entails.

3

Computer Vision: A 'Period Eye' for the 21st Century?

KATHRYN BROWN

IN *PAINTING & EXPERIENCE in Fifteenth-Century Italy*, Michael Baxandall posited the existence of a 'period eye' that captured a set of relationships between artist and public, individual expression and social context.[1] In his use of this term, Baxandall sought to elucidate the patterns, categories, inferences, and analogies that a viewer brings to an image for the purposes of deriving meaning from it. In the context Baxandall explored, these interpretative skills ranged from sensitivity to an artist's use of specific colours to the appreciation of narrative backgrounds for different scenes, recognition of the signifying power of gestures, and understanding of the ways in which geometrical forms stand in relation to each other and symbolise concepts relevant to everyday experience. The ability of audiences to recognise and interpret such elements of a visual image (all of which may be said to pertain to the work's style) comprised, for Baxandall, ways of seeing that exemplified the kind of creative production associated with a specific historical 'period'. In this account, 'cognitive style' maps onto 'pictorial style' to make pictures both intelligible to audiences and, in consequence, explicable in language.[2]

In this chapter, I want to test the extent to which Baxandall's account of a 'period eye' has relevance for contemporary practices of art history following the advent of computer vision as a tool for analysing and understanding artworks. My approach to this topic does not consist in investigating further the techniques for determining style that Baxandall himself examined or the art historical traditions that informed Baxandall's approach to this subject. Rather, I consider whether computer vision as a branch of artificial intelligence (AI) suggests new ways of seeing, engaging with, and interpreting pictorial artefacts. For the purpose of this analysis,

[1] Michael Baxandall, *Painting & Experience in Fifteenth-Century Italy: A Primer in the Social History of Pictorial Style*, 2nd edn (Oxford: Oxford University Press, 1988), pp. 29–45.
[2] Baxandall, *Painting & Experience*, pp. 36 and 40.

Proceedings of the British Academy, **285**, 51–68, © Authors 2025.

I will focus my discussion on paintings, though many of the points are relevant to works in a wider range of media. In similar fashion to the 'Quattrocentro cognitive style' that Baxandall posited as a common ground between the makers and viewers of artworks, is AI capable of introducing a new set of shared interpretative precepts in the 21st century and, if so, with what consequences for art worlds?

Before continuing, it is important to clarify why the question of a period eye is important in a contemporary context, particularly in light of the fact that the interpretation of artworks has long been affected by technological developments.[3] In Baxandall's account, social facts informed the development of visual skills and habits. If this premise is accepted, it can be argued that connections between cognitive and pictorial styles can be elucidated for any time period or community of makers and viewers. In light of the social changes being wrought by the widespread adoption of AI (ranging from the integration of AI into personal technologies to changes in work forces and developments in the relationship between individual and state through new surveillance systems), it is worth considering whether quantitative methodologies are prompting a revolution in the relationship between viewers and images that is similar to the cultural impact of early cinema or photography. In this chapter, I will argue that the implications of using computer vision to reveal and model the detailed structure of visual artefacts run even deeper than the impact of earlier technologies on the production and reception of art. By promoting the idea that computers 'see' – a metaphor for a variety of computational operations used to analyse the visible qualities of artworks – much scholarship encourages the idea that humans now share an interpretative space with autonomously functioning machines. This supposed extension of visual literacy to algorithms suggests a fundamental shift not just in how meaning is derived from visual artefacts, but in who (or what) has agency to produce that meaning.

The advent of computer vision also prompts reflection on the functioning of art history as a discipline by opening new questions about the relationships between visual perception, interpretation, and machine 'seeing'. Investigating these relationships problematises the role of the viewing subject in fashioning the range of interpretations derived from art. Whereas Baxandall's focus was on the social encounters that underpinned and guaranteed an interpretative apparatus for visual artefacts, it is now necessary to examine the implications of crafting such a framework with the assistance of non-human agents. This, I will argue, represents more than a change in the epistemic practices of art history. Rather, the integration of AI into art history opens a new set of social conditions that have the potential to influence the trajectory of the discipline as a whole.

[3] One of the most important of these was Walter Benjamin's discussion of the introduction of cinema and mechanical techniques for reproducing images, notably photography, in 'The Work of Art in the Age of Mechanical Reproduction' (first published in 1935). Walter Benjamin, *Illuminations: Essays and Reflections*, edited by Hannah Arendt, translated by Harry Zorn (London: Pimilico, 1999), pp. 211–44.

I shall examine these issues by pursuing three themes. First, if the possibility exists for computer vision to shape a new period eye, it is important to locate this debate in histories of vision and, from there, to explore how humans and machines interact to derive information from, and make sense of, artworks. Does computer vision have the capacity to reshape audiences' approaches to images and the kinds of question that might be asked about art? Second, an important, but underexplored part of Baxandall's analysis concerns the connection between vision and language. For Baxandall, it was not merely the case that a shared set of concepts informed the content and interpretation of artworks. Rather, those concepts gave rise to a discursive framework that generated a common written and verbal language about art. This leads me to ask how computer vision impacts not just ways of seeing, but also ways of talking and writing about art. Third, in the social history of the Quattrocento proposed by Baxandall, the roster of protagonists consisted of patrons, artists, artists' assistants, and educated viewers. To the extent there was a 'period eye', it was not generalisable over an entire populace. To what extent does the introduction of computer vision in contemporary settings mirror this point by instigating a new set of exclusive social relationships that shape the interpretation of art? In short, what new social contract has computer vision brought to bear on the intellectual environment of art history?

Addressing histories of vision

To understand whether computer vision plays a role in crafting a period eye for the 21st century, it is first necessary to define an important set of parameters that frame the debate, namely, the ways in which this kind of computational functioning relates to human seeing and ideas about its histories. Scholars have pointed out that use of the term 'vision' in the context of machines is, in fact, a metaphor and that computers do not 'see'. Instead, computers run sophisticated statistical models to extract and compare data about the visible features of artworks.[4]

Elsewhere, I have debated whether computer vision might be understood as the latest development in a history of lens-based looking on the part of humans (e.g., an extension of the use of glasses, microscopes, and other technologies that enhance human vision).[5] Although viewers do not physically look 'through' the computer in the way they would through an optical device, algorithmic analysis may be said to serve as a visual prosthetic that substantially increases the amount of visual information that can be extracted from the artwork and used by humans to make sense

[4] See Kathryn Brown, 'After Art History? Artworks as Data', *The Art Bulletin*, 106:2 (2024), pp. 33–6 (p. 33); Harald Klinke, 'Big Image Data within the Big Picture of Art History', *International Journal for Digital Art History*, 2 (2016), p. 21, https://doi.org/10.11588/dah.2016.2.33527; Nuria Rodríguez-Ortega, 'Image Processing and Computer Vision', in *The Routledge Companion to Digital Humanities and Art History*, edited by Kathryn Brown (New York: Routledge, 2020), pp. 338–57 (p. 341).

[5] Brown, 'After Art History? Artworks as Data', p. 34.

of visual data. In this case, computer vision functions as a new kind of 'lens' that enhances rather than displaces human vision, and the input of machines operates in relation to human experience as an 'augmented' rather than 'artificial' intelligence.[6]

Pursuing a different perspective, Mitra Azar, Geoff Cox, and Leonardo Impett wonder how computational technologies 'change the way we see the world'.[7] Drawing on John Berger's 1972 television series and accompanying book *Ways of Seeing*, and comparing ideas from these studies with David Marr's analysis of computational and human visual systems, *Vision*, published a decade later, the authors examine various perceptual, social, and political implications of 'machine seeing'.[8] Moving productively beyond debates about the potential harms and benefits of AI in this context, they suggest that computer vision, at the very least, 'gives us a new, precise set of metaphors with which to think about vision differently – in computational, biological, aesthetic, and consequently *political* terms'.[9] Taking up Baxandall's terminology, this equates AI with the emergence of a new 'cognitive style' that impacts not just on the making and interpretation of art, but on the ways in which humans conceive of their visual relationship to art and, indeed, to the world around them.

Elizabeth C. Mansfield, Zhuomin Zhang, Jia Li, John Russell, George S. Young, Catherine Adams, and James Z. Wang pursue a different metaphor in their argument that computer vision operates as a 'disinterested but visually attentive interlocutor' who engages the art historian in new dialogues.[10] In this case, the authors argue that machines reveal distinctive aspects of human seeing (including its perceptual biases and assumptions) rather than changing seeing itself. Adopting a similar stance, Peter Bell and Fabian Offert posit the existence of a computer-based 'artificial observer' capable of providing 'a deliberately "alien" point of view' that accompanies human seeing.[11]

[6] The term 'augmented intelligence' as opposed to 'artificial intelligence' is often used in clinical practice. See, for example, George Bazoukis, Jennifer Hall, Joseph Loscalzo, Elliott Marshall Antman, Valentín Fuster, and Antonis A. Armoundas, 'The Inclusion of Augmented Intelligence in Medicine: A Framework for Successful Implementation', *Cell Reports Medicine*, 3:1 (2022). See also Frank Pasquale's defence of human expertise in *New Laws of Robotics: Defending Human Expertise in the Age of AI* (Cambridge, MA: The Belknap Press of Harvard University Press, 2020), pp. 3–7.

[7] Mitra Azar, Geoff Cox, and Leonardo Impett, 'Introduction: Ways of Machine Seeing', *AI & Society*, 36 (2021), pp. 1093–194.

[8] Azar *et al.*, 'Introduction: Ways of Machine Seeing', p. 1103. John Berger, *Ways of Seeing* (London: Penguin, 1973); David Marr, *Vision: A Computation Investigation into the Human Representation and Processing of Visual Information* (Cambridge, MA: The MIT Press, 2010).

[9] Azar *et al.*, 'Introduction: Ways of Machine Seeing', p. 1093.

[10] Elizabeth C. Mansfield, Zhuomin Zhang, Jia Li, John Russell, George S. Young, Catherine Adams, and James Z. Wang, 'Techniques of the Art Historical Observer', *Nineteenth-Century Art Worldwide*, 21:1 (Spring, 2022), pp. 1–13 (p. 4) https://www.19thc-artworldwide.org/spring22/practicing-art-history-techniques-of-the-art-historical-observer.

[11] Peter Bell and Fabian Offert, 'Reflections of Connoisseurship and Computer Vision', *Journal of Art Historiography*, 24 (2021), pp. 1–10 (p. 2).

In the models of interpretative sociability defended in these two views, computer vision retains and exhibits an autonomous strangeness that encourages humans to see the world differently or, at least, test assumptions about human seeing. More specifically, computer vision is understood as making a discursive contribution to art history by extracting and analysing the formal features of artworks at scales that are unattainable for humans acting alone. By extending the viewer's epistemic resources in this way, machines seem to usher in a new set of conditions and opportunities for the interpretation of art. Yet Mansfield and her collaborators reject the idea that this culminates in the creation of a new 'prosthetic "period eye"'. Their more cautious view – similar to that of Azar, Cox, and Impett – is that there is simply 'potential for computer vision to aid art historians in gaining a better understanding of perception as well as vision'.[12]

Two themes concerning the relationship between technology and human vision run throughout the above-mentioned literature. The first, fairly uncontentious, idea is that computers encourage art audiences to think 'differently' about human vision and its metaphors. The second, more adventurous thought is that computer vision can bring about actual changes in human seeing. The latter has led to the claim that machines are capable of changing 'the *nature of seeing* and hence our knowledge of the world' (emphasis added).[13] The idea that computer vision is capable of triggering a change in human perception and its concomitant epistemologies is the latest example in a line of thinking that seeks to identify a relationship between techno-industrial development and alterations to the perceptual structure of the human mind.

One of the most famous proponents of this idea was Walter Benjamin who – taking his cue from Alois Riegl – argued that human sense perception 'is determined not only by nature but by its historical circumstances'.[14] For Benjamin, significant changes to perception were occasioned by technological developments associated with late 19th-century modernity. This claim from Benjamin's 1935 essay, 'The Work of Art in the Age of Mechanical Reproduction' has, like the essay itself, had a significant impact on art history, and it is unsurprising that it should inflect ideas arising from more recent revolutions in visual technologies.[15] Jonathan Crary, for example, discusses the history of vision as a 'hypothetical possibility', arguing that what changes 'are the plural forces and rules composing the field in which

[12] Bell and Offert, 'Reflections of Connoisseurship and Computer Vision', p. 8.

[13] Geoff Cox, 'Ways of Machine Seeing', *The Photographers' Gallery: Unthinking Photography* (24 November 2016), https://unthinking.photography/articles/ways-of-machine-seeing [accessed 28 May 2024]..

[14] Benjamin, 'The Work of Art in the Age of Mechanical Reproduction', p. 216. Developing this line of thinking from Benjamin, Geoff Cox made the argument in 2016 that 'we should discuss how machines have changed *the nature of seeing* and hence our knowledge of the world' (emphasis added). Geoff Cox, 'Ways of Machine Seeing: An Introduction', *The Photographers' Gallery: Unthinking Photography* (2016), https://unthinking.photography/articles/ways-of-machine-seeing [accessed 4 December 2024].

[15] Jonathan Crary, *Techniques of the Observer* (Cambridge, MA: The MIT Press, 1992), p. 6.

perception occurs'.[16] Yet Crary takes this idea a step further when he suggests that external factors comprising a 'collective assemblage of disparate parts on a single social surface' are capable of 'determining' vision in any particular historical moment.[17] This leads him to argue that 'a new kind of observer' came into being during the early decades of 19th-century Europe, one that was 'made adequate' to the events, forces, and institutions that are typically associated with the advent of technological modernity.[18] Might it then be argued that an even newer kind of observer – equipped with a new way of seeing – has come into being in the 21st century in response to the emergence of computer vision?

The idea that human vision has a history that is determined by wider social, technological, and environmental changes has been contested, most notably in the field of analytic aesthetics.[19] Developing Jerry Fodor's conception of the modularity of the human mind, Arthur C. Danto argues that human visual processes are 'cognitively impenetrable' and therefore unaffected by what is known or believed.[20] Danto does not deny that 'at a level higher than that of optical reality ... people see the same things differently at different cultural moments', but he argues that this does not equate to a claim that seeing itself changes throughout history.[21]

Defending a middle position that does not completely dispense with connections between human perception and the impact of social context, Noël Carroll draws a distinction between seeing and noticing.[22] Instead of insisting that human seeing changes in response to its environment, Carroll argues that factors including technological change (for example, cinema and photography) impact on how people attend to their worlds. New technologies might, for example, stimulate people to organise their visual field differently and to highlight specific features of it, much like close-ups or panning shots might direct the viewer's perspective on events that unfold in a film.[23]

Like Carroll, Bence Nanay productively moves the discussion away from a history of vision as a change in human sense perception to a history of attention, positing Baxandall's 'period eye' itself as a compromise position.[24] Nanay notes Baxandall's own attempt to maintain a modularity of mind while retaining the impact of social circumstances on acts of interpretation. In this case, it is argued that

[16] Crary, *Techniques of the Observer*.
[17] Crary, *Techniques of the Observer*.
[18] Crary, *Techniques of the Observer*, p. 9.
[19] Bence Nanay, 'The History of Vision', *The Journal of Aesthetics and Art Criticism*, 73:3 (2015), pp. 259–71.
[20] Jerry A. Fodor, *The Modularity of Mind* (Cambridge, MA: The MIT Press, 1983); Arthur C. Danto, 'Seeing and Showing', *The Journal of Aesthetics and Art Criticism*, 59:1 (2001), pp. 1–9 (p. 8).
[21] Danto, 'Seeing and Showing', p. 1.
[22] Noël Carroll, 'Modernity and the Plasticity of Perception', Symposium: The Historicity of the Eye, *The Journal of Aesthetics and Art Criticism*, 59:1 (2001), pp. 11–17 (p. 14).
[23] Carroll, 'Modernity and the Plasticity of Perception', p. 15.
[24] Bence Nanay, 'The History of Vision', *The Journal of Aesthetics and Art Criticism*, 73:3 (2015), pp. 259–71.

the formation of retinal images is universal, but all that follows from that (including how retinal images are interpreted) is historically contingent.[25] In similar vein, Hal Foster and Robert S. Nelson draw a distinction between 'vision' and 'visuality', the former a 'physical operation' and the latter a 'social fact'.[26] Michael Squire makes a similar point in his discussion of attempts to understand 'ancient sight', drawing attention to the distinctive ways in which seeing was envisaged and empirically experienced in antiquity.[27] Following these approaches, it is possible to defend the view that a period eye is a way of seeing that is responsive to a range of social factors without having to accept the wider, more contentious claim that technology prompts a change in the nature of visual perception itself.

There are three reasons why I have dwelt on this debate about whether human vision has a history. First, if the concept of a period eye is to be defended, it is necessary to take a position on the extent to which the social factors that obtain in any given period impact on human seeing and the ensuing interpretation of visual information. Second, the debate opens useful questions about the kinds of convention that shape the 'organization of visual material' as Carroll puts it. These range from the recognition of specific symbols, materials, and economic structures in the case of Baxandall to the impact of visual technologies in the cases of Benjamin and Crary. If, following Carroll's view, cinema and photography encouraged viewers to attend to aspects of the world as if they were close-up shots, computer vision opens an even closer, comparative view of the micro-details of numerous visible surfaces and might thereby effect a change in patterns of human attention. The compromise position entails, therefore, the possibility that a technology such as computer vision might well impact on ways of interpreting and talking about art, but without altering, or even functioning as a substitute for, human seeing. The third point is that by moving discussions of computer vision away from analyses of perception and debates about histories of vision, we might gain a better understanding of how AI technologies might reshape contemporary visual literacy.

New technologies; familiar questions?

With this background in place, I turn to the first question posed above: does computer vision have the capacity to change audiences' approaches to images and the kinds of question that might be asked about art? If so, how might this come about? While computer vision continues to develop in ways that facilitate increasingly

[25] Nanay, 'The History of Vision', p. 262.

[26] Hal Foster, 'Preface', in *Vision and Visuality*, edited by Hal Foster (Seattle: Bay Press, 1988), pp. ix–xiv (p. ix); Robert S. Nelson, 'Introduction: Decartes's Cow and Other Domestications of the Visual', in *Visuality Before and Beyond the Renaissance: Seeing as Others Saw*, edited by Robert S. Nelson (Cambridge: Cambridge University Press, 2000), pp. 1–21.

[27] Michael Squire, 'Introductory Reflections: Making Sense of Ancient Sight', in *Sight and the Ancient Senses*, edited by Michael Squire (Abingdon: Routledge, 2016), pp. 1–35 (p. 2).

more nuanced studies of form and pattern in visual images, one noticeable trend in the field is the use of this technology to operationalise and test older models of art historical analysis. Insightful work has, for example, been undertaken on how to extend the analysis of gesture proposed by Aby Warburg in his *Pathosformel* of 1905; to teach concepts about style derived from Heinrich Wölfflin's *Principles of Art History* published in 1915; or to expand examples used by Baxandall himself by modelling the physical poses and gestures of the archangel Gabriel in depictions of the Annunciation in European art produced from 1300 to the mid-18th century.[28]

As noted above, the principal advantage of computer vision in such cases is its ability to work at scales that are not available to the individual researcher.[29] Computers are typically able to extract features from a far larger number of artworks than an individual, often drawing comparisons across thousands of images and thereby providing significantly more raw data for analysis than would typically be available to, or even comprehensible by, an individual researcher. This way of operating has led Harald Klinke to examine differences between the traditional act of close looking practised by art historians, and the emphasis on big data that is a hallmark of computer vision. He notes 'the introduction of *quantitative* methods into a field that has used exclusively *qualitative* methods throughout its existence', but stresses that the former are not a substitute for the latter.[30] Instead, they are an addition to the methodological repertoire of the historian who seeks to 'create new hypotheses for qualitative research'.[31] Klinke's observation is fair, but the implications of working at scale and creating digital data for art historical analysis warrant further consideration.

One question that arises from this new methodology is whether the computational methods for operationalising existing analytical models yield new art historical knowledge. In their analysis of Annunciation images, Bell and Impett conclude that their methodological experiment 'confirms old truths', but might also open new ideas 'in the development of an iconography of the longue durée that does not resort to historical sparsity (such as extrapolating from a small canon) or temporal

[28] Leonardo Impett, 'Analyzing Gesture in Digital Art History', in *Digital Humanities and Art History*, edited by Kathryn Brown (New York: Routledge, 2020), pp. 386–407; Ahmed Egammal, Marian Mazzone, Bingchen Liu, Diana Kim, and Mohamed Elhoseiny, 'The Shape of Art History in the Eyes of the Machine', *Proceedings of the AAAI Conference on Artificial Intelligence*, 32:1 (2018), https://doi.org/10.1609/aaai.v32i1.11894; Peter Bell and Leonardo Impett, 'The Choreography of the Annunciation through a Computational Eye', *Histoire de l'Art*, 87 (June 2021), pp. 61–76.

[29] In their study of John Constable's cloud imagery, Zhuomin Zhang, Elizabeth C. Mansfield, Jia Li, John Russell, George S. Young, Catherine Adams *et al.* created a fairly modest dataset of 2,543 to train their classification model. See 'A Machine Learning Paradigm for Studying Pictorial Realism: How Accurate Are Constable's Clouds?', *IEEE Transactions on Pattern Analysis and Machine Intelligence*, 46:1 (2024), pp. 33–42. In 'The Choreography of the Annunciation', Bell and Impett used 4,806 images of the Annunciation from their working corpus of 23,018 images.

[30] Harald Klinke, 'Big Image Data within the Big Picture of Art History', *DAH Journal*, 2 (2016), pp. 15–36 (p. 28). https://doi.org/10.11588/dah.2016.2.33527

[31] Klinke, 'Big Image Data within the Big Picture of Art History'.

simplifications (e.g. by using gross periodizations)'.[32] Here, too, the point of working at scale (in contrast to 'historical sparsity') is posited as a key advantage. The idea that computer vision works to correct 'temporal simplifications' in art history is, however, more difficult to defend in light of approaches in art history that work to challenge familiar canons, including the temporal and epistemic categories on which they are based.[33] By contrast, emphases on temporal periodisations abound in the emerging computer vision literature, where broad stylistic categories – often contested in art historical literature – have been imposed on diverse corpora of work.[34]

This leads to the question whether new technologies may operate to reinforce existing biases in art history. If this were the case, an algorithmically informed period eye may, in fact, rely on and extend interpretative assumptions of the past rather than the present. Although the use of machines to test earlier approaches to the study of images is both computationally challenging and interesting in its own right, some of the interpretative models used by computer scientists appear methodologically outmoded in contemporary art historical terms, as other contributors to this volume have noted: studies turn repeatedly to examples from the canon of European art, for example, or reinforce traditional stylistic assumptions that have been challenged by more recent thinking.[35] If computer vision is able to stimulate the creation of a new period eye, the epistemic resources being used to fuel its conceptual apparatus often appear to be anchored in the past.

A further criticism that has been levelled at uses of computer vision in art history is that it introduces a new focus on the formal qualities of artworks (typically paintings), thus underestimating both the wider social contexts in which artefacts function and the variety of theoretical approaches that can be used to understand their capacity to generate meaning. Amanda Wasielewski, for example, argues that art history has now been engulfed by 'computational formalism', an approach to images that searches for the individual components of style and pattern or that prioritises 'matching games' between images and their constituent elements.[36] As Wasielewski goes on to point out, such approaches do not always yield art

[32] Bell and Impett, 'The Chorography of the Annunciation', p. 73.

[33] For an overview of relevant debates about periodisation see Lawrence Besserman, 'The Challenge of Periodization: Old Paradigms and New Perspectives', in *The Challenge of Periodization: Old Paradigms and New Perspectives*, edited by Lawrence Bessermann (New York: Routledge, 2013), pp. 3–28.

[34] Consider, for example, the range of works associated with 'Primitivism' in David G. Stork, 'Computer Vision, ML, and AI in the Study of Fine Art', *Communications of the ACM*, May 2024, 675, pp. 68–75 (p. 71).

[35] See Kathryn Brown, 'Humanist-in-the Loop: Machine Learning and the Analysis of Style in the Visual Arts', in *Modeling Visual Aesthetics, Emotion, and Artistic Style*, edited by James Z. Wang and Reginald B. Adams (Cham: Springer, 2024), pp. 219–30; Mansfield *et al.*, 'Techniques of the Art Historical Observer', p. 3.

[36] Amanda Wasielewski, *Computational Formalism: Art History and Machine Learning* (Cambridge, MA: The MIT Press, 2023), pp. 59–60, 138.

historically salient information that advances understanding about visual artefacts or their capacity to convey complex meaning.[37]

In response, it can be argued that sourcing data about purely visible components of style with the help of machines does not necessarily ringfence art historical enquiry from social or other theoretical perspectives. It would, for example, be possible to eliminate consideration of wider social or theoretical concepts in cases of stylistic analysis *without* the use of computers. The distrust of formalism as an art historical method had already come to the fore by the 1960s in critiques of approaches that had been championed by Clement Greenberg and Roger Fry.[38] Against the backlash that developed against such methodologies, the rise of computational methods that emphasise the formal qualities of paintings can easily be made to sound like a return to an outmoded art history.

The use of computer vision to reinforce the explanatory role of formalism in deriving meaning from artefacts is, therefore, capable of suggesting an approach to visual art that is, in effect, stripped of a period eye. Developing Baxandall's terms, subordinating the act of seeing to an algorithmic encounter might seem to sever important connections between the visible and cognitive content of images that, together, create meaning. To find a positive way through this impasse, it is helpful to develop further the theme of visual attention discussed earlier.

In his exploration of spectatorship in *Painting as an Art*, Richard Wollheim proposed the concept of 'two-foldness', a process of seeing in which the viewer simultaneously experiences the representational content of the work (what it shows) and the object qualities of the artefact (e.g., brushmarks, fingerprints, material damage, characteristics of a piece of paper, weave of the canvas, etc.). These physical features of the object may be essential to the work's aesthetic impact, but may have nothing to do with its representational content. In some cases (e.g., the presence of craquelure in painting), they may, in fact, trouble appreciation of the work.[39]

Bence Nanay takes up Wollheim's ideas in his exploration of histories of human attention, arguing that two-foldness became aesthetically relevant to the appreciation of artworks in Europe around the mid-16th century, notably in the complex brushwork of paintings by Titian.[40] Nanay explores the essential role in pictorial appreciation played by the complicated surface structure of Titian's paintings and contrasts this with a focus on representational content in 15th-century painting. Developing Baxandall's concept of the period eye, Nanay argues that visual skills which enabled appreciation of the artefact properties of the painted surface itself were not relevant to the enjoyment of Quattrocento painting and that, in consequence, two-foldness (as a form of aesthetic appreciation) only came into being in

[37] Wasielewski, *Computational Formalism*, p. 48.

[38] Matthew Bowman, 'The Experience of Formalism', *Art History*, 43:3 (2020), pp. 662–6. https://doi.org/10.1111/1467-8365.12515

[39] Richard Wollheim, *Painting as an Art* (London: Thames & Hudson, 1987).

[40] Nanay, 'The History of Vision', p. 266.

the 16th century.[41] Nanay uses this idea to defend the view that human visual attention (as opposed to vision itself) has a history.

Regardless of whether one agrees with the historical moment that Nanay associates with the advent of two-foldness as a determining factor in the aesthetic appreciation of paintings, his strategy of connecting directions (and intersections) of visual attention to particular historical moments is compelling and has important repercussions on the use and significance of contemporary computer vision.[42] I noted earlier that computer vision extracts, compares, and analyses the visible components of painted surfaces. This implies a focus of the machine on either the representational content of the work (high-level semantic features such as objects or scenes) or on specific aspects of its content (e.g., low-level semantic features such as corners, edges and angles of brushmarks, colour, and shape patterns).[43] The analysis results in the creation of discrete informational units about these various factors. One could describe this kind of vision as a 'single-foldness' – or the extraction of data pertaining to individual sub-components – that differs from the simultaneous twofold attention practised by humans and explored by Wollheim and Nanay in their respective works.

Countering the idea that computer vision functions as an autonomous, but alien visual agency that challenges the ways in which humans see visual artefacts (or, indeed, reveals something about human seeing), my argument is that it reduces the kind of synthetic seeing involved in twofoldness and encourages, instead, a form of visual attention that focuses on compartmentalised features of artworks. While, taken on its own, this might reduce the range of factors that, in combination, shape the aesthetic appreciation of painted surfaces, the data derived from computer vision can, however, be productive for art historical analysis. Returning to a point I made earlier, computer vision can, for example, add to the stock of data about an artwork by enabling humans to 'see' – in an extended sense – at hitherto unattainable scales.

Developing an argument proposed by Fred Dretske, it can be argued that computer vision is capable of telling observers 'facts about objects [they] do not perceive'[44] – in this case, micro-surface information about an artwork that derives from statistical models surveying a vast number of images. As Dretske puts it:

[41] Nanay, 'The History of Vision', p. 268.

[42] In a counterargument to Nanay, one might argue that the artefact properties of artworks extend to their placement and that, in consequence, the architectural location of artworks (including in sacred or secular settings) has a bearing on their aesthetic impact.

[43] David Stork makes the argument that computers will, one day, be able to extract more complicated meanings from artworks that, presumably, will bridge the gap between different semantic features of the image. Even this would not, however, translate into the kind of two-foldness envisaged by Wollheim. See David Stork, *Pixels & Paintings: Foundations of Computer-Assisted Connoisseurship* (Hoboken, NJ: John Wiley & Sons, 2024), p. 531.

[44] Fred Dretske, 'Introspection', *Proceedings of the Aristotelian Society*, 94 (1994), pp. 263–78 (p. 263).

> One looks at a fuel gauge to discover how much gas remains in a tank one cannot see; listens for the sound of a timer to learn when the cake in the oven is done; and reads the newspaper or watches television to see what is happening on the other side of the world.[45]

In similar fashion, one might understand the data yielded by computer vision as a conduit to information about an analogue visual artefact derived from, as Dretske puts it, an act of 'displaced perception'.[46] In this regard, computer vision neither alters nor replaces human seeing; nor does it constitute a new visual 'interlocutor'. Rather, computer vision is an extended informational channel about artworks, but one that does not constitute a new 'period eye' in its own right because it does not function as a 'cognitive style' in Baxandall's sense.

New languages of art?

If computer vision does not constitute a new period eye in a purely visual sense, might it nevertheless generate a new language for talking about art that reflects a different aspect of the concept as understood by Baxandall? The preceding section opened a question about the object of analysis in computer vision and, by extension, how contemporary viewers talk about that object. I noted above that in Baxandall's account of the period eye, 'cognitive style' maps onto 'pictorial style', but that this has trans-medial significance: paintings are made intelligible to audiences through concepts shared by artist and audience, but importantly, those paintings also become explicable in language.

Lev Manovich has defended the idea that computers offer not just a new, but a more precise vocabulary for describing the characteristics of analogue cultural artefacts.[47] In Manovich's view, the language of numbers is a 'better fit' than human languages in the measurement of artefact features such as sounds, colours, and spatial forms. This way of thinking about the impact of computer vision revives another old debate – one that concerns the relationship between word and image in hierarchies of the arts.[48] While this topic reached a height in Renaissance debates about the *paragone*, it is an issue that has come to the fore in various guises throughout histories of European art and art criticism. A recurring idea throughout the discussion is that human language can neither keep pace with aesthetic innovations in the plastic arts nor fully articulate the wide range of imaginative and sensory responses to them.

[45] Dretske, 'Introspection'.

[46] Dretske, 'Introspection'.

[47] Lev Manovich, 'Computer Vision, Human Senses, and Language of Art', *AI & Society*, 36 (2021), pp. 1145–52.

[48] See Linda Goddard, *Aesthetic Rivalries: Word and Image in France, 1880–1926* (Peter Lang, 2012).

Rather than debating a competition between human and computational languages, it is worth considering what it is that language is being asked to capture and express about the objects under discussion. Other chapters in the present volume examine the role of language in creating prompts for generative AI and extracting image descriptions from visual data.[49] Whereas text-to-image generation still entails the use of ordinary language as a stimulus for, or descriptor of, artworks or their style, Manovich champions the capacity of *mathematical* languages to articulate the characteristics of analogue artworks that are dematerialised into various data structures. Nuria Rodríguez-Ortega worries that the transformation of material objects into digital counterparts for this kind of analysis (and description) 'entails a dramatic change in the way we understand images considering that, until now images have been presented to our consciousness as visual entities unto themselves'.[50]

Rodríguez-Ortega is right to highlight a change in the artefact that is studied and ultimately described, but it must also be acknowledged that the use of a digital object in computational analysis is not an end in itself. Rather, the digital object can be understood as a surrogate that is used for the purpose of providing insight into its analogue counterpart, namely, the artwork. In consequence, it can be argued that there is no fundamental change in the object of analysis and that the digital surrogates studied by computer vision are merely ciphers of the analogue artwork that facilitate the gathering of enhanced information about that work.

How does this impact on Manovich's claim that computer vision offers a 'better' language for talking about art? One response is that it gives us a language for talking about the digital counterparts of art or, at least, a language that derives from such counterparts. This would make the computer vision study of data akin to conservation studies of the chemical composition of, say, a painted surface. Conservation studies have their own vocabularies and symbols for analysing and communicating information about the material qualities of artworks, yet these are not set in competition with other uses of language to articulate human sensory engagement with those objects. Indeed, conservation studies are alert to both interdisciplinarity and to different uses of language (metaphor, analogy, figurative language) to articulate the complexities of creating knowledge about artworks.[51] Why, then, are the languages of computer vision being set in competition with the diverse

[49] See, in particular, Nuria Rodríguez-Ortega (Chapter 5 of this volume) and Amalia Foka (Chapter 6 of this volume).

[50] Nuria Rodríguez-Ortega, 'Image Processing and Computer Vision in the Field of Art History', in *The Routledge Companion to Digital Humanities and Art History*, edited by Kathryn Brown (New York: Routledge, 2020), pp. 338–57 (p. 341).

[51] See, for example, Rebecca Gordan, 'Figurative Language, and the Artist's Voice in Contemporary Art Conservation', *Art Matters International Journal for Technical Art History*, 1 (2021), pp. 36–46; Robyn Sloggett, 'Expanding the Conservation Canon: Assessing Cross-Cultural and Interdisciplinary Collaborations in Conservation', *Studies in Conservation*, 54:3 (2009), pp. 170–83. https://doi.org/10.1179/sic.2009.54.3.170

ways in which humans typically use language to express their understanding of art and its meanings?

One reason this occurs in the emerging body of secondary literature on computer vision is the need to justify the use of technology in art historical analysis and to demonstrate how computers enhance the existing interpretative apparatus for the study of art. Often machines are posited as offering better insights than humans on the grounds that the information they receive eliminates human bias or even perceptual imprecision. David Stork argues, for example, that artworks pose 'profound problems that require sophisticated methods beyond those in traditional digital humanities' and that computer image analysis can, in some cases, solve art historical problems that defeat humans; in similar fashion, Bell and Offert argue that computer vision is ' "pure" vision, without any synesthetic interference'.[52] On the one hand, such statements stake a claim for the relevance of computer vision in the contemporary discipline of art history. On the other, they fuel a tension between the merits of human and machine analysis – one in which the human typically falls prey to sensory distortion and broad generalisations in the (inevitably failed) pursuit of 'objective' analysis.

The title of this section recalls Nelson Goodman's *Languages of Art*, a book that was published four years before Baxandall's *Painting & Experience in Fifteenth-Century Italy*.[53] In his book, Goodman developed a taxonomy of symbol systems. While it is beyond the scope of this chapter to discuss Goodman's work in detail, the point I want to make for the purpose of the present discussion is that, like Baxandall, Goodman mapped cognitive and visual information onto each other and, in so doing, embedded seeing in a wider social context. Advancing the view that the eye is never 'innocent', Goodman went further than Baxandall in defending a 'relativity of vision and of representation'.[54] Importantly, as noted by Alessandro Giovannelli, Goodman's elaboration of linguistic and non-linguistic symbols can be understood as 'having broken, in a non-superficial and fruitful way, the divide between art and science'.[55] The metaphors, similes, and symbols that humans typically apply in their interpretation of artworks are used in similar ways and purposes for crafting scientific descriptions of the world. Viewed in this light, computer vision may be an additional 'language of art', but not one that replaces, challenges, or diminishes the need for existing languages.

[52] Stork, 'Computer Vision, ML and AI in the Study of Fine Art', pp. 1–3; Bell and Offert, 'Reflections on Connoisseurship and Computer Vision', p. 3.

[53] Nelson Goodman, *Languages of Art: An Approach to the Theory of Symbols*, 2nd edn (Indianapolis: Hackett Publishing Company, 1976).

[54] Goodman, *Languages of Art*, p. 10. On this point, Goodman defers to the arguments of Ernst Gombrich in *Art and Illusion* (New York: Pantheon Books, 1960).

[55] Alessandro Giovannelli, 'Goodman's Aesthetics', in *The Stanford Encyclopedia of Philosophy* (Fall 2017), edited by Edward N. Zalta, https://plato.stanford.edu/archives/fall2017/entries/goodman-aesthetics

The new issue that does arise in this context, however, is one of intelligibility. In cases where art history is written by computer scientists, descriptions and analyses of artworks draw on concepts, symbols, and terms that, at first sight, are impenetrable to humanities researchers. This is often the case even where the goal of the investigation is understood and the artwork itself is familiar. This issue is more than a point about the challenges of interdisciplinary research. Rather, it raises questions about the kinds of speech community that are being developed to express the experience, description, and meaning of artworks. If Goodman's elaboration of the languages of art suggested a conceptual – and therefore linguistic – bridge between the arts and sciences, does the contemporary use of computer vision reinstate a divide between the ways in which audiences engage with and describe collective cultural heritage? The question is relevant to the role of computer vision in creating a 21st-century period eye because it raises an important point about the social conditions of art interpretation.

A new social contract?

If the case can be made that computer vision has introduced a new art historical episteme, who has the ability to bring that knowledge to bear on the interpretation of cultural artefacts and with what consequences for the practice of art history? On the one hand, the uses of AI in museum contexts have been associated by some commentators with a democratisation of historically elite spaces. This is clearest in literature about the integration of artificial conversational agents – chatbots – into museum settings. In these cases, the ability of audiences to talk to machines rather than humans and to curate their own experience of art collections has been connected to ideas of audience 'empowerment' and the avoidance of embarrassment in a potentially hierarchical educational setting.[56] It would go beyond the scope of the present chapter to debate this line of thinking, but it is worth noting the paradox that this 'democracy' reduces the plurality of voices in cultural communities where museums are transformed from social spaces into institutions that promote solitary experiences determined by machine functions.

Developing the idea that computer vision might nevertheless represent a democratisation of art history, it might be argued that because machine analysis works with digital images of artworks as opposed to physical artefacts, researchers are freed from the need to access objects that are in private collections, that are lost, or that require expensive travel for the purpose of study.[57] Not only can historians

[56] See, for example, O. Gustke, S. Schaffer, and A. Ruß, 'Exploring and Explaining Museum Objects with Speech-Based AI', in *AI in Museums: Reflections, Perspectives and Applications*, edited by S. Thiel and J.C. Bernhardt (Bielefeld: Transcript Verlag, 2024), pp. 357–64; G. Gaia, S. Boiano, and A. Borda, 'Engaging Museum Visitors with AI: The Case of Chatbots', in *Museums and Digital Culture: New Perspectives and Research*, edited by T. Giannini and J.P. Bowen (New York: Springer, 2019), pp. 309–29.

[57] See Brown, 'After Art History', pp. 33–4.

expand the range of works included in their research, but the financial playing field is levelled between researchers themselves, as there is less reliance on the need to view objects in situ. Yet this line of thinking quickly confronts limits. Conducting effective computer vision analyses of artworks requires the use of advanced technical resources (often supercomputers for greater speed), cloud computing, significant hours of collaboration between computer scientists and humanities scholars, and research funding. This means that the use of computer vision in arts subjects can only take place in those institutions with enough staff time and technical resources to undertake such projects.[58] Does this change the social fabric of art history as it is practised today? The question is relevant to the present discussion because it raises the final issue of whether computer vision is or is not generalisable over a wide enough demographic to constitute a 'period eye'.

While the aforementioned line of literature in discussions of AI and museums focuses on democratisation, other disciplines have shown a greater degree of scepticism on this subject. Jürgen Habermas has associated the rise of 'world dominating digital corporations' and the ensuing 'platformization' of political speech as a threat to the 'deliberative character of public opinion'.[59] Shifting the focus to the impact of technology on capital, Yannis Varoufakis uses the term 'technofeudalism' to address the power of multi-national tech businesses that have replaced owners of 'traditional capital' such as machinery, buildings, and infrastructure.[60] The new 'feudal overlords' are, he argues, the owners of cloud capital whose power derives from 'the epic ransacking of the internet commons, made possible by politicians, and then a sequence of spectacular technological inventions – from Sergey Brin's search engine [Google] to the dazzling array of today's AI applications'.[61]

As the use of computer vision in art historical research relies on the technologies, infrastructure, cloud computing services, and labour practices of large technology companies, the question arises as to whether the independence and ethics of art historical research may be compromised by the agendas of such companies (even where open-source resources are made available by them).[62] Yet Azar, Cox, and Impett argue that '[t]aking issues with the corporate machinery of machine vision is, for at least two reasons, an intrinsically slippery task'.[63] The first reason they identify lies in the difficulty of isolating and identifying the relevant pieces of corporate machinery; the second is that the

[58] See also Mansfield *et al.*, 'Techniques of the Art Historical Observer', p. 2.

[59] Jürgen Habermas, *A New Structural Transformation of the Public Sphere*, translated by Ciaran Cronin (Cambridge: Polity, 2023), pp. 38 and 59.

[60] Yannis Varoufakis, *Technofeudalism: What Killed Capitalism* (London: Vintage, 2024), p. xiii.

[61] Varoufakis, *Technofeudalism*, pp. 68–9.

[62] For further discussion, see Hito Steyerl's discussion of some of the ethical issues involved in the creation of image data sets such as LAION-5b (used to train Stable Diffusion) and other models including DALL·E and ChatGPT systems in 'Mean Images', *New Left Review*, 140/141 (March/June 2023), pp. 82–97.

[63] Azar *et al.*, p. 1102.

> demarcation lines of academia-versus-industry are blurred in this particular case (in contrast to, say, the denial of scientific results by the tobacco industry or the obscuring of connections by the oil industry to climate change, big tech has acknowledged – and in some cases tried to ameliorate – ethical issues around bias, inclusivity, though continues to play a major role in the defence industries).[64]

For Azar, Cox, and Impett, the result is an 'irresolvability' of the ethical, social, and political issues arising at the intersection of AI and humanities research.

On the one hand, the debate veers towards a techno-utopianism in which computer vision, machine learning, and AI are capable of driving art history forward, creating new languages for talking about art, and resolving 'art-historical debates that have proved resistant to traditional art-historical methods'.[65] On the other hand, more sceptical views suggest a need to reimagine the aims, styles of collaboration, and framing of computer vision in art history. For Amanda Wasielewski, this entails moving digital art history 'outside the technology-specific paradigm in which it has been placed'.[66]

For the purpose of the present chapter, the faultlines in this debate resonate, paradoxically, with one of the key social ideas that informs Baxandall's conception of the period eye, namely, the socially exclusive nature of that concept. If, as Baxandall argues, paintings are 'fossils of economic life', so too they are the means (technical, conceptual and social) of analysing them.[67] In the present context, researchers' ability simply to use AI technologies effectively in art historical analysis provides insight into contemporary features of economic life in and beyond the academy.

I noted above Baxandall's point that a Quattrocento cognitive style did not imply 'all fifteenth-century people, but … those whose response to works of art was important to the artist – the patronizing classes, one might say'.[68] To the extent that computer vision overlaps with Baxandall's notion of a period eye, it does so in the narrowness of the demographic capable of practising and accessing the interpretative precepts it sustains. The exclusivity of the period eye may be consistent from the 15th to the 21st century insofar as the use of computer vision is not a way of working that is open to all researchers, but it is no longer the artist who makes the demand for intelligibility. Rather, under current conditions, a period eye derived from computer vision likely emanates from computer science research and the funders (whether tech companies or research bodies) who promote that research. In this regard, it remains as exclusive as the period eye of the 15th century.

[64] Azar *et al.*, pp. 1102–3.
[65] Stork, 'Computer Vision, ML and AI in the Study of Fine Art', p. 68.
[66] Wasielewski, *Computational Formalism*, p. 138.
[67] Baxandall, *Painting and Experience*, p. 2.
[68] Baxandall, *Painting and Experience*, p. 38.

Conclusion

This chapter has debated whether computer vision can be understood to have inaugurated a new period eye for the 21st century. In order to make sense of that question, it has been necessary to understand some of the claims that are being made about the uses and possibilities of computer vision, including how the underlying technology relates to histories of human vision. I have argued that these two lines of thinking about human and machine vision need to be disentangled and that, by doing so, it is possible to arrive at a better understanding of how they relate to each other.

While the upshot of such disentanglement might suggest that computer vision does not shape or even mirror human vision such that it would constitute a 21st-century period eye, it might nevertheless be understood as a technology that is increasingly shaping research priorities and ways of approaching the interpretation of art. Much research in this field successfully and honestly confronts the limitations as well as the potential of undertaking AI-driven analyses of artworks. While computer vision is often described as an enhancement of the art historian's analytical toolkit, understanding its limitations becomes particularly important in order to avoid shaping research questions that only the machine can answer. As in other branches of AI (including the interpretation of the outputs of conversational agents), the data yielded by computer vision depend on further acts of human interpretation. Quantitative data thus add to a stock of visual information and do not constitute a definitive or reliable interpretation of an artwork in their own right. While the relationship between machines and humans continues to unfold and the possibilities of AI expand, the ambitions of imaginative, synthetic meaning-making derived from direct human engagement with visual artefacts remains paramount.

4

Digital Art History for Datasets: For an Iconology of AI

LEONARDO IMPETT

The cultural turn in artificial intelligence

A YEAR BEFORE the introduction of the iPhone, the art historian T.J. Clark asked what the role of art history might be in what he called the *age of image-machines*.[1] Today, screens and cameras are in our workplaces, our offices, our pockets – you may well be reading this text on such an image-machine, perhaps while its camera is pointed back at you, and it has certainly been written on one.

What do these machines see, and what do we see in and through them? Computer vision algorithms, which process visual information in an 'intelligent' way, have been the driving force behind the recent explosion in artificial intelligence (AI) technologies; and thus understandably a central focus of current debates on bias in AI.[2] But as soon as we consider the question of bias in vision – human or machine – we realise that the category of bias itself quickly becomes too narrow, or at least under-ambitious. In language models, bias is implicitly understood as the set of convictions and assumptions that the imaginary electronic author of an AI-generated text might be assumed to have. Culturally specific visual perception is always more insidious, having to do with subcutaneous ideology rather than stated opinion.

[1] Timothy J. Clark, 'Art History in an Age of Image-Machines', *EurAmerica*, 38:1 (2008), pp. 1–30; this is a published version of an oral presentation given in 2006.

[2] Computer vision is sometimes called machine vision; though this term often suggests a robotics or systems approach (i.e., an embodied machine with automatic vision, for instance in factory automation). Though current debates have shifted towards large language models, the 'deep learning' revolution is most often seen as having started in computer vision in the early 2010s; most famously with AlexNet, a deep convolutional neural network for image classification which won an image recognition challenge in 2012.

Proceedings of the British Academy, **285**, 69–86, © Authors 2025.

But situating the cultural vision of AI requires us to consider the visual culture of the millions, even billions, of example images from which such AI models 'learn' to see: so-called training datasets. Thankfully, past decades have seen the emergence of a set of practices precisely for studying the visual culture of millions of images: not just dataset critique, but digital art history. This chapter will ask whether, and how, these emergent practices of digital art history might help us address the enormous challenge of the visual culture of training data.

The ideological opacity of AI systems – the so-called 'black box' problem – often has to do with purposeful obfuscation, as in the invisible labour of data workers. Silicon Valley is continuously playing out the myth of the Mechanical Turk: the most recent of many such examples is *builder.ai*, a $1.5bn Microsoft-backed startup which collapsed in May 2025 when it was revealed that requests to its code-writing AI service were actually sent to a group of 700 coders in India.

But this opacity also speaks to the necessary complexity of the algorithms themselves. Computer vision was for decades the prime example of Moravec's Paradox, a phenomenon in AI research where apparently intellectual tasks (such as playing chess) are relatively easy to automate, while the 'simpler' cognitive skills of children or animals (navigating a room) were far more resistant to automation. Raw pixel values fed from cameras into computers appear, on the surface at least, to be relatively meaningless. Read them as a spreadsheet and you will struggle to say more than how bright and what colour the average pixel is. Highly sophisticated algorithms are required to go from pixel values to even the most basic forms of image recognition or understanding, though computer scientists are never quite sure what they mean by understanding or recognising an image. It is this group of systems that we call computer vision, and research into computer vision has long served as the main motivation for the connectionist (i.e., self-organising) neural network approaches to pattern recognition that have, since 2012, become synonymous with AI.[3]

Until recently, the majority of tasks computer vision had been expected to automate appeared to be relatively objective. Take, for instance, automatic vehicle registration plate (number/licence plate) recognition, first developed in the 1970s. We might be interested in studying the cultural biases of these systems – a system developed in the UK, say, might struggle to read a registration plate in Cyrillic or Arabic. But the clear definition of success and failure makes it straightforward to devise experiments that quantify these kinds of cultural biases. Though far more contested, facial recognition behaves, in this limited but important sense, in much the same way. The public debate around the ethics of facial recognition, which has started to lead to political pressure and even legislation,[4] emerges partly from

[3] James E. Dobson, *The Birth of Computer Vision* (Minneapolis: University of Minnesota Press, 2023).
[4] At time of writing, public use of face recognition has been banned in several parts of the US and partially banned (with exceptions for law enforcement) in the EU; several high-profile NGOs have supported a ban, including Amnesty and the Electronic Freedom Foundation.

several high-profile cases of mis-detected faces and subsequent wrongful arrests,[5] and partly from the well-documented racial bias in the accuracy of these systems.[6] The characterisation of bias, then, is built upon the epistemic clarity of the notion of 'mis-detection' (and therefore also accuracy) in facial recognition. A classifier which never makes mistakes – so the logic goes – would be without bias.

With the success of deep convolutional neural networks in the early 2010s, computer vision suddenly seemed able to detect new kinds of objects in photographs. In datasets such as PASCAL-VOC, ImageNet, and Microsoft COCO, computer vision systems trained on thousands or millions of images of objects (manually sorted into a pre-established taxonomy) learn to recognise these objects in unseen images, even in apparently new visual contexts. Computationally, object recognition is an extremely challenging task – we went to the Moon around four decades before we had reasonably robust visual object detection – but again, it is usually fairly straightforward to see when a particular algorithm has failed. In 2019, a team from Facebook AI Research found that common object recognition systems tend to perform better on images of household objects from the global North than those from the global South: it was suggested that, for instance, when attempting to detect tubes of toothpaste, the systems were implicitly also looking for the kind of tiled bathroom walls they had seen in their (Western) training data.[7] Here too this ability to characterise errors, or more precisely to agree on a definition of what an error might be within a particular task, has been the basis for many of the ways we have tackled bias in computer vision systems and AI more widely.

This line of reasoning has several important consequences which I would like to call into question. First, that bias is essentially to be found in the explicit *errors* of a computational image classifier. This is a practical definition for a computer scientist aiming explicitly to measure, and therefore perhaps reduce, the bias in a system; but it limits our view of biases to systems which can make mistakes (or more precisely, tasks for which the notion of a 'mistake' is relatively uncontroversial). Second, the solution to this kind of bias is also conceptually straightforward: to add to the training data many more examples from the underrepresented categories. This way of thinking about bias leads quickly to an extractivist position – the case of the Facebook image-recognition algorithm, for instance, might well be taken as a call to add to the training data millions of photographs of household objects taken

[5] One especially high-profile early case was the wrongful arrest of Robert Julian-Borchak Williams, a Black American man based near Detroit, which was claimed at the time to be perhaps 'the first known account of an American being wrongfully arrested based on a flawed match from a facial recognition algorithm'; see Kashmir Hill, 'Wrongfully Accused by an Algorithm', *New York Times*, 24 June 2020. https://www.nytimes.com/2020/06/24/technology/facial-recognition-arrest.html

[6] Joy Buolamwini and Timnit Gebru, 'Gender Shades: Intersectional Accuracy Disparities in Commercial Gender Classification', *Conference on Fairness, Accountability, and Transparency. Proceedings of Machine Learning Research*, 81 (2018), pp. 77–91.

[7] Terrance De Vries, Ishan Misra, Changhan Wang, and Laurens van der Maaten, 'Does Object Recognition Work for Everyone?', *Proceedings of the IEEE/CVF Conference on Computer Vision and Pattern Recognition Workshops* (2019), pp. 52–9.

in the global South. (In any case, we might be sceptical that a for-profit company would go to the expense; especially as there is a proven mathematical trade-off between overall performance and bias.)[8]

Bias, then, might be an insufficiently expansive term for the sort of situated perception we are dealing with. In truth, Facebook's study hinted at something far deeper, with wider consequences for how we understand AI: that all perception, and vision most of all, is always historically, socially, culturally, bodily, and politically contingent. This is no less true for machine visual perception than it is for our own; only the stakes in the case of a single computer vision algorithm, which might be deployed at huge global scale, are arguably far higher than those for a single person. In the case of object detection based on the 1,000 categories of the ImageNet-1k image classification challenge, for instance, even a system which performed equally well on images of the global South (but also by race, gender, age, income bracket) would be bound to the taxonomy of possible categories, which are largely either biological species or industrially manufactured consumer goods: 'Laptop', 'Truck', 'Polaroid Camera', and even 'Model T'. Thus – at least for the many instances trained in some way on ImageNet – computer vision systems have a fundamentally Fordist understanding of images. These systems' visual ideologies are informed by the structure of the taxonomy of the dataset, by the images chosen to represent it, and of course by the particular algorithms and architectures they choose to compress it.

Much excellent critical work has been done on the taxonomy of computer vision training datasets;[9] but in the past few years we have seen two shifts in the implicit epistemology of computer vision systems which complicates this understanding of algorithmic bias. First, a shift away from strictly taxonomic training data, with lists of possible objects to be detected. And second, away from problems which have even the pretence of objectivity. Computer vision research now attempts to automate tasks which seem to sit quite explicitly in the realm of subjective experience. Automatic visual aesthetic algorithms, for instance, try to estimate (on a scale from 1 to 10) how pretty a photograph will appear to the average viewer.[10] This task turns out to be automatable to a high degree of accuracy; though computer science's understanding of the term accuracy is unsettled in a paradoxical attempt to mechanise the most individual of human judgements. The algorithm's performance is perhaps better understood as a predictor of social psychology than of aesthetics.[11] I have argued elsewhere that this might have something to do with the stylistic

[8] Jon Kleinberg, Sendhil Mullainathan, and Manish Raghavan, 'Inherent Trade-offs in the Fair Determination of Risk Scores', arXiv preprint, arXiv:1609.05807 (2016).

[9] Kate Crawford and Trevor Paglen, 'Excavating AI: The Politics of Images in Machine Learning Training Sets', *AI & Society*, 36:4 (2021), pp. 1105–16.

[10] See Leonardo Impett, 'Prettiness Algorithms: Smartphones and the Manipulation of Taste', *Theory & Struggle*, 123:1 (2022), pp. 72–9.

[11] I am grateful to the anonymous peer reviewer for pointing out this formulation.

predictability of the photographers and image-labellers in the training data, the largest group of whom are middle-aged male amateur photographers from the US.[12]

But perhaps the clearest, and most widespread, example of this post-objective and post-taxonomic computer vision system is in multimodal networks, which associate pictures with sentences or digital image files with strings of letters. Systems such as OpenAI's CLIP are able to estimate the 'similarity' between any text string – 'a chair in the shape of an avocado', '$100', ':)' – and a digital image. It learns to do so from a dataset of images with free-text 'natural' language descriptions, often scraped from Alt Text (which describes an image for accessibility reasons, including for the figures in this chapter). These text–image similarity estimators then serve as the backbone of text-to-image generation systems, such as DALL·E and Stable Diffusion, and text-to-video systems such as SORA.

As Fabian Offert and I have argued at length elsewhere, 'multimodal' (text–image) AI thus completely overturns the epistemic foundations on which the discussion of bias in computer vision had been built, as there is clearly no right or wrong arrangement of pixel values that should correspond to a particular input text.[13] There are obviously more and less successful solutions, but in truth the image-generating system might choose from a huge family of possible images, each with their own cultural associations and nuances, and none quite free of bias, of a cultural viewpoint. A taxonomic image classifier might be free from 'bias' (in the technically limited sense) if it never made mistakes, but multimodal AI always carries with it a computational visual culture. There is no longer a computational view from nowhere.

Where is computer vision's somewhere, then? Northern California, perhaps, is too simple an answer. The most widely used open-source image-generation model, and therefore the model about which most is known, Stable Diffusion, is trained on the gargantuan LAION-5B dataset – itself named after its five billion images (in truth the figure is closer to six). It is then fine-tuned (tweaked) with an algorithm for automatic visual aesthetics, in order to make the output prettier.[14] For-profit systems tend to have more systems in place for reducing apparent 'bias', though they tend to operate not in terms of the model itself, but rather in terms of the interface. OpenAI's DALL·E, for instance, would at one point add keywords including 'woman', 'Africa', 'black', 'Asian', and 'female' to a user's input prompts, after concerns raised around the racial and gender stereotyping of much of its output (Figure 4.1).[15] As the result of what I suspect is a similar system, Google apologised

[12] See Leonardo Impett, 'Computation and Beauty', *The Photographers' Gallery: Unthinking Photography* (2024). https://unthinking.photography/articles/computation-and-beauty

[13] Leonardo Impett and Fabian Offert, 'There Is a Digital Art History', *Visual Resources*, 38:2 (2022), pp. 1–24.

[14] Impett, 'Computation and Beauty'.

[15] Fabian Offert and Thao Phan, 'A Sign that Spells: DALL-E 2, Invisual Images and the Racial Politics of Feature Space', arXiv preprint, arXiv:2211.06323 (2022).

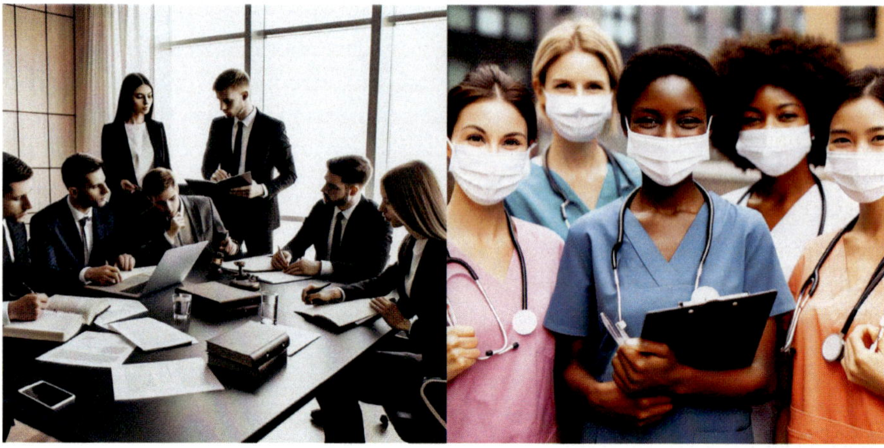

Figure 4.1 Bing image generator (based on OpenAI's DALL E 3) results for 'a group of lawyers' (left), 'a group of nurses' (right).

after its Gemini image generator seemed to add physiognomic diversity in any context, in what was referred to in the media as the 'Black Nazi' incident.[16]

Uncovering the visual ideologies behind complex computer vision algorithms entails, among other things, a deep exploration of the example images they 'learn' from: their training datasets. But how can we begin to study the implicit visual culture distributed through a computer vision's training dataset? Over the past decade, we have seen a rich development of practices and discourses around *dataset critique* which try to tackle this question – which have often emerged from artists or artist-scholar collaborations, rather than solely from within the academy.

Training data as photographic archive

In early 2021, I received a letter from Brazil. In it were two postcard-sized photographs. They were sent by the artist-scholars Gabriel Pereira and Bruno Moreschi, who were experimenting with new forms of engaging with large AI training datasets: they sent different images to a number of people during the COVID-19 pandemic whom they would go on to interview a few months later.[17] On the back of each photograph was the text: '1 imagem de 1.590.611 imagens'.[18]

[16] Nico Grant, 'Google Chatbot's A.I. Images Put People of Color in Nazi-Era Uniforms', *New York Times*, 22 February 2024. https://www.nytimes.com/2024/02/22/technology/google-gemini-german-uniforms.html

[17] Gabriel Pereira and Bruno Moreschi , 'Living with Images from Large-scale Data Sets: A Critical Pedagogy for Scaling Down', *photographies*, 16:2 (2023), pp. 235–61.

[18] One image of 1,590,611 images.

Pereira and Moreschi managed to convince me of something critical AI scholars had often hinted at, but rarely quite committed to: the continuity between the photographic archive and the AI image dataset. In doing so, they drew on the work of previous artists working to highlight, surface, expose, or materialise the 'raw' training data of computer vision models. Two exhibitions in London in 2019, for instance, showed large slices through the ImageNet dataset on its tenth anniversary; Trevor Paglen's 'From "Apple" to "Anomaly"' presented it spatially, with about 30,000 printed images, while Nicholas Malevé's 'Exhibiting ImageNet' showed all 14 million images on a computer screen over a period of about two months, giving each image less than a tenth of a second.[19]

Others have used computer vision to look through its own training datasets, turning it back on itself. The 'ImageNet Roulette' face recognition app, made by artist-scholars Trevor Paglen and Kate Crawford for an exhibition at the Fondazione Prada, used a model trained only on the many racist, misogynistic, and offensive training categories in ImageNet ('Orphan', 'Creep'); it generated sufficient public interest to lead to the removal of 600,000 images from the dataset.[20] Adam Harvey and Jules LaPlace's Exposing.AI, meanwhile, serves as a kind of search engine for training datasets – highlighting Flickr images used in training datasets for applications ranging from facial synthesis (i.e., deepfakes) to age, gender, or ethnicity detection.

Artists, then, have been at the forefront of the development of dataset critique; but it would be wrong to think that the technical research community has produced nothing of note. Scholars from Google Research have proposed data cards to accompany AI datasets,[21] based on Mitchell *et al.*'s notion of Model Cards[22] for trained AI models: standardised documents which outline the motivation, composition, and intended use of a model or dataset, with at least some consideration of possible ethical implications. Model and data cards have found some traction within industry, and a number of large technology companies – including Huggingface and OpenAI – currently publish cards for their trained models or datasets.[23] Very occasionally, datasets have even been released with their own exploration interfaces. Before its problematic categories came under closer public scrutiny following Paglen and Crawford's work, the ImageNet website featured a searchable interface that allowed users to browse images associated with specific labels.

[19] The arithmetic here might seem wrong; but the screen will regularly pause on a random image for a few seconds, otherwise switching every 90 ms.

[20] Crawford and Paglen, 'Excavating AI'.

[21] Mahima Pushkarna, Andrew Zaldivar, and Oddur Kjartansson, 'Data Cards: Purposeful and Transparent Dataset Documentation for Responsible AI', *Proceedings of the 2022 ACM Conference on Fairness, Accountability, and Transparency* (2022), pp. 1776–826.

[22] Margaret Mitchell, Simone Wu, Andrew Zaldivar, Parker Barnes, Lucy Vasserman, Ben Hutchinson *et al.*, 'Model Cards for Model Reporting', *Proceedings of the Conference on Fairness, Accountability, and Transparency* (2019), pp. 220–9. https://doi.org/10.1145/3287560.3287596

[23] The nurse/lawyer example shown in Figure 4.1 was first introduced in the datacard for the DALLE-2 model.

The LAION-5B dataset, on release, provided an image-search interface using the multimodal CLIP model.

Together these form, broadly speaking, two tendencies in dataset critique. One group of approaches turns its attention to the dataset's 'ontology': its structured set of categories, which usually underpin the training labels.[24] This strategy, adopted for instance by Paglen and Crawford, offers insights into the hierarchical organisation of knowledge within the dataset. It necessarily provides only a fragmentary glimpse into the dataset's visual culture, focusing on what the dataset is depicting (or rather what it claims to depict) and not how: tracing the form, rather than the content, of the training data. The second group attempts to delve into a specific subset of images, promising a kind of hermeneutics of a fragment of the dataset; this is the approach promised by Pereira and Moreschi, by Malevé, by Paglen's 'From "Apple" to "Anomaly" '. The obvious challenge becomes one of selection: which images do we choose and what do we look for within them?

We might attempt to reframe the question by reminding ourselves of the stakes; we are interested in the biases, in the culturally and historically situated mode of vision, and thus in the visual ethics and politics of computer vision systems. We are, in other words, attempting to reconstruct a particular way of seeing from a dispersed, distributed archive of visual evidence.

This sounds a lot like the foundational challenge of art history. 'Seeing as such has its own history', wrote Wölfflin in the *Grundbegiffe*, 'and uncovering these "optical strata" has to be considered the most elementary task of art history'.[25] Wölfflin's elementary task has been retheorised and reframed into a dozen other forms since: the period eye (Baxandall), ways of seeing (Berger), 'modes of human sense perception' (Benjamin), the history of artistic perception (Vygotsky), the scopic regime (Metz).[26] I have myself been involved in a research network called *Ways of Machine Seeing*;[27] and in this volume, Kathryn Brown explores and questions the notion of a machinic period eye.[28] Not only has art history long been interested in the history of vision, but in developing a practice for reconstructing a social history of perception through historical artefacts: pictures, yes, but also (for instance in the work of Svetlana Alpers or Jonathan Crary) optical machinery.[29]

[24] This refers to a specific technical meaning of ontology (the taxonomy of possible relations that can be saved in a dataset) rather than, say, as a branch of metaphysics.

[25] Heinrich Wölfflin, *Principles of Art History: The Problem of the Development of Style in Early Modern Art*, translated by Jonathan Blower (Los Angeles: Getty Publications, 2015), p. 93.

[26] Michael Baxandall, *Painting and Experience in Fifteenth-Century Italy* (Oxford: Oxford University Press, 1972); John Berger, *Ways of Seeing* (London: Penguin Books, 1972); Walter Benjamin, 'The Work of Art in the Age of Mechanical Reproduction', in *Illuminations*, edited by Hannah Arendt, translated by Harry Zohn (New York: Schocken Books, 1969, originally published 1935); Lev Vygotsky, *The Psychology of Art* (Cambridge, MA: MIT Press, 1971, originally published 1925); Christian Metz, *The Imaginary Signifier* (Bloomington, IN: Indiana University Press, 1986, originally published 1976).

[27] Mitra Azar, Geoff Cox, and Leonardo Impett, 'Introduction: Ways of Machine Seeing', *AI & Society*, 36 (2021), pp. 1093–104.

[28] Kathryn Brown, Chapter 3 of this volume.

[29] Jonathan Crary, *Techniques of the Observer* (Cambridge, MA: MIT Press, 1990).

What I am proposing, then, is to no longer see datasets through the tired and highly depoliticised conceptual categories of AI ethics (fairness, accountability, or transparency), but rather to dig a little deeper into the culturally situated perception of computer vision: into its immanent ideology of vision. This requires an investigation into the visual culture of training datasets which penetrates beyond mere questions of *what* is depicted (as is often tackled in technical discussions of dataset bias), but rather takes this as a starting point for their symbolic and ideological values. After dataset critique, we need dataset iconology.[30]

The dataset as atlas

Malevé's 2019 work at the Photographer's Gallery took two months to cycle rapidly through ImageNet's 14 million images. LAION-5B would take around 70 years at the same pace. Nicholas Mirzoeff has long cited the analogous problem for photographic historians that more photographs are taken every two minutes in the United States alone than in the entire 19th century.[31]

Even if we accept the basic resonance between the task of art history and that of dataset critique – the cultural analysis of a large and somewhat heterogenous image corpus – the inhuman scale of contemporary training datasets constrains our methodological options. We cannot hope to uncover the visual culture of a neural network by becoming connoisseurs of the six billion images in LAION; what we need instead is an art historical practice for reading across millions or even billions of images. An art history of the dataset, in other words: precisely the challenge that *digital art history* has been attempting to tackle.

The relationship here is reflexive, in that digital art history often uses computer vision to arrange the objects of its analysis.[32] Method and object of study become dangerously entangled: if we are going to use computer vision to study training datasets, will we not be limited to studying phenomena that are, so to speak, already inside the visual logic of the neural network? Here we might try to think through the convergence between the *fototeca* (the art historical photographic archive) and

[30] The definition of iconology is notoriously slippery; it is the final stage of symbolic analysis (after recognition and iconographical) in Erwin Panofsky, *Studies in Iconology* (Oxford: Oxford University Press, 1939), although more influential in contemporary discussions is Aby Warburg's more capacious – but perhaps more slippery – notion of a 'critical iconography' in Aby Warburg, 'Italian Art and International Astrology in the Palazzo Schifanoia', in *The Renewal of Pagan Antiquity: Contributions to the Cultural History of the European Renaissance*, translated by David Britt (Los Angeles: Getty Research Center for the History of Art and the Humanities, 1999; originally published 1912), pp. 563–91 (p. 569). For a more detailed discussion on the relationship between computer vision and iconography and iconology, see Peter Bell and Leonardo Impett, 'Ikonographie und Interaktion: Computergestützte Analyse von Posen in Bildern der Heilsgeschichte', *Das Mittelalter*, 24:1 (2019), pp. 31–53.

[31] Nicholas Mirzoeff, *How to See the World* (London: Pelican, 2015).

[32] Although it may just as well use human annotations, image metadata, or indeed lower-level image processing algorithms.

the training dataset in the other direction. When we look at an art historical archive through a computer vision algorithm, we learn something not just about the archive and the objects therein, but about the algorithm itself. In digital art history, we are, in fact, studying *two* visual corpora through each other: the art historical collection and the visual training dataset.[33] If, as in the most exciting current computer science research into fairness and bias, we simply turn computer vision back on itself – for instance, by automatically classifying the gender bias of LAION – we risk assessing computer vision only on its own terms, collapsing this fruitful tension. Instead, we must try to invert it: seeing the training dataset, if not through an algorithm trained on an art historical collection, then at least with an attentiveness to modes of reading that run against the taxonomies of training datasets.

This may all sound rather abstract, and a practical example might be useful. My first experiment in digital art history, with the literary scholar Franco Moretti, was on the subject of gesture; we had attempted to 'operationalise' Aby Warburg's theory of the Pathosformel, a sort of contagious gestural formula for the expression of pathos. We established an algorithm for the Pathosformel; one which we applied on Warburg's own image collection, the *Bilderatlas*, to which we will return.[34] At first this was done manually; but eventually, the algorithm used computer vision to study the articulations of bodies in images.[35] By taking it as, so to speak, an art historical algorithm, we might use it to read the gestural iconography of the reference datasets of computer vision (LAION, COCO, ImageNet).

It is impossible to imagine 'reading' features over image datasets today without thinking, in some way, through the work of Lev Manovich over the past two decades. Manovich has often worked through what he has called direct visualisation, which can be thought of at the most basic level as a plot in which data points are replaced by the images they represent. The method itself draws upon works of media art such as Brendan Dawes' *Cinema Redux* (2004), which chains together film stills taken every second into a kind of feature-length film strip.

Scale is a recurring protagonist in his work: in his 2015 paper 'Data Science and Digital Art History', for instance, Manovich presents a number of methodological approaches for dealing with one million manga images, one million artworks of non-professional artists, and over 13 million Instagram images – almost the size of ImageNet.[36] When others have developed Manovichian visualisations

[33] For a more detailed development of this argument, see Leonardo Impett, 'Digital Art History as Critical AI', *The Art Bulletin*, 106:2 (2024), pp. 11–14; and Impett and Offert, 'There Is a Digital Art History'.

[34] Curiously enough, one of the few times I have not relied on some kind of direct visualisation: Leonardo Impett and Franco Moretti, 'Totentanz: Operationalizing Aby Warburg's Pathosformel', *New Left Review*, 107 (2017), pp. 68–97.

[35] Leonardo Impett, 'Analyzing Gesture in Digital Art History', in *The Routledge Companion to Digital Humanities and Art History*, edited by Kathryn Brown (Abingdon: Routledge, 2020), pp. 386–407. Valentine Bernasconi later developed the technique to study hand gestures. See Valentine Bernasconi, Eva Cetinić, and Leonardo Impett, 'A Computational Approach to Hand Pose Recognition in Early Modern Paintings', *Journal of Imaging*, 9:6 (2023), p. 120.

[36] Lev Manovich, 'Data Science and Digital Art History', *International Journal for Digital Art History*, 1 (2015), pp. 13–35.

of datasets, they have often done so through an interest in scale: Cyril Diagne and Simon Doury's Curator Table for Google Arts and Culture (2017) shows six million images from the Google Arts and Culture collection.[37]

The most surprising echoes of Manovich's work, however, are found beyond digital art history (Figure 4.2). Possibly without knowing it, computer scientists are already effectively borrowing Manovich's techniques, or at least developing analogous ones in a kind of convergent evolution. Google's Tensorboard, a visualisation tool for training neural networks which is part of the popular Tensorflow deep learning platform, includes a direct visualisation of images in an embedding-space which might not look out of place in a digital humanities journal. Once again, the gap between digital art history and the cultural analysis of computer vision systems is far smaller than we have tended to assume.

In 2020, researchers from OpenAI working on 'structural phenomena' in early-stage visual processing within neural networks produced, once again, something approaching a cultural analytics of an image corpus. In this case we have a subsequent evolution where the images do not come (directly) from a training dataset; rather they are synthetic images created to show the maximum activations of particular neurons. This is an exciting way of probing a neural network, since its visual perception is influenced not only by its training dataset, but also by its architecture. They are what the German filmmaker Harun Farocki called *operational* images – images which, in Trevor Paglen's formulation of Farocki's concept, rather than 'simply representing things in the world … "do" things in the world'.[38] These synthetic diagnostic images capture both, as do the huge numbers of images computed by recent diffusion-based multimodal generative models (DALL·E, Stable Diffusion, etc.). The boundary between these pictures and training datasets is itself blurred by the common use of synthetic images as training data. An iconology of AI, then, will have to deal with image-expanses of both real and synthetic images, which appear at *every* stage of a neural network.

My own 2DCLIP project[39] (Figure 4.3) attempts to play on this resonance by showing a direct visualisation embedding of any image dataset in the same tool – though users can upload their own images, preloaded examples consist of both art historical collections and AI training datasets (including subsets of both ImageNet and LAION). Though I remain committed to the potential of multimodal image features, they face the same basic challenge as the image-maps I have discussed above: the scale has slipped away from us. We can reasonably explore a map of tens of thousands of images through a computational interface, as in Yale's PixPlot, glancing at each one. Rendering a few million (as in Google's Curator Table) is technically possible,[40] but we start to treat it like the Earth on Google Maps, zooming into a few potentially interesting corners but relying on ourselves rather than on

[37] https://experiments.withgoogle.com/curator-table

[38] Trevor Paglen, 'Operational Images', *e-flux*, 59 (2014).

[39] Impett and Offert, 'There Is a Digital Art History'.

[40] Already a challenge for direct visualisation – as Manovich (2015) notes, 'no popular commercial or free image management or sharing software or web service can even show that many images together in a single screen'.

(a)

(b)

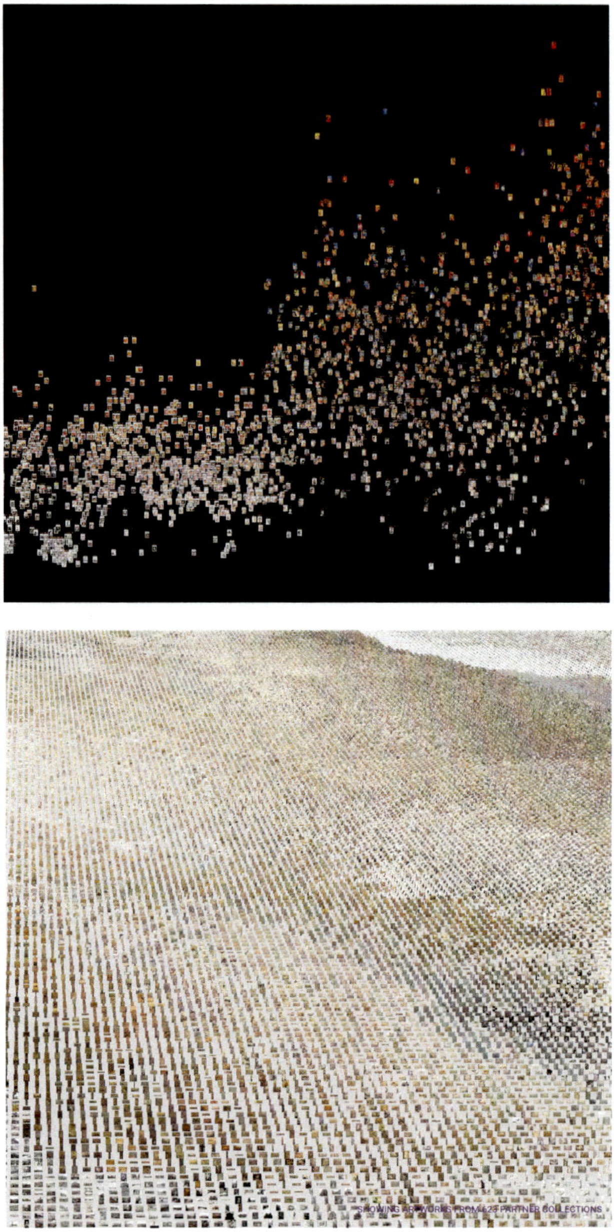

Figure 4.2 Direct visualisation, (a) Lev Manovich's visualisation of *Time Magazine* covers (2009)[41]; (b) Google Arts and Culture's Curator Table (2017); (c) OpenAI's Neural Activation visualisations (2021)[42]; (d) Google Tensorboard's embedding projector.[43]

[41] Lev Manovich, 'What Is Visualization?', *Visual Studies*, 26:1 (2011), pp. 36–49.

[42] Chelsea Voss, Gabriel Goh, Nick Cammarata, Michael Petrov, Ludwig Schubert, and Chris Olah, 'Branch Specialization', *Distill* (2021). https://distill.pub/2020/circuits/branch-specialization/

[43] https://github.com/seraj94ai/TensorBoard-Embedding-Visualization-TensorFlow-MNIST-/

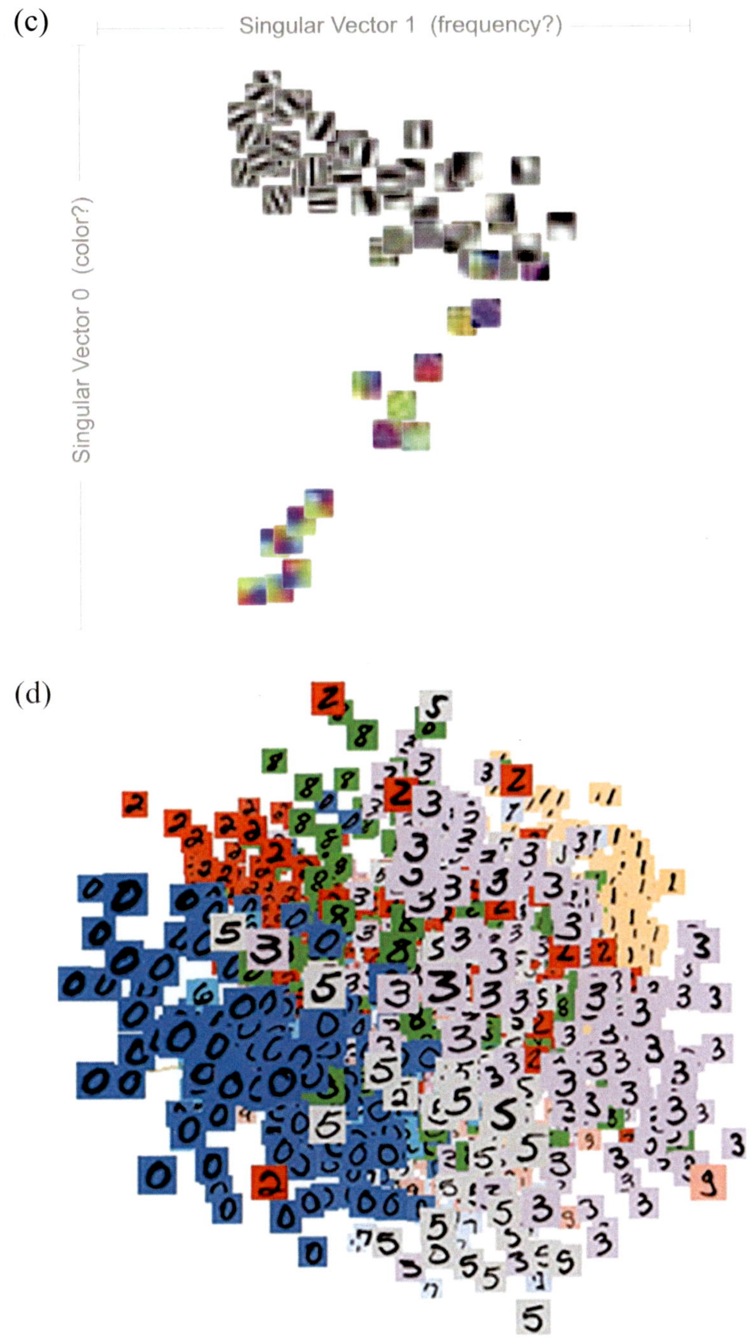

Figure 4.2 (*Continued*)

(a)

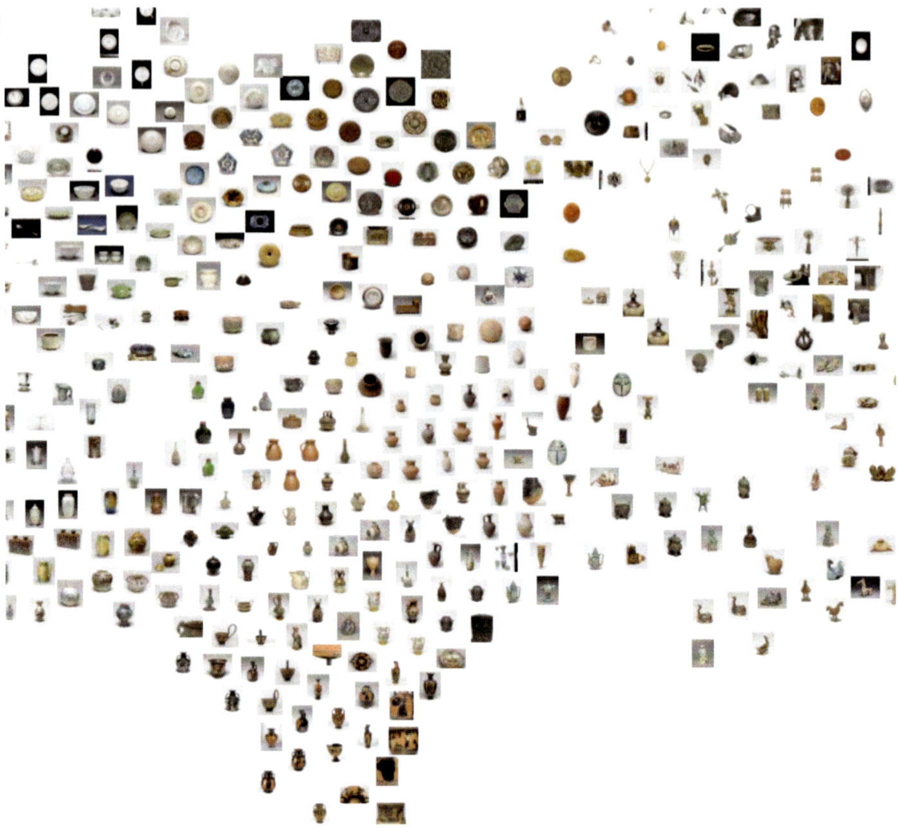

Figure 4.3 2DCLIP visualisations of subsets of (a) the digitised collection of the Fitzwilliam Museum, University of Cambridge, and (b) the ImageNet-1k training dataset, arranged by UMAP-reduced CLIP embeddings.

the large-scale topography – which has been computed for us – for our understanding of the dataset as a whole. Even if we could load six billion images onto one webpage, we would – ironically enough – have to effectively place our trust in the arrangement of images by a computer vision algorithm.

W.J.T. Mitchell, the great proponent of *Bildwissenschaft* (image sciences) in the Anglosphere, has attempted to trace the intellectual antecedents of Manovich's work and of other image-assemblages. Mitchell sees echoes of André Malraux's *musée imaginaire*, which Nicholas Malevé had already connected to AI training datasets.[44] Malraux comments, for instance, on the amnesia of scale in photography,

[44] Nicolas Malevé, 'On the Dataset's Ruins', *AI & Society*, 36:4 (2021), pp. 1117–31.

(b)

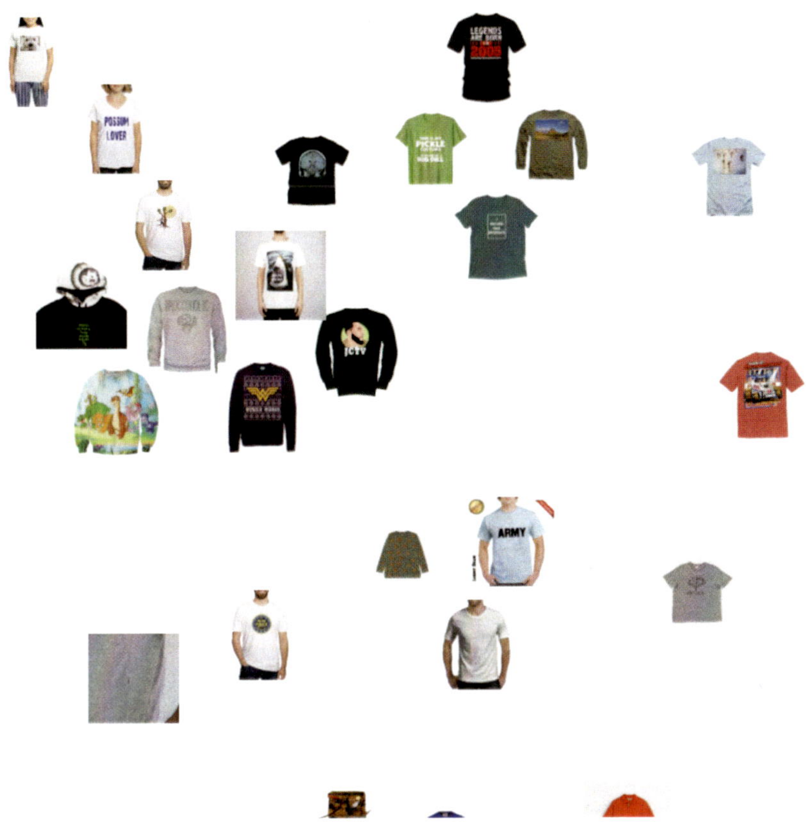

Figure 4.3 (*Continued*)

such that 'works of art use their relative proportions; a miniature bulks as large as a full-size picture'.

The central precursor of Manovich and cultural analytics, for Mitchell, is Aby Warburg and his unfinished *Bilderatlas*, a set of roughly 1,000 images assembled over 60 panels in the late 1920s. Mitchell is by no means the first to emphasise the resonance between Warburg and the digital humanities. In the years since my own computational work on Warburg, Amanda du Preez echoes Griselda Pollock in declaring Warburg a 'thinking machine' for Digital Art History,[45] with the *Bilderatlas* as a kind of prototype for computational methods; while Naja le Fevre Grundtmann reads the 'monistic' digitisation of the *Bilderatlas* as a cautionary

[45] Amanda Du Preez, 'Approaching Aby Warburg and Digital Art History: Thinking through Images', *The Routledge Companion to Digital Humanities and Art History,* edited by Kathryn Brown (Abingdon: Routledge, 2020), pp. 374–85 (p. 374).

case: 'Automated pattern recognition across large quantities of images is irreconcilable with Warburg's comparative juxtaposition of images.'[46] But Mitchell is interested in the nature of the spaces, including Manovich's computational image-maps, in which images are displayed *en masse* – what is the nature of the *Bilderatlas* as a space? Warburg is often lauded for reaching beyond 'high' art – studying, as he saw it, not merely the flowers, but the subterranean roots, of visual culture – and his source material is often as eclectic as a training dataset: coins, stamps, newspaper photographs of zeppelins, adverts, and so forth. In an important early lecture on the astrological cycle of Palazzo Schifanoia, Warburg called for an 'extension of the methodological borders of our study of art, in both material and spatial terms'; and part of this extension was to see all registers of visual culture as 'equivalent documents of expression'.[47] Already on this level there is something Warburgian about a concern with the visual culture of training datasets – not just Hito Steyerl's 'poor images'[48] but the mundane, the quotidian, the banal: the many millions of screenshots of presentation slides, for instance, that make up a large chunk of LAION.[49]

But the connections to critical AI, in truth, run much deeper than a concern with visual culture beyond art. A key concept for Warburg – according to Didi-Huberman, the *central* concept – is the notion of a '*Nachleben*' (after-life) of images. We are not dealing here with images that survive because of an historical coincidence, or with motifs or styles resurrected out of nostalgia; the *Nachleben* is, rather, a kind of spectral renewal, 'ghostly and symptomatic'.[50] How better to describe the training images which are occasionally regurgitated, half-remembered, by glitching neural networks (Figure 4.4)? Less visually striking but perhaps more important is the wider and subtler *Nachleben* in training datasets: the many millions of images forming a space of visual possibility from which the worldview of the neural network emerges.

In the unfinished introduction to the *Bilderatlas*, also called the *Atlas Mnemosyne* (after Mneme, the muse of memory), Warburg talks of uncovering the relationship between a highly distributed, interconnected form of image-memory (the '*Eindruckserbmasse*', something like an inherited mass of impressions) and the historical psychology of expression. For Kurt Forster, Warburg understood the Mneme as emerging 'from a sea of forgetting' into an 'archipelago of data'. The *Bilderatlas*, then, is an experimental apparatus for building upon a vast image-expanse in order to reconstruct historically situated modes of imaging. The basic challenge of critical computer vision scholarship today is to reconstruct the *Eindruckserbmasse* of training data.

[46] Naja le Fevre Grundtmann, 'Digitising Aby Warburg's Mnemosyne Atlas', *Theory, Culture & Society*, 37 (2020), pp. 3–26.

[47] Warburg, 'Italian Art and International Astrology in the Palazzo Schifanoia', p. 585.

[48] Hito Steyerl, 'In Defense of the Poor Image', *e-flux*, 10:11 (2009).

[49] See Christo Buschek and Jer Thorp, *Models All the Way Down*, Knowing Machines Project. https://knowingmachines.org/models-all-the-way

[50] Georges Didi-Huberman, Vivian Rehberg, and Boris Belay, 'Artistic Survival: Panofsky vs. Warburg and the Exorcism of Impure Time', *Common Knowledge*, 9:2 (2003), pp. 273–85 (p. 274).

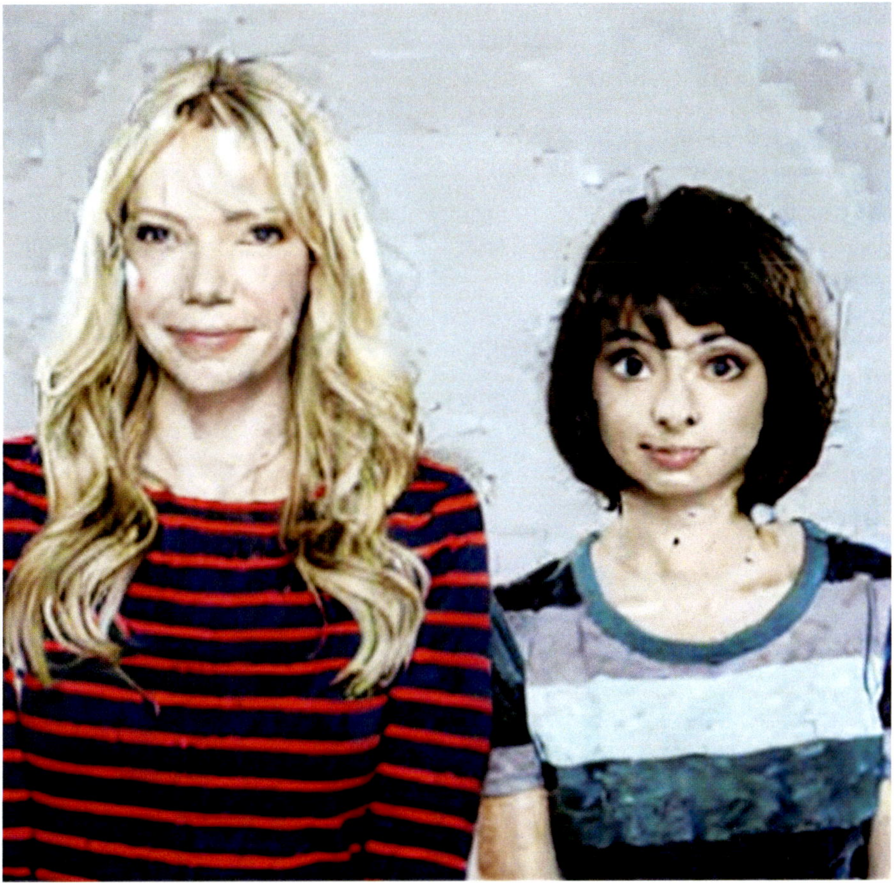

Figure 4.4 *Nachleben* in the neural network: a photo of comedy duo Garfunkel and Oats, one of many images found by researchers to have been partially remembered by a diffusion model from its training dataset.[51]

My intention here is not to claim a false equivalence between the *Bilderatlas* and the project of dataset critique. Most of the *Bilderatlas*'s thousand or so images, after all, are images from European art history – while Warburg's own writing (and thinking) is often so contradictory and ambiguous that the meaning of a 'Warburgian' approach is still highly contested. But I am suggesting that as digital art history asserts its usefulness for dataset critique, and thus for critical AI more generally, it must face up to the problem of scale in a new way. Rather like Borges' famous joke about a map so detailed it could not be made smaller than the size of

[51] Nicolas Carlini, Jamie Hayes, Milad Nasr, Matthew Jagielski, Vikash Sehwag, Florian Tramèr *et al.*, 'Extracting Training Data from Diffusion Models', *32nd USENIX Security Symposium* (2023).

the empire, much of our current work in digital art history relies on simulating a space large enough to map out every image in the corpus we are working with. This basic assumption is now untenable. At the scale of modern training datasets, with each datapoint represented by an ever-smaller image and eventually a single pixel, our atlases and direct visualisations collapse back into regular scatterplots. In confronting the vast scale of contemporary training datasets, we must abandon our panoptic ambition – itself an uncomfortable echo of the colonial project of a universal museum – and instead navigate these image-corpora through partial, interdependent perspectives. Instead, an iconology of training datasets might therefore proceed, like the *Bilderatlas*, from an assemblage of highly detailed views, embracing the fragmentary and the situated.

5

Ekphrasis Reloaded: An Enquiry into the Word–Image Relationship in the Post-Semiotic Era

NURIA RODRÍGUEZ-ORTEGA

THE PROMPT AND the corresponding AI-generated image depicted in Figure 5.1 represent one of my initial encounters with generative text–image models. Upon observing the outcome, my immediate impression was that I was confronted with an inverted form of traditional ekphrasis, the verbal description of an image or visual object. Indeed, the word–image relationship appears to be structured in such a way: the text serves as the starting point for the production of an image, with the latter presented as its visual representation or materialisation. This initial observation prompted a series of questions: Is this a genuine ekphrastic relationship, but in reverse? Is the generative image really a visual representation of a verbal description? What role does the linguistic text play in the generation of the image? Are we still dealing with an image, or has a different kind of semiotic sign emerged, albeit of a visual nature?

As I explored these questions, I found myself revisiting intellectual problems that were central to debates that emerged during the so-called linguistic turn and, later, the visual turn in art history. I came to realise that multimodal models (text-to-image and image-to-text), beyond their generative capabilities, offer a privileged field for re-problematising the word–image relationship, the interaction between the linguistic and the visual, through a new AI-mediated lens. This perspective is far from trivial, especially when considering Vilém Flusser's postulation that language and image are not merely two systems of representation, but two distinct modes of mediation between human beings and their environment – two ways of understanding the world.[1]

[1] Vilém Flusser, *Towards a Philosophy of Photography*, translated by Anthony Mathews (London: Reaktion Books, 1999).

Proceedings of the British Academy, **285**, 87–115, © Authors 2025.

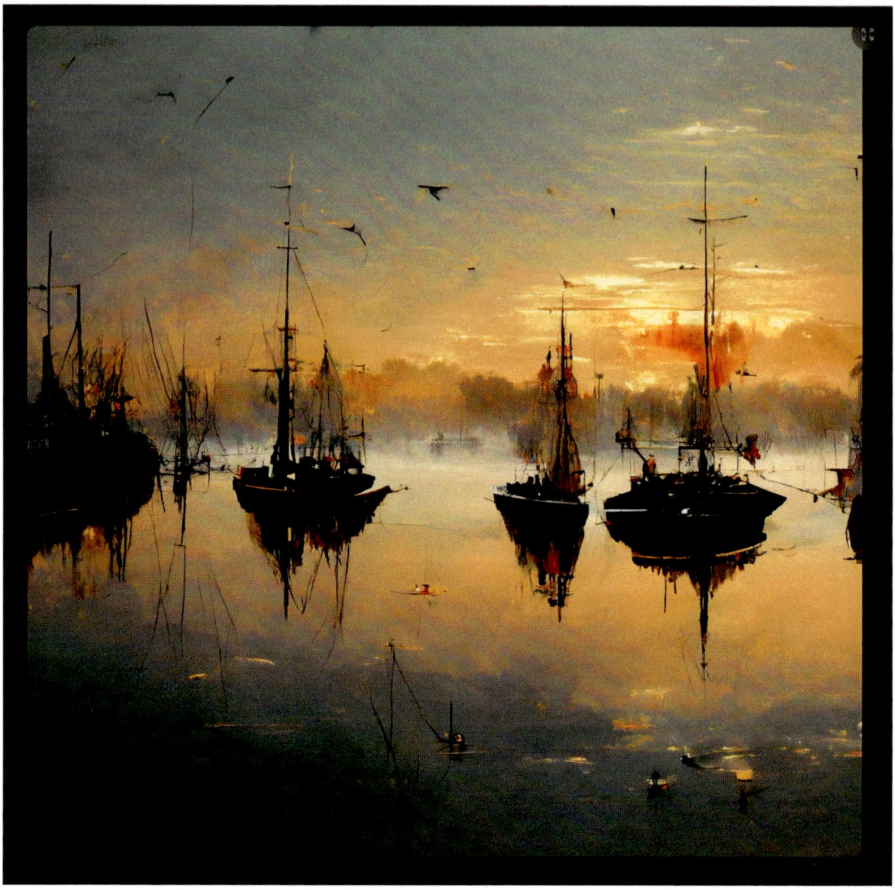

Figure 5.1 Image generated with Midjourney from the prompt 'A harbour at sunset, with several sailboats anchored on calm waters, and seagulls flying over the boats'. Source: Author. © Nuria Rodríguez-Ortega

The emergence of generative AI models has sparked considerable intellectual discussion regarding new modes of producing cultural objects, especially images, which directly affects the field of art history as the discipline dedicated to the cultural study of images (among other issues). Since multimodal models gained popularity with the launch of text-to-image systems such as DALL·E, Midjourney, and Stable Diffusion in 2022, reflections and research on AI generative models have multiplied. However, one perspective that has received less attention – and which is the focus of this chapter – is the reformulation of the theoretical framework concerning the word–image relationship and its implications for art historical research. In this context, the aim of this chapter is to explore some of the conceptual transformations that the word–image relationship is undergoing within a new semiotic framework, which I term *post-semiotic*. This analysis is grounded in the concept of ekphrasis, understood as the dialectical relationship between words and images.[2]

Ekphrasis as a theoretical problem: a brief overview

According to the conventional definition, ekphrasis is a rhetorical device employed in classical literature that uses language to describe images or visual artefacts, thereby creating a vivid mental representation in the receiver's imagination. This form of ekphrasis, conceived as a tool for visual evocation through language, has been practised throughout history, from antiquity to the present day, and constitutes one of the central objects of research in the field of art history. However, this chapter builds on the broader concept of ekphrasis articulated during the last third of the 20th century, namely, a dialectical relationship between semiotic systems – particularly linguistic and visual. This expanded understanding extends the concept of ekphrasis beyond the realm of poetic-literary descriptions of visual works to encompass any interaction or correspondence between visual objects and verbal texts, ultimately becoming a constitutive pillar of the discipline of art history and art criticism.

In the course of the 20th century, ekphrasis was re-examined within various theoretical frameworks, including language theory, hermeneutics, representation critiques, and visual and media studies. This led to a reconceptualisation of ekphrasis, moving away from its exclusive literary dimension towards a perspective that emphasised its status as a problem of intersemiotic relations. As a result, the concept of ekphrasis evolved from a literary technique used to describe visual works into an intellectual tool for investigating the complex semiotic relationships between diverse media and representational systems at a time when the boundaries between media were becoming increasingly permeable and fluid.

In his seminal 1991 work, James A.W. Heffernan defined ekphrasis as 'the verbal representation of a visual representation'.[3] As observed, in this definition the concepts of poetry, literature, and artistic work were subsumed within a broader contextual framework. In his monograph *Museum of Words* (1994), Heffernan further argued that ekphrasis is not merely a descriptive strategy or technique; rather, it is a mediating practice between two forms of representation – visual and verbal – that are inherently in tension due to their distinct medial natures.[4] In this new era,

[2] It was only after the completion of this text that Hannes Bajohr's recent publication 'Operative Ekphrasis: The Collapse of the Text/Image Distinction in Multimodal AI' (*Word & Image*, 40:2 (2024), pp. 77–90), came to my attention. Therefore, the proposals on ekphrasis discussed in that work could not be incorporated into the discussions in this chapter, although other ideas presented by Bajohr in earlier writings have been considered.

[3] James A.W. Heffernan, 'Ekphrasis and Representation', *New Literary History*, 22:2 (Spring 1991), pp. 297–316.

[4] James A.W. Heffernan, *The Museum of Words: The Poetics of Ekphrasis from Homer to Ashberry* (Chicago, IL: The University of Chicago Press, 1994).

the scope of ekphrasis expanded theoretically as well. Understanding ekphrasis as a mediating practice prompted a shift away from its traditional directionality (from image to text) toward a focus on interactions, tensions, convergences, and negotiations – areas of enquiry that would become central in the years to come. In this way, the problem of ekphrasis evolved into a subfield within the broader investigation of the relationship between words and images.

A key contribution to this field came from W.J.T. Mitchell, whose foundational work *Picture Theory* (1994) delves deeply into the relationship between language and image.[5] Mitchell's approach understands ekphrasis as one manifestation of a broader phenomenon: the constant interaction between language and image that occurs in all forms of visual and textual art. His now-classic concept, 'iconotextuality', which described the interdependent coexistence of word and image, responded to this idea. Mitchell argued that the relationship between the visual and the verbal is not a straightforward act of translation from one medium to another. Instead, it is a complex dialectic characterised by a dynamic interplay of power and competition between two semiotic systems that interact, create tension, complement, or contradict each other in intricate ways. As Derrida had also argued in his deconstruction of the limits between word and image, the relationship between these two semiotic systems is not rigid but dynamic and full of tensions – an interdependent 'game' in which the impossibility of an absolute separation between the forms of representation is constantly manifested.[6]

As a consequence of this approach, the issue of distinction, equivalence, or similarity between words and images became pivotal, not solely as a means of demarcation, but rather as an exploration of their diverse forms of interaction and intersection. Mitchell asserts that no medium is entirely autonomous. The notion that there are 'pure' semiotic systems or media – such as a purely visual image or a purely linguistic word – turned into a fallacy. All media or semiotic systems are inherently mixed, incorporating visual and/or linguistic features, even if these are not explicit or immediately apparent.

From another perspective, in his 1967 work *Grammatology*, Derrida had already posited that writing should be considered a form of 'image' due to its representational capacity, just as images possess a 'textual' quality in their ability to communicate and signify.[7] This explains why both Mitchell and Derrida argue that the problem of the word–image relation cannot be established on the basis of intersemiotic comparisons between distinct and independent systems. Instead, it must be understood through the lens of their complex interplay and the effect (or production of meanings) to which this dialectic gives rise. As a logical consequence, ekphrasis was no longer regarded as a mere act of description, but as an act of meaning production in which language and image intertwine, generating a hybrid

[5] W.J.T. Mitchell, *Picture Theory: Essays on Verbal and Visual Representation* (Chicago, IL: The University of Chicago Press, 1994).

[6] Jacques Derrida, *The Truth in Painting*, translated by Geoffrey Bennington and Ian McLeod (Chicago, IL: The University of Chicago Press, 1987).

[7] Jacques Derrida, *De la grammatologie* (Paris: Les Éditions de Minuit, 1967).

visual-verbal experience. In this manner, meaning is understood as an emergent phenomenon, arising from the interactions and negotiations between media through a dialogic process.[8]

Art history and criticism as forms of ekphrasis

The new formulation of ekphrasis also extended to the fields of critical discourse and art historical interpretation. Defining ekphrasis as the dialectic relationship between different representational or media systems, particularly between language and image, led to the logical corollary that art history and art criticism could be conceived as forms of ekphrastic practice. After all, art history and art criticism have always been an attempt to interpret, understand, and render visual works intelligible through text and language. In other words, there has always been an interaction between the visual and the written, layered with multiple levels of meaning.

In the 1990s, this approach converged with postmodern and post-historical approaches in Hayden White's *Metahistory*, a study that understood history as a narrative construction inextricably linked to the act of writing and thus to language.[9] In this context, it was argued that the discipline of art history was inherently tied to the linguistic and narrative processes that underpin it.[10] Donald Preziosi posited that the act of 'reading' visual images in art history is, in fact, a process of textual and discursive construction.[11] Similar to ekphrasis, historiographic discourse in art creates a 'textual image' of visual works, combining descriptive, explanatory, and interpretative elements that imbue the image with new meaning. Michael Baxandall asserted that 'we explain pictures only to the extent that we have considered them in the light of some kind of verbal description or specification'.[12] David Carrier

[8] See, among others, Roland Barthes, *Image, Music, Text* (New York: Hill and Wang, 1977); Mieke Bal, *Double Exposures: The Subject of Cultural Analysis* (New York: Routledge, 1996); Juan Antonio Ramírez, *Historia y crítica del arte: fallas (y fallos)* (Madrid: Ediciones del Serbal, 1998); Jean-Luc Nancy, *Au fond des images* (Paris: Galilée, 2003).

[9] Hayden White, *Metahistory: The Historical Imagination in Nineteenth-Century Europe* (Baltimore, MD: Johns Hopkins University Press, 1973).

[10] Michael Baxandall, *Patterns of Intention: On the Historical Explanation of Pictures* (New Haven, CT: Yale University Press, 1985); Donald Preziosi, *Rethinking Art History: Meditations on a Coy Science* (New Haven, CT: Yale University Press, 1989); David Carrier, *Principles of Art History Writing* (University Park, PA: The Pennsylvania State University Press, 1991); Juan Antonio Ramírez, *Ecosistema y explosión de las artes* (Barcelona: Anagrama, 1994); Michael Ann Holly, *Past Looking: Historical Imagination and the Rhetoric of the Image* (Ithaca, NY: Cornell University Press, 1996); James Elkins, *Art History as Writing: Our Beautiful, Dry, and Distant Texts* (University Park, PA: The Pennsylvania State University Press, 1997); Keith Moxey (ed.), *The Art of Art History: A Critical Anthology* (Oxford: Oxford University Press, 1998); Michael Baxandall, *Words for Pictures: Seven Papers on Renaissance Art and Criticism* (New Haven, CT: Yale University Press, 2003).

[11] Preziosi, *Rethinking Art History*.

[12] Baxandall, *Patterns of Intention*, p. 15: 'Every developed explanation of a picture includes or implies an elaborated description of that picture. This description is the mediating object of the explanation. The description is constituted by words and concepts in relation to the picture, a relation that is complex and sometimes problematic'.

noted that '[a]rt history writing is a *verbal representation* (emphasis added) whose argumentation can be understood only by analysing its narrative structure'.[13] For James Elkins, the problem of art historiography can be defined as the problem of how meanings are constructed and modified through the act of writing.[14] Regarding art criticism, Noël Carroll stated: 'Criticism as I am using the term is a genre of verbal discourse. Art criticism is the verbal act of criticising artworks.'[15]

At that time, there was a shared recognition of the inevitability of language in the explanation and understanding of images. For example, Mitchell asserted that 'visual representation cannot represent itself; it has to be represented by discourse', while Lyotard had earlier stated: 'The work of art needs to be spoken.'[16] For Lyotard, the phenomenon of ekphrasis is a direct pragmatic effect of the artwork's existence. Given this inevitability, ekphrasis (in its expanded form as word–image convergence) was presented as a constitutive, foundational condition of possibility for art history and criticism. Therefore, in the final third of the 20th century, the problematisation of art history and art criticism as fields of knowledge became a discussion on the intricate relationship between language and image, and how both art historical and critical meaning are produced through this interplay.

The case of interpretation as an ekphrastic problem

In this context, the act of writing was immediately understood as a form of meaning-making that articulates specific visions and cultural perspectives. The mediating function of language resituated the question of art historical interpretation and art criticism as a problem derived from the dialectical relationship between words and images as differentiated semiotic systems whose dialogical interplay had the potential to affect the visual object (the object of interpretation and criticism) in different manners.

This 'effect' was understood in terms of transformation into a new work, as Lyotard posited:

> Critical works are language games, correlated with plastic games. ... This is not fundamentally a problem of reference but of transformation. The corresponding theory, which underlies and supports the exercise of criticism, serves as an authentic device

[13] Carrier, *Principles of Art History Writing*, p. 5. However, it should be noted that Carrier's understanding of ekphrasis is somewhat limited. He defines it as 'verbal re-creations of the visual artwork', suggesting that its purpose is merely to substitute the original work (in this case, the book's illustrations). Consequently, in his view, it cannot be regarded as a form of interpretation, which is the actual objective of modern art history writing (Carrier, *Principles of Art History Writing*, p. 8).

[14] Elkins, *Art History as Writing*.

[15] Noël Carrol, *On Criticism* (New York: Routledge, 2009), pp. 12–13.

[16] Jean-François Lyotard, 'L'Opera come propia prammatica', in *Teoria e pratiche della Critica d'Arte, Atti del Convegno di Montecatini*, edited by Egidio Mucci and Pier Luigi Tazzi (Milan: Feltrinelli, 1979), pp. 88–109. Similar assertions are reiterated by Heffernan in *Cultivating Picturacy: Visual Art and Verbal Interventions* (Waco, TX: Baylor University Press, 2006), who posits that words are indispensable to understanding paintings.

> of transformation, enabling and facilitating the transition between the plastic work and the descriptive, narrative, or explanatory work that comments on it.[17]

It was also conceived as a process of meaning production that expands, modifies, or modulates the comprehension of the object, generating a mental image or concept in the receiver.[18]

The word–image relationship was also understood as a process of displacement or alienation, in that ekphrasis tends to make the visual object disappear in favour of a textual image produced by the ekphrastic act. This idea underpins Krieger's 'ekphrastic principle', which presents the image as an 'absence' in the text, something that can only be evoked or summoned.[19] It also informs Susan Sontag's critique of interpretation as an oversaturation of meanings that impedes direct engagement with the object.[20]

Alternatively, this relationship was also seen as a process of destruction. Flusser expressed this notion in a radical way: ekphrasis, understood as the translation of an image into words, constitutes the destruction and disintegration of the image. Texts analyse, decompose, and penetrate images with historical and rational consciousness, ultimately leading to their disintegration.[21] As Elkins also observed, when attempting to describe an image, that language inevitably betrays what is essentially a visual phenomenon, given the inherent limitations of language in fully capturing visual details. Thus, in the process of describing or representing an image through language, the integrity of the image is compromised.[22]

The semiotic difference-distance

As observed, tension between the two distinct semiotic systems – language and image – underpins all theoretical approaches. While the fluidity and permeability among media are recurrent ideas in discussions about the convergence between words and images, the notion of semiotic 'difference' remains a fundamental concept. It is important to note that this fluidity or porosity refers to the dynamic capacity of images and words to influence and reconfigure in relation to each other, but

[17] Jean-François Lyotard, 'L'opera come propia prammatica', p. 93.

[18] Preziosi, *Rethinking Art History*; Baxandall, *Patterns of Intention*; Elkins, *Art History as Writing*. For Preziosi, art history, in its broader scope, operates as an extended form of ekphrasis, where language not only describes but also transforms the visual work, thus generating new layers of meaning with each interpretative act. In *Patterns of Intention*, Michael Baxandall develops theoretical approaches aimed at understanding how art historians and critics use language to describe, interpret, and explain images. These approaches also examine how this process entails a transformation of the image's meaning through language. Consequently, for Baxandall, art historiography is also the history of how these works are being described and explained, and how words shape our perceptions of them.

[19] Murray Krieger, *Ekphrasis: The Illusion of the Natural Sign* (Baltimore, MD: Johns Hopkins University Press, 1992).

[20] Susan Sontag, *Against Interpretation and Other Essays* (New York: Farrar, Straus & Giroux, 1966).

[21] Flusser, *Towards a Philosophy of Photography*.

[22] Elkins, *Art History as Writing*.

always within the framework of differentiated semiotic systems. Consequently, the problem of intersemiotic translation persists – though now in a more complex form rather than a linear one. The meaning produced through the dialectical relation between words and images cannot be separated from their medial determinations; they are meanings embodied in their respective media. Words and images signify *because of* and *through* their medial characteristics.

This inevitable difference or distance between both semiotic systems underpins the fundamental problem at the core of the ekphrasis: whether it is possible to express and represent the visual through language and vice versa. What W.J.T. Mitchell terms 'ekphrastic indifference, hope, and fear' lucidly encapsulates this intellectual discussion, where the medial differences and distinct natures of both semiotic systems serve as a central axis.[23]

This conflicting relationship is particularly evident in the limitations (or impossibility) of language to represent the visual, as discussed by Krieger, Derrida, Sontag, and Nancy, among others.[24] Derrida's concepts of distance, *différance*, and displacement are also relevant. For Derrida, the relationship between words and images resembles a 'game' in which the visible and the legible intersect, but never fully align. Any attempt to translate an image into words necessarily involves a certain degree of restructuring, whereby part of the essence of the visual is lost in the verbal and vice versa.[25]

Similarly, the practices of art history and art criticism are predicated on an inherent tension: while language is seen as an inevitable dispositive for representing, understanding, and/or explaining images, there is also an acknowledgement of its intrinsic limitations. As Elkins observed, art history is inherently constrained by the limits of language in describing the visual.[26] In the same vein, Baxandall argued that, while language is the primary means through which art is analysed and discussed, there will always be a discrepancy between what is seen and what can be said about what is seen.[27] This is also the reason why Preziosi characterised art history as 'a coy science', a science acutely aware of its inherent interpretative constraints.

And yet, this tension arising from the distance and difference between word and image is precisely what endows them with their interpretative potential. The word–image relationship is characterised by constant mediation, wherein images, which cannot be fully translated into words – and vice versa – exist within a space of creative and interpretative tension. As Derrida argues, the interplay between words and image is one of coexistence within a network of meanings that is never completely

[23] Mitchell, *Picture Theory*, pp. 151–64.

[24] Krieger, *Ekphrasis*; Derrida, *The Truth in Painting*; Sontag, *Against Interpretation*; Nancy, *Au fond des images*.

[25] Derrida, *The Truth in Painting*.

[26] Elkins, *Art History as Writing*.

[27] Baxandall, *Patterns of Intention*.

stable or definitive.[28] It is precisely this margin of indeterminacy that opens new fields of creative and interpretative possibilities.

Against the background of this scenario, a central question emerges: How is this theoretical approach reformulated when the semiotic difference between the linguistic and the visual – upon which the disciplines of art history and criticism as forms of ekphrastic knowledge production are founded – disappears within what may be termed a *post-semiotic era*? Does this era, and its reliance of processes of mediation by algorithmic agencies, call into question the very concepts of word and image as we have understood them thus far?

Defining a post-semiotic era

Vectorial culture–vectorial semiotics

The advent of AI systems over the past decade has given rise to a new phenomenon: the vectorisation of culture. As neural networks are only capable of processing vectors of numerical characteristics, the growing reliance on AI systems for the processing, classification, analysis, and generation of cultural objects inevitably leads to their conversion into vectors and the mapping of cultural domains into types of vector spaces, known as latent spaces. A latent space, like a numerical vector, is a mathematical concept that can be informally defined as a type of n-dimensional space made up of vectors distributed in accordance with distances that quantify the similarity of their characteristics. These distances are calculated by algorithmic agencies.

If latent spaces are now the spaces in which cultural objects 'exist' as a consequence of their increasing transformation into vectors, one of the priorities we must address – as with previous research on books, archives, museums, and databases – is how to develop a rigorous and nuanced understanding of the specific characteristics and implications of vectors and vector spaces in order to advance our knowledge and enquiry in this domain. In this regard, it is of particular importance to investigate how cultural objects signify within the contexts in which they currently exist, and how they signify in their novel mode of existence, that is, as vectors or latent embeddings in a space configured by mathematical relations.

The phenomenon of cultural vectorisation gives rise to a number of epistemological, critical, and narrative implications. However, the one I wish to emphasise here is the emergence of a new representational order in the cultural domain, where the vector is established as a novel 'representational entity'. In the process of algorithmic vectorisation, certain characteristics of the cultural object are extracted and encoded as numerical features in a vector. This then becomes a specific representation of that object. The process of algorithmic vectorisation extracts and encodes

[28] Derrida, *The Truth in Painting*.

certain characteristics of the cultural object in a vector, thereby creating a representation of that object. In other words, in the context of AI, cultural objects are represented as and by vectors.[29]

Consequently – and this is one of the key arguments of this chapter – it can be said that the vector is the new cultural sign of the AI era. Signs, according to Charles Sanders Peirce's classic definition, are entities that represent something beyond their mere form.[30] In the context under discussion, the vector represents the cultural object through a set of numerical values that relate to it in terms of mathematical abstraction. This representation is not addressed to human subjects but to algorithms.

Moreover, vectors are not merely mathematical descriptions; they function as the medium through which AI processes, analyses, and generates new cultural objects. These cultural objects include both the vector itself (as a new cultural sign) and the generative signs derived from it – later, it will be argued that what emerges is a new type of sign entity. Therefore, vectors serve not only as a means of representing cultural objects, but also as operational entities within AI systems that enable the generation of new ones. This generative dimension endows them with an active role in the creation of meaning within the framework of digital cultural production. This dual status as both representational and generative entity – the latter operating based on its representational quality – also endows them with a new level of complexity as a cultural sign.

For their part, latent spaces, as mathematical structures that algorithmically encode the characteristics of an entire cultural domain (previously transformed into mathematical abstractions or vectors), also become a specific representation (both mathematical and algorithmic) of that cultural domain, encapsulating a particular understanding of it. In other words, latent spaces are specific interpretations of cultural realms. As with the vector, the latent space is not only a representational entity; it also has a productive or generative quality, as it can be modelled or explored to produce new cultural forms.

The cultural value of vectors and vectorial spaces lies not only in their ability to encode cultural information in the form of numerical values, or in their function as representations of other cultural objects, or even in being the entities that enable the generation of new cultural forms. Rather, its cultural value stems from its consolidation as a central *dispositif* that generates cultural practices of the present moment,

[29] For a more extended discussion, see Nuria Rodríguez-Ortega, 'Techno-Concepts for the Cultural Field: n-Dimensional Space and Its Conceptual Constellation', *Multimodal Technologies and Interaction*, 6:11 (2022).

[30] 'A sign is something which stands to somebody for something in some respect or capacity. It addresses somebody, that is, creates in the mind of that person an equivalent sign, or perhaps a more developed sign. That sign which it creates I call the interpretant of the first sign. The sign stands for something, its object'. Charles Sanders Peirce, *The Collected Papers of Charles Sanders Peirce*, edited by Charles Hartshorne and Paul Weiss, 8 vols (Cambridge, MA: Harvard University Press, 1931–58), vol. 2, para. 2.228, p. 135.

having become the dominant form of representation in contemporary digital systems stemming from the pervasive expansion of AI. In light of these considerations, the term 'vectorial culture' describes a cultural phenomenon in which cultural objects are represented as vectors in a latent space with the potential to become new cultural forms.

If it can be argued that the vector is a cultural sign that represents another cultural sign, it seems clear that the process of vectorisation can be understood as a form of mathematical and algorithmic ekphrasis. In this process, a sign (linguistic or visual) is transformed into a vector sign that represents it numerically and mathematically. This mathematical and algorithmic ekphrasis is not without interpretation. The vectorisation process is not a simple transfer of the cultural object into a numerical form; rather, it involves the selection and reformulation of certain characteristics of the object according to the patterns that the AI has learned to detect and process.

Developing this argument, if vectors are the new cultural signs, the latent space can be understood as a system of signs articulated through a grammar of mathematical relations, through which meaning is produced. I will return to this point later. In this context, the concept of a 'vectorial semiotics' could be proposed, as both representational and generative. Within this framework, vectors and latent spaces constitute a new bifunctional sign system, where algorithms operate as mediating agents. These signs are not constrained by the materiality of any particular medium. Rather, they exist as abstract, numerical representations in AI systems, while simultaneously serving as the foundation for the generation of new cultural signs.

This implies that when addressing the question of how the production of cultural meanings occurs in the AI era, or how cultural systems and modes of representation (both linguistic and visual) converge, relate, and interact with each other, we must consider not only the surface of what appears to our sensory experience – that is, the visual or linguistic sign displayed on the computer screen – but also its full ontological depth, which includes the vector and latent spaces where vectors and embeddings (the latent signs) exist or are produced, as well as the computational processes involved. It is impossible to understand digital or digitised objects without referring to the entire network of interactions and processes involved in their production and generation.

This gives rise to a new form of cultural understanding that necessitates a re-evaluation of traditional categories of semiotic analysis and meaning-production processes. It also leads us to question how the human subject and the subjective practices of meaning-making are redefined in a context where signs and their relations are produced by algorithmic agencies operating under logics alien to human reasoning. This calls for an inevitable post-anthropocentric theoretical framework. This chapter does not seek to address this ambitious question. Instead, it will focus further on the ekphrastic processes that occur within these new semiotic systems (or latent spaces) to gain insight into their new or renovated conceptual and research-related implications.

AI multimodal models and the emergence of a pansemiotic system

One of the pivotal consequences of cultural vectorisation is what we might term the 'ontological flattening' of traditional semiotic systems. From a computational perspective, there is no substantive, material, or ontological distinction between words, images, sounds, and other forms of cultural objects. They all share the same nature and mode of existence: they are vectors of numerical characteristics that function as representations in the form of mathematical abstractions of cultural objects. This levelling effect is an inherent consequence of the digital realm, where everything becomes information. As Hookway stated, in digital culture, modality becomes an effect of the interface.[31] However, this circumstance has particular implications in the context of AI multimodal models where the vectors representing linguistic and visual objects converge. These are the models of interest for the purposes of this chapter.

This new scenario is far from trivial. The immediate and almost obvious question arises: can we still talk about multimodality in a context where different semiotic systems no longer exist? It could be argued that multimodality, traditionally defined as the existence and interaction of different semiotic systems, vanishes in latent spaces and is replaced by a continuity of vectors. In this light, it might be proposed that multimodal latent spaces become a form of 'pansemiotic' system where linguistic and visual systems are subsumed into a unified vectorial continuity devoid of medial differences.[32] In this sense, when discussing linguistic and visual vectors, it is important to clarify that they are not inherently different entities. These terms merely refer to the cultural objects they encode or represent. Linguistic and visual vectors are essentially identical in their nature; their difference lies solely in the mathematical information (their meaning) they encode.

This circumstance has significant implications for the concepts of word and image, their respective linguistic and visual values, and their diverse modes of interaction, especially intersemiotic processes. It compels us to reconsider the issue of the blurred and fluid boundaries between semiotic systems from a new angle – an issue that, as examined earlier, has been central to the field of ekphrasis and word–image studies. Furthermore, it demands a re-evaluation of the very concept of ekphrasis.

To develop this analysis, it is necessary to examine how this pansemiotic scenario is configured. This will allow us to elucidate the convergence between the linguistic and the visual as encoded in mathematical vectors. To gain more in-depth

[31] Branden Hookway, *Interface* (Cambridge, MA: MIT Press, 2014).

[32] Other researchers have also highlighted this issue. Hannes Bajohr, for instance, proposes the concept of 'panmodality': 'multimodality at the neural level, promising to be panmodality, suggesting a semantics without clearly differentiated sign systems', Hannes Bajohr, 'Dumb Meaning: Machine Learning and Artificial Semantics', *Image: The Interdisciplinary Journal of Image Sciences*, 37:1 (2023), pp. 58–67 (p. 66). This idea is also addressed by Jack Merullo, Louis Castricato, Carsten Eickhoff, and Ellie Pavlick, 'Linearly Mapping from Image to Text Space' (2022), arXiv:2209.15162 [accessed 10 July 2024].

insight, we will explore the operation of CLIP (Contrastive Language-Image Pretraining) and generative models, particularly diffusion models.[33] Both models aim to align linguistic and visual vectors through statistical correlations, yet each follows a distinctive operational logic when processing and 'understanding' this relationship, offering us a comprehensive view of this new semiotic landscape.[34]

CLIP: alignment as spatial contiguity in a shared representational space

CLIP aligns linguistic and visual vectors through spatial contiguity to return the most appropriate or coherent linguistic or visual representation in response to a given input. Trained on billions of image-description pairs, the model uses statistical correlations to maximise the similarity between semantically 'correct' vectors (e.g., a vector representing the word 'death' and a vector representing an image related to death), while minimising 'incorrect' pairs and distributing the vectors in a latent space according to their mathematically computed degree of similarity. Essentially, CLIP creates a shared representational space configured by semantic regions where similar linguistic and visual vectors coexist in contiguity or proximity. These semantic regions, trained with billions of cultural data points, encapsulate collective cultural concepts. When prompted with a linguistic vector such as 'death', the system correlates it with the nearest visual vector in the region and makes a prediction, returning the image with the highest statistical probability of accurately corresponding to that linguistic concept among those existing in the latent space.

Accordingly, ekphrasis does not manifest in CLIP as a phenomenon of intersemiotic translation. Instead, it operates as a process of spatial coexistence and contiguity within a shared semantic continuity that embeds both visual and linguistic characteristics, culturally constructed. Indeed, evidence suggests that CLIP contains multimodal neurons that activate in response to both the classifier label (text) and the corresponding image, implying the existence of a fused 'multimodal' representation. In this regard, it has been proposed that these are 'conceptual neurons', where the distinction between image and text is fully overcome.[35] Nevertheless, this fusion phenomenon becomes even more evident in diffusion models, as will be discussed subsequently.

[33] CLIP comprises two models: one for image processing (typically a convolutional neural network (CNN) or a variant of the vision transformer) and one for text processing (usually a transformer).

[34] Alignment is the process through which AI models associate, compare, or adjust visual and linguistic vectors in the latent space. The goal of alignment is to maximise the correspondence between these vectors when they describe the same concept or content. Statistical correlation is the process by which common patterns or associations between linguistic and visual representations are identified based on large volumes of pre-trained data. This process enables the model to learn associations between different types of data (textual and visual), using statistical relationships to correctly align their numerical representations or vectors within a shared latent space.

[35] Gabriel Goh, Nick Cammarata, Chelsea Voss, Shan Carter, Michael Petrov, Ludwig Schubert *et al.*, 'Multimodal Neurons in Artificial Neural Networks', *Distill*, 6:3 (2021).

Diffusion models: text as condition and transductive fusion processes

Diffusion models, which are a central example of text-to-image generative models, as seen in applications such as DALL·E or Midjourney, introduce a different approach from CLIP. While CLIP primarily aligns vectors by comparing their semantic characteristics within a latent space, diffusion models generate images from text through an iterative refinement process. The process follows a thermodynamic-like logic. It starts by turning the visual dataset into Gaussian noise, creating a random distribution of features that serves as the starting point for generating a visual vector.[36] This vector is then progressively transformed, conditioned by a linguistic vector that encodes the semantic attributes of the input text (or prompt) and guides the generation process over several iterations. This ultimately results in a visual vector (or image embedding) that coherently aligns with the initial prompt – a process known as the 'inverse diffusion'.[37] Essentially, the linguistic vector acts as the guiding force that extracts an image from noise or, metaphorically, imposes order on chaos through probabilistic calculations.

Like CLIP, diffusion models are grounded in probability. They learn to predict the range of potential image variations corresponding to a given text by modelling the probabilistic distribution of images conditioned on the prompt. Instead of generating a single image, the model captures a spectrum of possible images that could accurately correspond to the description.

However, the process is more complex when it comes to the relationship between visual and linguistic characteristics. During the inverse diffusion process, the text influences the distribution of visual features, with linguistic information being incorporated at each iteration. This process modifies and adjusts the visual vector in line with the semantic features of the linguistic vector. The final result is the latent image, which emerges from the dynamic integration of visual features and the linguistic instruction provided by the prompt into a single unit. In other words, the latent space is shaped by the text, meaning that linguistic features are implicitly embedded within the latent representation of the image. Therefore, the final decoded image represents visual features, while also incorporating subtle linguistic elements that may not be directly visible, but introduce details or nuances that were not explicitly mentioned in the text and were implicit in its semantics. These semantic features were induced by the linguistic vector.

[36] In the context of diffusion models, 'Gaussian noise' refers to random perturbations added to visual data that follow a normal or Gaussian distribution (also known as a 'bell curve'). This noise simulates a random scattering of features, which is progressively reversed during the image-generation process, transforming the noise into a coherent and ordered representation based on a given text or prompt.

[37] This conditioning can be implemented in various ways, including cross-attention, direct concatenation, FiLM, and latent control, among others. See, among others, Aditya Ramesh, Mikhail Pavlov, Gabriel Goh, Scott Gray, Chelsea Voss, Alec Radford *et al.*, 'Zero-Shot Text-to-Image Generation, *Proceedings of the 38th International Conference on Machine Learning* (2021), pp. 8821–31 and Chitwan Saharia, William Chan, Saurabh Saxena, Lala Li, Jay Whang, Emily Denton *et al.*, 'Imagen: Text-to-Image Diffusion Model' (2022), arXiv preprint, arXiv:2205.11487 [accessed 13 July 2024].

Consequently, it can be argued that the outcome is an embedding that iteratively and conditionally fuses visual and linguistic features. Given these considerations, it seems reasonable to propose that sign generation in latent spaces operates as a process of transductive fusion. Here, transduction refers to the transformation of one sign, signal, or piece of information into another through the integration of external features that drive this transformation.[38]

Image-to-text models that generate texts from visual vectors, whether in the form of simple descriptions or more elaborate narratives or interpretations, are not diffusion models. However, their operating logic is similar, and they can also be understood as forms of transductive processes. These models, such as CLIP (in its inverse version) or Vision Transformers, when combined with language models (such as GPT), are capable of statistically correlating a visual vector with a linguistic text that is consistent (coherent) with the image.[39] This process is not merely a straightforward translation from image to text; rather, it is a transductive integration of visual information into a different semantic format: language. Throughout this process, visual features are transformed into linguistic semantics through a continuous process that integrates visual and textual semantics within a shared latent space. Consequently, the resulting text is not a mere linguistic translation of the visual input, but rather a synthesis of the visual information at the conceptual level, which transforms and creates new meanings.

Thus, it can be stated that in diffusion models, ekphrasis takes the form of transductive fusion. It is neither an intersemiotic translation nor a case of semiotic syncretism (the blending of different semiotic systems to create a unified sign, as in W.J.T. Mitchell's 'imagentext').[40] Instead, it is best described as a process of transduction, in which a new type of sign is generated through the transformation of meaning and form, represented as mathematical abstractions within latent space.

This new cultural scenario driven by AI multimodal models thus suggests the advent of a post-semiotic era – a post-linguistic and post-visual epoch characterised by new cultural signs that extend beyond the traditional categories of words and images as distinct and discrete signs. The operativity of the sign in AI does not necessarily indicate the overcoming of semiotics; rather, it suggests a necessary reconfiguration of semiotics. This is evidenced by the transformation of analytic categories into dimensions of a continuous space. For example, whereas Peirce describes iconicity

[38] For a more detailed explanation of this transductive process, see Nuria Rodríguez-Ortega, 'Exploring the Concept of Transduction to Interpret AI-Generated Images', in *From Hype to Reality: Artificial Intelligence in the Study of Art and Culture*, edited by Eva Cetinić and Darío Negueruela del Castillo, Hertziana Studies in Art History, 3 (2024), pp. 23–8.

[39] In models that generate text from images, the image is first processed by a neural network, typically a convolutional neural network (CNN) or a vision transformer, which extracts visual features, including colours, shapes, and structures. These features are then transformed into a numerical representation, or vector, within a latent space. Subsequently, this representation is used as input for a language model, such as GPT or an alternative transformer, which generates descriptive or narrative text corresponding to the visual features.

[40] The term 'imagentext' designates composite, synthetic works that combine text and image in a unity of meaning (Mitchell, *Picture Theory*, p. 89).

as resemblance and indexicality as causal contiguity, in a model like CLIP those distinctions merge: a single vector coordinate can simultaneously represent the visual form of a tree, its verbal designation 'tree', and myriad associated semantic contexts. Although the semiotic tradition of Saussure, Peirce, and their successors has already theorised the notion of the sign beyond the mere word–image dichotomy, in multimodal AI systems these signs cease to be discrete categories and become statistical vectors within a latent space. This mutation – operative and quantitative, not merely theoretical – demands a redefined understanding of the generation and interpretation of signs, hence the use of 'post-semiotic'. This is not to deny the semiotic tradition or herald its overcoming, but to signal the emergence of a phase in which its foundational premises are no longer sufficient. This era is also characterised by new semiotic relations and production of meaning (mathematical and algorithmic, governed by a probabilistic-predictive logic, alien to intentionality, subjectivity, and human cultural context) within vectorial spaces operating as pansemiotic systems.

Spheres of conceptual problematisation and displacements

As previously argued, an examination of ekphrastic phenomena in this post-semiotic scenario must be contextualised within a solid and well-established tradition of enquiry, research, experimentation, and reflection on the convergence, porosity, and permeability of both semiotic systems. The next question that arises is whether we are witnessing continuity or discontinuity: is this simply a new reformulation of ekphrasis as a dialectical relation between words and images or does it represent an actual paradigm shift? The following considerations do not aim to provide a definitive answer to this question; rather, they are intended to offer some clarity and avenues for further enquiry.

To delineate the scope of this problem, it can be claimed that the shift introduced by multimodal models – where words and images are represented as numerical feature vectors in a shared mathematical space (the latent space) and probabilistic and predictively related through statistical correlations based on patterns extracted from vast amounts of cultural data – concerns the reformulation of their very nature as signs. This extends to the interaction between linguistic and visual values and the incorporation of algorithmic agencies into the convergence processes. This shift brings forth specific areas of conceptual problematisation and displacements that demand further reflection and the posing of new questions.

From mediality to intervectoriality – from intermediality to intersemanticity

The ontological equalisation resulting from algorithmic vectorisation, along with the coexistence of cultural objects as numerical representations within the same mathematical space, shifts the focus away from the traditional problem of 'mediality' – the analysis of their differentiated media or semiotic characteristics. In latent space, what defines a linguistic or visual vector is not its mediality (which, strictly speaking, no longer exists), but rather its position, namely, its dynamic mathematical distance to other vectors, and its potential to algorithmically converge through statistical correlations. This can be called its 'intervectoriality'.[41]

Intervectoriality also determines the semantics codified in latent spaces and in the vectors themselves – what the linguistic and visual vectors 'represent' in terms of meaning. As mentioned earlier, spatial contiguity between vectors in the CLIP model shapes semantic regions of shared meanings, just as the transductive fusion process induced by prompt conditioning (which might, in fact, be characterised as a form of 'transvectoriality') shapes the characteristics of the final embedding. This ultimately determines what the resulting image or text 'expresses' or 'represents'.

Consequently, vectorial systems foster a shift towards an approach grounded in semantic relationships (visual and linguistic) that are represented as numerical abstractions in the form of vectors. The ekphrastic problem, thus, is no longer one of translation between two distinct media, but rather the relationships between abstract representations of meaning that traverse or extend across a semantic continuity that embeds both visual and linguistic characteristics. In my view, the term 'intersemanticity' is an appropriate term to describe this phenomenon. It can be argued that from intervectoriality – understood as a quality of latent spaces conceived as dynamically entangled semiotic systems – emerges an intersemanticity, which consists in relationships between abstract representations of meaning. The term 'intersemanticity' captures this capacity of pansemiotic systems to navigate across linguistic and visual meanings without requiring translation between different media.[42] This, of course, carries significant conceptual and research implications.

First, this scenario suggests that semantic relations can be understood independently of medial determinations, thereby opening the possibility of meaning beyond the traditional separation of media signs. This raises an intriguing line of enquiry into whether these medial determinations could be obliterated – determinations that, however, remain inextricable from human experience, as our interaction with meanings is always mediated through the material embodiment of a sign (whether a word or an image). Even conceptual art has not been able to entirely forgo its manifestation within a medial object. I will return to this point in the conclusion.

More interesting is that both modalities are rooted in a shared field of underlying meanings because they share abstract representations within the latent space.

[41] The term 'intervectoriality' denotes the notion that vectors, which encode linguistic and visual representations, do not interact as discrete entities but rather as constituents of a unified numerical representation system. Vectors do not function in isolation; rather, they interact continuously, aligning or correlating to generate a shared semantic representation that emerges from the connections, fusion, and proximity between vectors.

[42] If intervectoriality describes the manner in which vectors relate to one another in latent space, intersemanticity refers to the way in which these relations give rise to meaning in that space.

This reinforces a notion already discussed in the literature on ekphrasis – that images and words are inherently interconnected in their meaning. However, this idea can now be materialised in a tangible artefact – the latent space or vectorial system – which can be directly explored and analysed.

Accordingly, the ekphrastic research focus shifts towards examining how both systems share a common meaning within the latent space. The primary object of this enquiry becomes 'semantic continuity', with the central question being how concepts and meanings traverse and manifest 'intervectorially'. However, we should not assume that this shift turns the study of ekphrasis into a purely semantic investigation. On the contrary, although it may seem paradoxical, it is precisely this abstract representation of semantic continuity that opens a path for the exploration – on a new scale and depth – of how meanings and complex concepts are intermedially constructed and transformed over time.

As mentioned earlier, the CLIP model's semantic regions, trained with billions of cultural data points, encapsulate collective cultural concepts. In fact, we could say that this latent space constitutes a map of the linguistic-visual relationships embedded in the cultural productions (images described through texts) with which the model has been trained.[43] Thus, for instance, CLIP might have encapsulated a visual concept of the linguistic sign 'death' (derived from the set of images described with the word death), that is not limited to explicit representations of death (the iconography of death), but also condenses the visual characteristics that have culturally constructed images of death. Similarly, CLIP might have encapsulated a linguistic concept of the images representing death, which condenses the semantic values of the words that culturally co-appear in the texts where such images are described. Therefore, the image that the CLIP model returns in response to the linguistic vector 'death' does not establish a 'direct' relationship with the word, but rather invokes a culturally constructed visual concept embedded 'in' the word 'death'. Likewise, the linguistic description it returns in response to an image does not establish a direct relationship with that image, but rather invokes a semantic-linguistic structure embedded in multiple visual representations.

Here, we cannot help but evoke fundamental concepts from intersemiotic studies, such as Derrida's 'trace', Bakhtin's 'heteroglossia', and Kristeva's 'intertextuality' – concepts that refer to the history of meanings and contexts. Though not explicitly present, these continue to influence the signification of cultural objects, raising the question of how these concepts become reformulated within a new semiotic context.

[43] Leonardo Impett and Fabian Offert, 'There Is a Digital Art History', *Visual Resources*, 38:2 (2022), pp. 1–24.

From a regime of differences to a regime of similarities

Another conceptual shift in the semiotic processes mediated by AI can be characterised as a transition from a regime of differences to one of 'sameness' and 'similarity'. This new scenario leads us to re-problematise the concepts of difference and similarity within the context of the ekphrastic relationship, requiring an examination of how the concept of 'difference' is being reconfigured.

In traditional semiotics, although the boundaries between semiotic systems and media are understood to be fluid and blurred, the conceptual distinction between language and image remains. The distinction between words and images is not simply a matter of degree; it is a fundamental difference, even though they may intersect in processes of syncretic fusion. Likewise, linguistic and visual values are not identical, despite the fact that, as Derrida discusses in his *Grammatology* (and as later authors such as Mitchell or Drucker examine from other angles), images can exhibit linguistic characteristics, and words can take on visual qualities.[44] Yet, despite this potential overlap, they remain distinct. In fact, their *raison d'être* is fundamentally grounded in 'difference'. Semiotic systems signify because of their differences, which can manifest through various forms of interactions, including convergence, conflict, or contradiction. It is this semiotic difference or distance that constitutes the fundamental axis of traditional problematisation of ekphrasis, as discussed earlier.

All of these considerations, however, are rendered moot in latent spaces. The vectorisation of linguistic and visual signs, and the transformation of their values into numerical characteristics, result in a regime of 'sameness', both conceptually and formally. In turn, AI operates fundamentally within a regime of similarity. AI algorithms are trained to detect patterns – essentially, commonalities – and establish statistical correlations that create relationships of similarity between vectors, as the operational logics of CLIP and generative multimodal models clearly evidence.

In the context of latent space, the traditional concept of semiotic distance is reformulated. It no longer implies 'distinction', but rather degrees of similarity. In the vector system, the distance between linguistic and visual vectors is not a semiotic distinction but a continuous, gradual mathematical 'spatial' distance that measures the degree of similarity between vectors based on statistical correlations. From this perspective, it could be argued that the concept of 'difference' as a caesura is no longer applicable in the context of latent spaces. What emerges instead is a semantic continuity where vectors are more or less similar to one another depending on their spatial contiguity, mathematically computed.[45]

It is important to recall that the primary goal of multimodal models is to align linguistic and visual vectors based on criteria of coherence and correspondence.

[44] Mitchell, *Picture Theory*; Johanna Drucker, *The Visible Word: Experimental Typography and Modern Art, 1909–1923* (Chicago, IL: University of Chicago Press, 1994).

[45] Rodríguez-Ortega, 'Techno-Concepts for the Cultural Field'.

The ultimate objective is statistical optimisation, referred to as maximising coherence – basically, achieving the most accurate correspondence between text and image. This regime of similarity prompts us to enquire how processes of meaning production and critical interpretation, which have traditionally emerged from the dialectical relationship between words and images are reconfigured in the context of AI-mediated systems. It also urges us to delve into their conceptual and research implications.

From the dialectical relationship to coherence and alignment

This new scenario suggests that, within latent spaces, meaning production is no longer shaped by an intricate dialectical interplay marked by contradictions, conflicts, tensions, and negotiations. Instead, meaning is determined by degrees of proximity, accurate alignment, and coherence. This shift introduces a new area of ekphrastic enquiry, focusing on the divergence between the notions of coherence based on statistical correlations of alignment and dialectical tension. In principle, it can be argued that, in the vector system, dialectical tension is replaced by statistical correlation, materialised in the concept of 'coherence' between visual and linguistic representations as the ultimate goal of multimodal models.

In traditional ekphrasis, there is always a discrepancy or an irreducible space of difference between the two media. AI models, however, aim precisely to minimise this gap by resolving tensions and ensuring a direct correspondence between linguistic and visual vectors, both representing the same content or concept in the vector structure. In doing so, they collapse the distance between the two media.

This circumstance not only redefines the word–image relationship in purely functional terms but also suggests that 'tension', as a mechanism of meaning production, is effectively eliminated within the vectorial system. Furthermore, since the processes are carried out by algorithmic agencies operating outside the framework of subjective intentionality or cultural consciousness, there is no longer any tension or dialectical relationship between human subjectivity and a cultural object that needs to be appropriated, described, interpreted, narrated, or discursively constructed for 'another human subjectivity' (the potential spectator-receiver).

However, the interesting point is that the concept of tension is not removed, but rather reframed within the vector system. It can be postulated that the optimisation of coherence does not entirely erase tension, but instead reallocates it to a new domain: statistical ambiguity. Rather than an ontological or media-based tension (word vs image), the tension now manifests as a range of probabilities in the statistical correlations that determine how linguistic and visual vectors align in latent space. Since AI does not generate a perfect match, but rather the most probable match based on its training data, an element of ambiguity is introduced into the process. For instance, if the system is tasked with generating an image from the word 'death', the linguistic vector for 'death' will correlate with the nearest visual vector in the latent space. However, given the probabilistic nature of this relationship, multiple images may represent the concept of 'death' with varying degrees of accuracy or fidelity. This lack of determinism introduces ambiguity into the correlation and image-generation processes, thus transforming the traditional ekphrastic tension based on difference-distance between systems and the impossibility of full suturing into a 'probabilistic tension', where the issue becomes one of varying degrees of precise correspondence or alignment.

This new dialectic is, therefore, not grounded in the irreducible limitations of translating-expressing-interpreting an image into words or vice versa, but rather in how levels of precision and ambiguity interact within a probabilistic space. We might posit that the relationship between the different levels of probabilistic correspondence is dialectical in nature, with degrees of ambiguity and accuracy at the core of the meaning-generation process.

As explained earlier, this probabilistic tension or statistical ambiguity implies that the model may produce an image or text that does not perfectly align with the user's expectations (which are shaped by their subjective and cultural frameworks), even though it remains statistically consistent with the linguistic description or image provided. Thus, this statistical ambiguity opens a new dialectical space between words and images when they are experienced by the human subject – that is, when we move from the latent space to the space of interaction between the subject and the AI-generated outcomes. Consequently, this dialectical tension no longer occurs between two human subjectivities mediated by a cultural object (image or word), but between a human subjectivity and algorithmic agency. This brings us into the framework of a post-human hermeneutic production, to which I will return later.

From open possibilities to predictive anticipation

The probabilistic nature of AI models also implies that algorithmic ekphrasis within vector systems operates under a predictive anticipation regime, marking a clear distinction from the 'possibilistic' regime that characterises traditional ekphrasis. This shift opens a space for re-examining and problematising the concept of the probable in the meaning-production processes based on word–image convergence.

In this discussion, I understand a 'possibilistic' regime as one in which the concept of the 'possible' aligns with the Deleuzian concepts of the 'virtual' and 'becoming'.[46] Thus, it refers to a context where creative or productive processes are open to indeterminacy and are not governed by the rules of what is predictable or what 'can' be represented. In this regime, the truly new emerges not as a variation within a set of pre-existing possibilities, but as something entirely distinct and singular, resulting from a process of differentiation.

[46] Gilles Deleuze, *Logique du sens* (Paris: Éditions de Minuit, 1969).

Traditional ekphrasis operates under a possibilistic regime because the ekphrastic text does not aim to capture the image in an exact or exhaustive manner, just as an image does not aspire to (nor can it be) a literal representation of a text. Rather, they serve as cultural mediations, with the objective of affecting meaning by producing a new one, which is open to indeterminacy. The production of meaning in traditional ekphrasis, grounded in the dialectical relationship between word and image, operates within a framework of indeterminate possibilities.[47]

As noted earlier, AI models are designed to predict the most probable 'correct' (i.e., coherent) images or texts based on a mathematical representation of all potential descriptions or images that could align with a given description or image. Accordingly, it can be argued that generative processes operate by constraining the space of possibilities – constituted by the latent space – into a reduced set of probabilities, guided by the coherence-correspondence principle. In other words, the output with the highest predictive index is the one that most accurately aligns with the source vector. Put differently, algorithmic ekphrasis works by contracting the space of possibilities to establish as tight correspondence as possible, thereby eliminating any indeterminacy.

Algorithmic ekphrasis, therefore, eliminates the potential for multiple meanings by selecting, through a predictive anticipation process, a statistically optimised option. It could be argued that this issue of reducing or limiting meanings is also an inherent part of traditional ekphrasis, as a consequence of the intrinsic limitation involved in encapsulating the image within a concrete linguistic framework (which functions through the fixation of meanings or oversaturation of interpretations). However, in traditional ekphrasis, the openness to new, indeterminate possibilities of meaning is not the result of a process of expanding or multiplying meanings. Instead, it is an effect or consequence of the inherent dialectical tension between language and image (what language attempts to capture from the image and what the image suggests beyond the words) and the inherent limitations of this relationship. It is precisely these limitations of language in fully encapsulating the nuances of the image and vice versa – thereby leaving space for the unsaid, the implicit, or the absent – that allow for a margin of indeterminacy or uncertainty.

It could also be argued that the algorithmic process is not entirely closed since, due to the probabilistic tension or statistical ambiguity mentioned previously, different images or texts can be generated for a single input. Nevertheless, probabilistic tension is precisely the reason why these possibilities are constrained to the range of the most probable options. It cannot be considered a framework of possibilities open to the indeterminacy of the unforeseeable. They are not indeterminate possibilities but probable alternatives.[48]

[47] Nevertheless, as Deleuze alerts, the creative act itself is not necessarily indeterminate. That is why cultural productions sometimes remain confined to a dynamic of repetition of the same (what already exists or can exist) with variations.

[48] In fact, there is an intrinsic conflicting relationship between indeterminacy and probability, as the ultimate aim of probability is precisely to tame indeterminacy through prediction.

From representation to probabilistic projection?

The probabilistic-predictive paradigm associated with algorithmic ekphrasis necessitates a reconsideration of the concept of representation, which is central to the traditional ekphrastic word–image relationship. It could be argued that this relationship is no longer 'representational' in the conventional sense, but is instead probabilistic and predictive, as discussed.

Traditionally, representation has been understood as a process of mediation between a sign (whether visual or linguistic) and its referent, within a context where all elements are ontologically distinct. In AI systems, however, there is no referent in the classical sense. Rather than 'representing' something external to itself, AI predicts and computes similarities between patterns of data, generating probabilities from statistical correlations. This shift transforms the notion of representation into a predictive act, where meaning is tied to what is most likely to occur in latent space, rather than to a connection with the referent world. In this context, the value of this 'representation' lies not in its referential correspondence to a specific object, but in its capacity to predict and adapt to other vectors with similar semantic properties. Thus, we could speak of a 'representation immanent' to a system of numerical relations, where semantics emerge from the interrelation of vectors.

While we may observe an apparent representational image (an image of a sunset with boats and seagulls), this image is neither representational in relation to the objects it depicts, nor in relation to the linguistic text upon which the generative process is based. Instead, it is the result of algorithmic data processing that involves no inherent ships, seagulls, or sunsets. The representation here does not refer to anything beyond the sign itself; it is a creation of algorithmic processing that calculates the visual configuration most likely to align with a linguistic vector in a space of mathematical relations.

As a result, it becomes necessary to reconsider what 'representation' means in this context – what, if anything, is being represented and whether the concept of representation remains applicable at all. Indeed, we might argue that what is generated in latent space is not a representation in any traditional sense, but rather a projection of possibilities within a mathematical relational space.

The potential redefinition of the concept of representation within this algorithmic-predictive framework is highly contentious and demands rigorous theoretical exploration. In the coming years, it will be necessary to debate whether we are witnessing a new way of understanding representation or an entirely distinct phenomenon that requires new terminology and theoretical articulation. One possible term could be 'probabilistic projection', referring to the idea that what is generated in latent space is no longer a 'representation', but rather a projection of possibilities based on statistical probabilities within a mathematical relational space.

The different regimens discussed in the previous paragraphs are expressions of the conceptual displacements that arise when focusing on the new semiotic scenario represented by latent spaces as pansemiotic systems. All of them involve epistemological reconsiderations and the formulation of new research questions. However, what I wish to emphasise here is that these different operational regimes do not, in my theoretical approach, imply a hierarchy of ekphrastic modes. On the contrary, they call for the recognition of different regimes of meaning and interpretation, which can be fertile grounds for a shared territory of hybrid hermeneutics. This brings up the penultimate question.

From algorithmic to post-humanist ekphrasis

For the time being, and until AI systems evolve to a further stage of autonomy, the operations taking place in latent spaces are meaningful only to the extent that they invade and penetrate the space of human experience. In other words, the significance of these systems is contingent upon the implications they hold for the human subject. Therefore, it is essential to examine how the ekphrastic processes operating within latent space manifest in human experience, how they reformulate the subject's relationship with cultural objects, and how they reshape interpretative practices. This is especially relevant for art historians and critics, given that – as noted earlier – art history and criticism are underpinned by ekphrastic forms of knowledge production.

This implies positioning systems of meaning production within the framework of an ecology of human–machine, where meaning and interpretation emerge from the complex interactions between them.[49] As N. Katherine Hayles notes, the generation of meaning in AI systems is not an internal process; rather, it emerges through the interaction between humans and algorithms.[50] This would constitute the domain of a post-humanist ekphrasis that produces hybrid hermeneutics or interpretations about visual works involving machine and human agencies. However, a post-humanist ekphrasis also refers to the proper convergence of two forms of representation: machine and human. What I mean is that assemblages, in which meaning emerges from the complex interaction between human and machine rationales could also be understood as an ekphrastic phenomenon, that is, as a problem of dialectical relation between two different systems of representation.

[49] This entanglement of diverse agencies and materialities that interact with each other can be explained under various theoretical frameworks and by invoking different concepts. However, my approach is based both on N. Katherine Hayles' concept of cognitive assemblage, where knowledge production emerges from the interaction of distributed human and non-human cognitive agencies (N. Katherine Hayles, *Unthought: The Power of the Cognitive Nonconscious* (Chicago, IL: University of Chicago Press, 2017)) and on Gilbert Simondon's ontogenetic theory of individuation, which posits that the formation of new individuals is a dynamic process arising from the interplay of different systems and scales, allowing for the continuous integration of the physical, biological, psychic, collective, and machinic realms (Gilbert Simondon, *L'Individuation à la lumière des notions de forme et d'information* (Paris: Jérôme Millon, 2005)).

[50] N. Katherine Hayles, 'Can Computers Create Meanings? A Cyber/Bio/Semiotic Perspective', *Critical Inquiry*, 46:1 (2019), pp. 32–55.

Consequently, in the context of AI, ekphrasis is no longer a concept circumscribed to the convergence between image and text, between the linguistic and the visual. It also becomes a complex interaction between algorithmic processes and human interpretative practices, where meaning is produced through their interplay. In this context, the role of the art critic or art historian is redefined, transforming into that of a critical mediator between algorithmic correlations generated by AI models and cultural and subjective human interpretations.

Hybrid human–machine hermeneutics

This scenario still requires us to address the central problem of the nature of interpretation and meaning production in the AI system, including whether interpretation is genuinely feasible. This question is fundamental, as it depends on how human agency will be understood in this complex ecology of meaning production: either as a process of endowing meaning to something that is intrinsically meaningless, or as a genuinely hybrid process of meaning construction.

As will have become apparent at this point, the arguments developed throughout this text rest on the premise that algorithmic ekphrasis produces meanings and can be considered a form of interpretation. However, this is a controversial assumption. In the traditional (pre-IA) semiotic approach, both words and images are regarded as cultural mediations that generate meaning through historical contexts and interpretative frameworks. Algorithmic ekphrasis operating in vector systems does not perform interpretations, nor does it 'understand' in a human, culturally informed sense; rather, it simply calculates correlations between vectors and optimises their coherence. At first glance, it appears that algorithmic ekphrasis reframes the relationship between words and images by replacing human-mediated interpretation with an automatic process of generating correlations based on mathematical patterns, thus calling into question the very possibility of interpretation and meaning production. Indeed, critiques of AI's ability to produce meanings and interpretations often focus on its lack of intentionality and the absence of a subjectively and culturally informed understanding of the visual and verbal worlds (the so-called 'grounding problem').[51] Critics argue that, without intention, cultural context, and subjective experience, AI outputs cannot be regarded as a form of interpretation. This positioning has resulted in the establishment of an antithetical binary between interpretation-hermeneutics and mere correlation. Furthermore, it is argued that any explanation or description generated by AI systems merely flattens concepts that

[51] See, for example, Emily M. Bender and Alexander Koller, 'Climbing towards NLU: On Meaning, Form, and Understanding in the Age of Data', *Proceedings of the 58th Annual Meeting of the Association for Computational Linguistics*, online (Association for Computational Linguistics, 2020), pp. 5185–98. https://doi.org/10.18653/v1/2020.acl-main.463 or Mercedes Bunz, 'The Calculation of Meaning: On the Misunderstanding of New Artificial Intelligence as Culture', *Culture, Theory and Critique*, 60 (2019), pp. 264–78.

are, in their cultural articulation, extremely complex (the debate on the oversimplification of the concept of style is a paradigmatic example).

However, in the context of this post-semiotic scenario – one inextricably linked to algorithmic agencies – it is not, in my view, a matter of disputing or delegitimising the concepts of algorithmic interpretation and hermeneutics. Rather, it is a question of resituating them within a new framework of cognition and meaning production, where a form of algorithmic (or artificial) semantics converges with cultural semantics. Evaluating the interpretative or meaning-producing capacities of AI from a human-centric perspective is a reductionist approach that may limit the exploration of new avenues of understanding. It is, therefore, essential to adopt a post-anthropocentric perspective when attempting to comprehend the concepts of meaning, semantics, and interpretation – one that moves beyond the clichés that 'AI does not understand', 'AI does not comprehend', 'AI does not produce intentional meaning', or 'AI flattens complex concepts'.

Various authors advocate for the legitimacy of an artificial semantics that is not bound by the concepts of intentionality, subjectivity, or cultural consciousness. They argue that AI's capacity for data correlation, coherent alignment, and predictive anticipation forms the basis of AI's approach to meaning production.[52] Therefore, this approach is concerned with the potential for a hybrid hermeneutic rather than the impossibility of algorithmic meaning production.

This is also my position. In my view, the issue that will require attention in the coming years is not to demonstrate the incapacity of AI to generate legitimate meanings and interpretations, but to explore the conditions under which a hybrid hermeneutic might emerge – one that goes beyond the notion of using AI-generated results merely as a complement or starting point. As has been previously mentioned, it is precisely at this level that the tensions, conflicts, contradictions, and negotiations, which seem to flatten within the latent space, can re-emerge within a new context of dialectical interaction between two rationales – or forms of representation and mediation: human and machine. For instance, the mismatch of expectations generated by the probabilistic ambiguity inherent in AI's operational logic could be of significant interest, both from a heuristic perspective (as it raises new research questions) and from a creative one. This will demand experimental research grounded in specific cases, as well as the development of new theoretical frameworks to guide and inform such enquiries, in the same way that artists are exploring the creative possibilities of human–machine convergence.

[52] In this regard, the contributions of N. Katherine Hayles are of paramount importance. In response to these criticisms, Hayles addresses the question of whether computers can participate in the creation of meaning from a cyber/bio/semiotic perspective in her article 'Can Computers Create Meaning?'. Hayles suggests that, although AI lacks intentionality and subjectivity, this does not preclude its capacity to engage in meaning-making processes. Hayles posits that meaning in AI systems is relational and functional, emerging from the model's capacity to correlate data and generate coherent results (effectively aligning with its objectives). This constitutes their method of generating meaning.

Generative ontogenesis and the phenomenological divide

As discussed throughout this chapter, the distinction between word and image becomes irrelevant in latent spaces where a regime of sameness emerges. However, this assertion needs to be qualified when placed within the context of post-human ekphrasis. The erasure of the distinction between words and images in latent space does not signify their complete disappearance. Conversely, this distinction remains fundamental to our everyday human experience and the way we still encode knowledge.

Yet, the traditional categories of word and image must also be called into question in this semiotic 'surface' – that is, where the final generative output that we see, read, or experiment is materialised – insofar as we are dealing with a new semiotic entity. In other words, although the sign produced at the end of the generative process (whether a decoded image or text) is perceived as either a visual or linguistic sign, it cannot be considered an image or text in the traditional sense. From an ontogenetic perspective, it is a transductive fusion of visual and linguistic characteristics. Its operational logic, moreover, puts into question its *apparent* representational nature (at least in the traditional sense). Therefore, generative processes and transductive fusion give rise to a new type of semiotic entity that is inherently visual and linguistic at the same time, a new form of cultural materiality, whose problematisation as such extends beyond its stochastic nature.[53] This is what I refer to as the phenomenological divide, resulting from the difference between the ontogenesis of AI generative signs and how they appear in human experience.

These nascent signs reformulate, with a new level of complexity, the problem that Vilém Flusser inscribed in his concept of the 'technical image', namely, the emergence of a new visual sign that is, at the same time, language.[54] Indeed, the idea that the generative processes associated with AI models engender a phenomenological divide – a disparity between the intrinsic nature of objects and their perceptual manifestation – already appears in Flusser's theory about the digital age. According to Flusser, 'technical image' refers to a new form of representation that is not simply an iconic representation in the traditional sense. Instead, these images are based on code (that is, written language) and, as such, demand critical reading and interpretation similar to that of a text. Therefore, Flusser argues that individuals must learn to interpret technical images not merely as visual representations but also as coded texts requiring decryption.

This divide also implies that a form of word–image tension arises between the operational logic of latent spaces and what is directly revealed to experience. For example, as Bajohr noted: 'The discussed tendency to eliminate the speech/image

[53] Emily, M. Bender, Timnit Gebru, Angelina McMillan-Major, and Shmargaret Shmitchell, 'On the Dangers of Stochastic Parrots: Can Language Models Be Too Big?', *Proceedings of the 2021 ACM Conference on Fairness, Accountability, and Transparency* (2021), pp. 610–23.

[54] Flusser, *Towards a Philosophy of Photography*.

distinction at the technical level is contrasted with the displacement of the image by speech at the interface level. The results of DALL·E could therefore also be understood as language art instead of being mere visual objects.'[55]

This phenomenological divide, in my view, places us in a new complexity when it comes to analysing how signs produce meaning and how they must be critically interpreted, since they cannot be analysed simply as images or texts, or even as forms of semiotic composite or syncretism. This divide is also critical because our experience of latent spaces can only be possible through these signs, which serve as an interface or mediator.[56] Humans cannot directly access latent spaces; they remain unknowable to us in a direct sense. It is thus imperative to examine what the implications of this phenomenological divide are for interpretation, and what new tools and categories of analysis must be developed to bridge or navigate the gap.[57]

Conclusion

Throughout this chapter, the concept of ekphrasis, understood as the space of dialectical relations between words and images, has been employed as an intellectual tool to explore the transformations that the convergence of the visual and the linguistic is undergoing within the framework of AI multimodal models, where both are ontologically equalised into a continuity of vectors. In latent spaces, the visual and the linguistic no longer function as distinct entities but coexist as abstract, mathematical representations, leading to the configuration of a pansemiotic system. This new pansemiotic scenario entails a series of conceptual shifts, leading us to move from the concept of intermediality to that of intervectoriality and intersemanticity; from dialectical tension to statistical ambiguity; from representation to probabilistic projection.

Yet, this ontological collapse in computational latent spaces does not translate directly into our embodied, perceptual experience. Human interlocutors never engage with vectorial encodings themselves, but rather with the visual and linguistic signs rendered from them. We continue to look at images and read words as distinct sign-systems, even when multimodal AI treats them interchangeably in latent spaces. It is precisely this mismatch – a disparity between the intrinsic nature of generative signs and their perceptual manifestation – that gives rise to what I term the phenomenological divide. This divide reframes classic ekphrasis as a triadic problem of (1) algorithmic vectoriality, (2) generated sign-forms,

[55] Bajohr, 'Dumb Meaning', p. 67.

[56] See, for example, Amalia Foka's discussion of the use of generative images employed as interfaces to better understand the structure and functioning of the latent spaces in text-to-image models, in Chapter 6 of this volume.

[57] See Nuria Rodríguez-Ortega, 'Exploring the Concept of Transduction', where it is proposed to explore the epistemological framework associated with Simondon's concept of transduction.

and (3) human meaning-making, adding a new layer of complexity to any analysis of word and image.

In this context, the ekphrastic phenomena operating within latent spaces, and the corresponding conceptual displacements explored throughout this chapter, suggest that traditional modes of enquiry into the word–image relationship are no longer adequate. A new analytical framework and theoretical apparatus must be adopted – one that can accommodate the AI generation of signs and meanings, based on the transductive fusion of visual and linguistic characteristics, and guided by principles of statistical correlation and predictive logic. The challenge for art historians, media scholars, and critics will be to navigate this hybrid terrain, where artificial and human rationalities converge in a novel form of dialectical tension. Likewise, it is crucial to explore the consequences of the phenomenological divide caused by the gap between the computational logics operating in latent spaces and the way that generated signs are perceived as a new tension between the linguistic and the visual arises. This new scenario calls for an expansion of ekphrastic theory and a redefinition of its scope to incorporate new realities and fields of enquiry alongside the development of a post-anthropocentric theoretical framework and a revised semiotic epistemology.

Acknowledgements

This study forms part of the outcomes of the R&D project PID2021-125037NB-I00, funded by the Spanish Ministry of Science and Innovation titled 'Study and Interpretation of the Art Exhibitions Domain as a Complex Cultural System through Data Analytics and Natural Language Processing'.

6

Experiments in the Relationship between Art History and Text-to-Image Models

AMALIA FOKA

THE ADVENT OF text-to-image models, capable of transforming written prompts into visuals, has revolutionised computer vision and opened new frontiers for artistic and scholarly exploration.[1] However, this remarkable capability has also sparked a critical debate. The very nature of the training data, often scraped from the internet and shrouded in secrecy, raises unresolved issues about copyright, bias, and the representation of diverse cultures and perspectives.[2] Moreover, the inner workings of these models remain a 'black box', with the mechanisms by which they interpret complex concepts and translate them into visual form still elusive.[3] As Brown and Wasielewski suggest in this volume, the opacity of such systems – akin to a 'locked gallery' or a sealed performance – raises critical concerns around authorship, representation, and the ideologies encoded in training data.[4]

[1] See Aditya Ramesh, Mikhail Pavlov, Gabriel Goh, Scott Gray, Chelsea Voss, Alec Radford *et al.*, 'Zero-Shot Text-to-Image Generation', *Proceedings of the 38th International Conference on Machine Learning* (2021), pp. 8821–31, for a foundational model that helped define this paradigm.

[2] The opacity surrounding training data is a major concern in AI image generation. While models such as DALL·E, Midjourney, and Imagen are trained on proprietary datasets, Stable Diffusion uses the open LAION dataset (Christoph Schuhmann, Romain Beaumont, Richard Vencu, Cade Gordon, Ross Wightman, Mehdi Cherti *et al.*, 'LAION-5B: An Open Large-scale Dataset for Training Next Generation Image-Text Models', *Advances in Neural Information Processing Systems*, 35 (NeurIPS, 2022), pp. 25278–94), offering partial transparency. Nevertheless, issues of copyright, dataset bias, and representational equity remain unresolved.

[3] See W. Samek and K.R. Müller, 'Towards Explainable Artificial Intelligence', in *Explainable AI: Interpreting, Explaining and Visualizing Deep Learning*, edited by W. Samek, G. Montavon, A. Vedaldi, L.K. Hansen, and K.-R. Müller (Cham: Springer, 2019), pp. 5–22, for an overview of challenges and approaches to making deep learning models more interpretable.

[4] Kathryn Brown (in the Introduction to this volume) outlines the stakes of critical AI, emphasising demystification, ethical scrutiny, and resistance to technodeterministic narratives. Amanda Wasielewski, in Chapter 1 of this volume, draws on Joseph Beuys's 'locked gallery' performance as a metaphor for the opacity of text-to-image models, highlighting their performative inaccessibility and the ideological charge of training data.

Proceedings of the British Academy, **285**, 116–148, © Authors 2025.

This chapter investigates those concerns through a focused, empirical approach, using prompts derived from art historical analysis to interrogate how these models 'understand' and render complex visual concepts. Art historians examine artworks and translate visual details into textual descriptions, especially when employing methods such as formal and iconographical analysis.[5] This process is fundamentally ekphrastic, as it attempts to render the visual into verbal form – what Jaś Elsner has described as the core operation of art historical writing itself.[6] Yet, as James Elkins argues, such translation is always partial and fraught, revealing the inherent inadequacy of language in fully capturing visual experience.[7] James Heffernan, too, emphasises the mediating function of ekphrasis, framing it as a site of interpretative tension between word and image.[8] Text-to-image models reverse that process. This mirroring process probes the interpretative logic of text-to-image models and resonates with Nuria Rodríguez-Ortega's concept of 'inverted ekphrasis', where description gives rise to image rather than the reverse.[9]

This methodology also relates to what Leonardo Impett calls an 'iconology of the dataset': a critical lens that sees the model not as a neutral translator but as a system imbued with aesthetic, ideological, and historical biases.[10] The images it produces reflect and reproduce the cultural conditions embedded in datasets. As such, this study contributes to the broader field of critical AI by offering empirical evidence of how such systems interpret (or misinterpret) canonical visual vocabularies. In doing so, it questions whether these models are simply recombinatory engines – remixing existing motifs – or whether they gesture towards new, albeit algorithmically constrained, modes of visual expression.

Ultimately, by confronting the limitations, distortions, and unexpected resonances that arise when machine vision encounters art historical language, this chapter seeks to reframe these models not only as tools, but also as subjects of aesthetic and epistemological enquiry. In doing so, it aligns with ongoing conversations in critical AI about transparency, demystification, and the ethical stakes of generative systems, while also exploring how the humanities might inform and reshape the evolving methodologies of computer vision.

[5] M. Hatt and C. Klonk, *Art History: A Critical Introduction to Its Methods* (Manchester: Manchester University Press, 2006), pp. 13–29 and pp. 73–112.

[6] J. Elsner, 'Art History as Ekphrasis', *Art History*, 33:1 (2010), pp. 10–27 (p. 11).

[7] J. Elkins, *On Pictures and the Words That Fail Them* (Cambridge: Cambridge University Press, 1998), pp. 3–15.

[8] J.A.W. Heffernan, 'Ekphrasis and Representation', *New Literary History*, 22:2 (1991), pp. 297–316 (p. 301).

[9] See also Nuria Rodríguez-Ortega (Chapter 5 of this volume). In her analysis of 'inverted ekphrasis', this inversion signals a broader transformation in representational logic, one that challenges established semiotic hierarchies and prompts a reconsideration of how meaning is produced when language becomes the origin rather than the outcome of visual expression.

[10] Leonardo Impett, in Chapter 4 of this volume, proposes an 'iconology of the dataset' as a method for interpreting the symbolic and ideological structures embedded in training data, treating datasets as culturally shaped visual archives.

Methodology

Defining art historical concepts

This methodology adopts a black box exploration strategy that leverages art historical research methods to investigate the inner workings of text-to-image models. A controlled vocabulary was defined to establish a shared understanding of key terminology in art historical discourse. This vocabulary serves as a bridge between the domain of art history and the field of text-to-image generation, creating a structured framework for crafting effective prompts and analysing the generated images. To this end, a list of frequently used terms and concepts was compiled from two key areas: formal analysis and iconographic analysis.

Formal analysis focuses on the visual components of an artwork. Analysing elements such as line, shape, colour, texture, space, and composition helps reveal the artist's technical skill, stylistic choices, and the overall aesthetic impact of the work. Iconographic analysis addresses the symbolic meanings and cultural significance embedded within an artwork's imagery. By decoding symbols, motifs, allegories, and situating the work within its historical context, this approach reveals deeper layers of meaning intended by the artist. Together, these methods provide a foundation for interpreting both the visual and symbolic dimensions of artworks.

Curating a diverse corpus of artworks

The second phase of this methodology focused on selecting artworks that have undergone extensive art historical analysis and represent pivotal moments in art history, across diverse media such as painting, sculpture, and installation. These works were chosen not only for their cultural significance, but also for their relevance to the research questions and the diversity of aesthetic parameters they encompass.

The first group of paintings spans the Renaissance to Abstract Expressionism and includes *The Arnolfini Portrait* (1434) by Jan van Eyck, *Impression, Sunrise* (1872) by Claude Monet, and *Autumn Rhythm (Number 30)* (1950) by Jackson Pollock. To expand the corpus into three-dimensional and installation art, the Hellenistic sculpture *Winged Victory of Samothrace* (*c.*190 BCE) and the contemporary installation *The Dinner Party* (1974–9) by Judy Chicago were included. This selection enabled an assessment of how text-to-image models handle a range of visual, spatial, and material complexities.

Each of these works explores a distinct dimension of the models' capabilities and limitations: *The Arnolfini Portrait* raises issues of symbolic misreadings and cultural bias; *Impression, Sunrise* exemplifies stylistic emulation; *Autumn Rhythm* introduces challenges of abstraction and symbolism; *Winged Victory* presents material representation; and *The Dinner Party* foregrounds gendered representation. Together, they form a methodological and conceptual continuum that supports a multifaceted investigation into how models interpret and generate images based on varied visual and cultural parameters.

While diverse in style and medium, the selected artworks share a common thread: they push the boundaries of traditional artistic representation, challenge perceptions of reality, and invite new forms of engagement with art. These qualities make them particularly relevant for research on text-to-image models.

To systematically analyse each artwork, the study drew on art historical sources such as academic publications, exhibition catalogues, and scholarly essays. The analysis identified key formal and iconographic terms used to describe each work's visual elements and their creation of meaning. For the formal analysis, terms related to line, colour, composition, perspective, and other visual aspects were recorded and examined in relation to each artwork. The iconographic analysis focused on symbolic content and cultural references, including symbols, motifs, allegories, and historical context. Relevant quotes and paraphrases from the literature were collected to guide the prompt crafting, ensuring the prompts reflected the essence of art historical interpretation.

Crafting prompts based on art historical analysis

To effectively probe the models' understanding of art historical concepts and assess their broader visual language comprehension, this study crafted prompts that are both informative and evocative, guiding the model to generate images that reflect specific artistic and historical ideas. These prompts are primarily constructed using paraphrases of art historical analysis to avoid overly specific wording that might lead to mere imitation of the original artworks. However, in cases where direct quotes are particularly succinct or capture a nuanced aspect of the analysis, they are selectively incorporated.

The goal was to balance the conveying of broader historical ideas with the avoidance of excessively specific references unique to each artwork. To achieve this, the prompt design prioritised terms and concepts that are widely applicable to a particular style, period, or movement. Special emphasis was also placed on visual and symbolic elements most salient to each artwork's received meaning and significance. This ensured that the prompts remained accurate and effective in guiding the models towards generating images that embody core historical concepts.

Prompt creation involved an iterative refinement process. Initial prompts were based on collected art historical analysis and then tested through multiple variations, introducing subtle changes in wording and phrasing. By analysing the models' outputs for each variation, the study gathered insights into how the models interpret and respond to different visual language cues.

This iterative process led to a set of prompts that are both specific enough to anchor interpretation and open-ended enough to allow for generative variation. Prompt design thus became a form of reverse-engineering, akin to what Impett describes as an iconological reading of the dataset. By observing what the model chooses to visualise in response to specific terms, one can begin to trace the outlines of its inherited visual logic.[11] Furthermore, crafting prompts involved more than mere descriptions; it encoded specific cultural semantics that the models interpret through latent vector spaces. As Rodríguez-Ortega notes, such prompts function as entry points into a 'vectorial semiotics', where linguistic and visual meanings converge within statistically organised latent spaces.[12] The final prompt variations used in the study are presented in Table 6.1 at the end of the chapter.[13]

Generating images with text-to-image models

To gain a comprehensive understanding of how different models interpret and translate art historical prompts, three text-to-image models were employed: DALL·E, Midjourney, and Stable Diffusion.[14] These models were selected for their prominence in the field, their differing strengths and limitations, and their distinct generative approaches which reveal important nuances in the interpretation of art historical concepts.

DALL·E, known for its photorealism and ability to render intricate visual detail, is trained on a vast dataset of text–image pairs and uses a transformer-based architecture. Midjourney, by contrast, does not disclose its technical architecture, but is widely believed to employ a diffusion-based process, with a strong emphasis on aesthetic stylisation and creative abstraction. Its outputs often exhibit a distinctive visual flair. Stable Diffusion, an open-source model, relies on a diffusion-based architecture and balances photorealism with stylistic flexibility, offering a wide range of visual interpretations.

Using identical prompts derived from art historical analysis, the study compared the outputs of these three models. This approach made it possible to identify variations in how each model interpreted the same concepts, shedding light on their respective strengths and limitations in representing specific elements of art history.

For each artwork in the curated corpus, a fixed number of images was generated per prompt across all three models. This accounted for variation within each model's output and provided a more robust and representative sample for analysis.

[11] Impett, Chapter 4 of this volume.

[12] Rodríguez-Ortega, Chapter 5 of this volume.

[13] For larger versions of the images and full prompts used for each text-to-image model, please visit https://amaliafoka.com/Experiments-in-Art-History-and-Text-to-Image-Models.html

[14] OpenAI, 'DALL·E 3' (2023), https://openai.com/index/DALL·E-3/ [accessed 9 May 2024]; Midjourney Inc., 'Midjourney' (2023), https://www.midjourney.com/home/ [accessed 9 May 2024]; Stability AI, 'Stability AI Image Models' (2024), https://stability.ai/stable-image [accessed 9 May 2024].

Evaluating model performance and understanding

The final stage of the methodology consisted of a qualitative evaluation of the text-to-image models' performance and understanding of art historical concepts, focusing on the formal and iconographic elements present in the generated images. These images were then analysed and compared to the original artwork and the prompt that guided their creation. The evaluation assessed the models' ability to capture and translate formal elements (line, colour, composition, perspective), their understanding and representation of iconographic elements (symbols, motifs, allegories). Additionally, the evaluation considered the models' capacity to generate novel and creative interpretations while remaining faithful to core art historical concepts.

Crucially, this stage also examined the interpretative variability observed across models, particularly when responding to abstract or symbolically dense prompts. Such variability may reflect what Rodríguez-Ortega describes as *intersemanticity*; a dynamic in which the boundary between verbal and visual signs becomes fluid, and meaning emerges from shared patterns across the linguistic and visual domains within the models' latent vector spaces.[15] This framework provided a valuable lens for understanding how AI models synthesise cultural knowledge and produce images that are not merely translations but transformations of textual input.

Experiments and analysis

The Arnolfini Portrait (1434) by Jan van Eyck

The Arnolfini Portrait (1434) by Jan van Eyck, an oil painting on oak panel, demonstrates meticulous realism and layered symbolic detail. The painting's balanced composition, refined use of light and shadow to create spatial depth, and vibrant colours convey a sense of opulence and social status.[16] Laden with iconography, the work invites multiple interpretations: the couple's clasped hands may signify *dextrarum iunctio*, the ritual joining of hands in marriage; the man's raised right hand has been read as a gesture of oath-taking; and the woman's pose and appearance have sparked debate regarding whether she is pregnant.[17] The convex mirror has been interpreted both as a symbol of divine omniscience and as a Marian reference.[18] Other objects reinforce the painting's symbolic complexity: the single lit candle (possibly evoking the all-seeing eye of God or the flame of life), the oranges (linked to fertility or wealth), and the small dog (symbolising fidelity). These elements have supported a range of interpretations. Panofsky viewed the painting

[15] Rodríguez-Ortega, Chapter 5 of this volume.

[16] C. Harbison, *Jan van Eyck: The Play of Realism* (London: Reaktion Books, 1991), pp. 13–23, 83.

[17] E. Hall, *The Arnolfini Betrothal: Medieval Marriage and the Enigma of Van Eyck's Double Portrait* (Berkeley, CA: University of California Press, 2023), pp. 20–40.

[18] E. Panofsky, 'Jan van Eyck's "Arnolfini" Portrait', *Burlington Magazine*, 64 (1934), pp. 117–19, 122–7 (p. 126).

as a visual marriage contract,[19] while Bedaux questioned the presence of hidden symbolism.[20] Harbison proposed a multivalent reading, combining symbolic and realistic elements,[21] Carroll emphasised legal authority,[22] and Koster suggested a memorial function.[23] Collectively, these views reflect ongoing debates about social roles and symbolism in 15th-century Bruges.

DALL·E interpretations

DALL·E's interpretations of *The Arnolfini Portrait* reveal a nuanced understanding of formal elements such as colour, lighting, detail, and texture, while its grasp of specific iconography and deeper meanings varies considerably depending on the prompt's phrasing and focus.

A highly detailed prompt emphasising object placement (Figure 6.1, DALL·E-*i*) resulted in an image with only the couple and a column, omitting key elements such as the chandelier and dog. This demonstrates DALL·E's difficulty in following explicit instructions, highlighting potential limitations in generating comprehensive scenes.

Conversely, using evocative language (Figure 6.1, DALL·E-*ii*) produced an image aligned with the portrait's overall aesthetic, yet lacked intricate symbolism and specific detail. A balanced prompt allowing for interpretation without 15th-century context (Figure 6.1, DALL·E-*iii*), yielded a complex, layered composition with multiple scenes, but again lacked religious symbols and detailed interpretations found in the original.

Removing historical context by specifying a 'modern time' setting (Figure 6.1, DALL·E-*iv*) introduced Neo-Renaissance or Neoclassical elements, such as twisted columns and sculptures, but omitted religious symbolism. Further emphasis on modernity by removing 'glazing' and 'oil painting' (Figure 6.1, DALL·E-*v*) led to geometric abstraction reminiscent of Modernism, again missing religious symbols. This suggests a potential disconnect in DALL·E's understanding of religious iconography in contemporary settings.

Surprisingly, refining the prompt to specify the '21st century' instead of the broader term 'modern time' produced an image (Figure 6.1, DALL·E-*vi*) with Orientalist elements in a historical setting. This underscores the model's difficulty associating religious symbols with contemporary contexts, and suggests biases in training data. It appears to default to Orientalism that depicted Eastern cultures and peoples in a stereotypical and often patronising way.

19 Panofsky, 'Jan van Eyck's "Arnolfini" Portrait', pp. 124–6.

20 J.B. Bedaux, 'The Reality of Symbols: The Question of Disguised Symbolism in Jan van Eyck's Arnolfini Portrait', *Simiolus*, 16 (1986), pp. 5–28 (p. 7).

21 Harbison, *Jan van Eyck*, p. 83.

22 M.D. Carroll, 'In the Name of God and Profit: Jan van Eyck's Arnolfini Portrait', *Representations*, 44 (1993), pp. 96–118 (p. 98).

23 M. Koster, 'The Arnolfini Double Portrait: A Simple Solution', *Apollo*, 158 (2003), pp. 3–14.

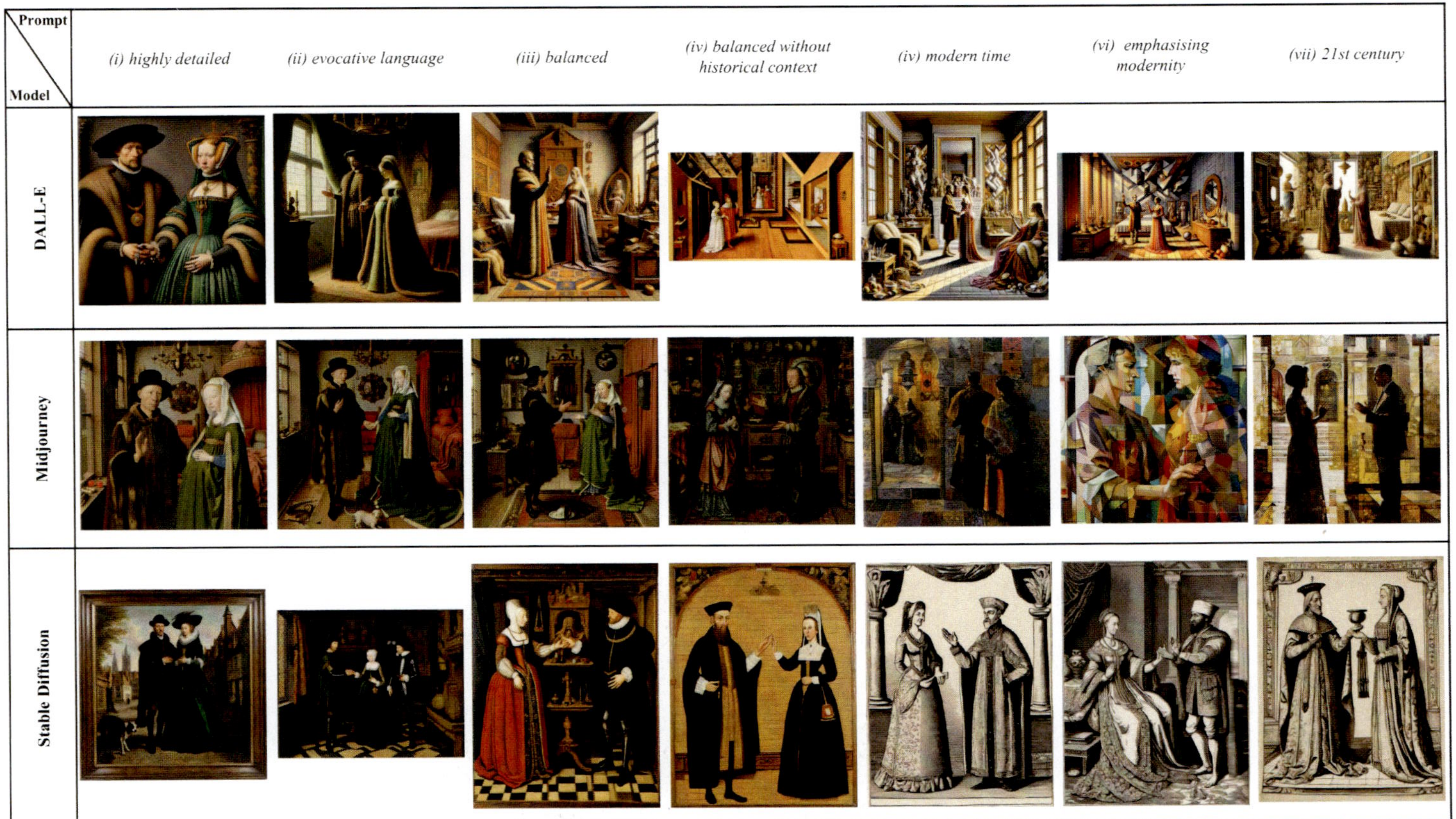

Figure 6.1 Interpretations of *The Arnolfini Portrait* by DALL·E, Midjourney, and Stable Diffusion across seven prompt variations. Rows indicate models; columns show variations across seven prompt types. Source: Author. © Amalia Foka

Midjourney interpretations

Midjourney's results demonstrate a refined understanding of formal artistic elements and a strong ability to capture the aesthetic essence and themes of wealth, status, and traditional gender roles. The first three prompts (Figure 6.1, Midjourney-*i, ii, iii*) consistently produced images that clearly resemble the original, indicating that Midjourney's training data include substantial information on historical artistic styles and artworks like *The Arnolfini Portrait* – a finding not observed in DALL·E.

Despite this, Midjourney shares with DALL·E limited understanding of symbolic interpretations and specific iconography. Even with detailed prompts and art historical terms, the generated images often lacked or misrepresented crucial religious symbols. For example, the single lit candle, a significant symbol in the original, appears as a candle-shaped bulb in some images (Figure 6.1, Midjourney-*i, ii*). This indicates a disconnect between Midjourney's ability to identify objects and its understanding of their symbolic significance.

When prompts removed historical context but retained composition-specific instructions (Figure 6.1, Midjourney-*iv*) the result resembled Flemish painting, yet failed to accurately depict the clasped hands or suggest the woman's body shape. This suggests a prioritisation of visual style over symbolic or narrative accuracy.

The 'modern time' prompt (Figure 6.1, Midjourney-*v*) resulted in an image with influences from Islamic art and Orientalism, similar to the bias observed in DALL·E. The addition of an archway and multiple figures, likely due to prompt instructions for depth and a reflective mirror, shifted the spatial and narrative focus.

Efforts to further modernise the setting (Figure 6.1, Midjourney-*vi*) by removing the prompt term 'glazing technique' led to geometric abstraction, echoing DALL·E's tendencies. The 21st-century prompt (Figure 6.1, Midjourney-*vii*) generated an image with a mosaic-like fragmentation and a blend of past and present elements. Architectural elements such as arches and stairs enhance depth, showcasing Midjourney's potential for creative reimagining. However, the absence of religious symbolism in both modernised outputs – similar to DALL·E's results – underscores Midjourney's struggle to associate such symbols with modern imagery.

Stable Diffusion interpretations

Stable Diffusion's interpretations of *The Arnolfini Portrait* reflect notable differences in training data and generative approach compared to DALL·E and Midjourney. While all three models exhibit limitations in understanding deeper symbolic interpretations and accurately depicting specific details, Stable Diffusion consistently struggles with intricate detail and the nuanced symbolic content of the original artwork. This may be due to a greater emphasis on basic compositional elements and core artistic principles in its training data, potentially at the expense of complex iconography and detailed symbolic references.

In response to a highly detailed prompt (Figure 6.1, SD-*i*), Stable Diffusion produced an image that, while effectively emphasising the figures and their status through composition and setting, lacked specific details and symbolism found in the original. A prompt utilising evocative language (Figure 6.1, SD-*ii*) further highlights Stable Diffusion's strength in composition, depth, and perspective, successfully conveying themes of wealth and status. However, it again struggled to accurately depict the specified setting and symbolic details, including a third figure and omitting the bedroom setting specified in the prompt.

When given a more balanced prompt with fewer details (Figure 6.1, SD-*iii*), Stable Diffusion incorporated some religious symbols. However, unlike DALL·E and Midjourney, it failed to include all objects and symbols described in the prompt (such as the bedroom setting) or to depict them with the same level of creativity and adherence to the prompt's instructions.

Surprisingly, the removal of historical context led to a relatively flat image (Figure 6.1, SD-*iv*) with minimal depth, primarily conveying wealth and status through clothing and gestures. This suggests that Stable Diffusion relies heavily on visual tropes and artistic conventions tied to specific historical periods when interpreting prompts. When contextualised in the 15th-century Flemish context, it seems to draw upon its art historical knowledge to reconstruct period-specific aesthetics. However, when stripped of that context, it struggles to generate novel visual elements or interpret scenes beyond familiar historical frameworks.

Prompts aimed at modernising the setting (Figure 6.1, SD-*v*, *vi*, *vii*) consistently produced images resembling engravings or woodcuts. This could indicate that Stable Diffusion's training data are heavily skewed towards historical imagery, or that the model has difficulty associating traditional symbolic meanings with contemporary visual languages.

Comparative analysis and discussion

In conclusion, DALL·E, Midjourney, and Stable Diffusion each demonstrate distinct strengths and limitations in their interpretations of *The Arnolfini Portrait*. While DALL·E effectively captures formal visual elements, it struggles with complex prompt structures and displays an inconsistent grasp of iconography. Midjourney excels in replicating visual aesthetics and conveying atmosphere, but falls short in interpreting deeper symbolism and rendering specific details accurately. Stable Diffusion, by contrast, emphasises compositional elements and foundational artistic principles, yet consistently struggles with intricate details and the layered meanings embedded in the original artwork.

Notably, none of the models effectively associates religious symbols with modern settings, revealing a shared shortcoming that may stem from training biases or representational gaps, and in some cases, results in the use of Orientalist aesthetics that displace or stereotype non-Western visual cultures. These findings align with Kathryn Brown's argument that computer vision systems tend to reproduce a technologically mediated 'period eye' rooted in canonical European art traditions, reinforcing stylistic hierarchies and overlooking alternative visual cultures.[24] This may help explain both the persistent omission of religious symbolism in contemporary settings and the appearance of Orientalist motifs when historical context is removed.

Impression, Sunrise (1872) by Claude Monet

Claude Monet's *Impression, Sunrise* (1872), a seminal Impressionist oil painting, captures a fleeting moment in the port of Le Havre.[25] The asymmetrical composition is dominated by the vibrant orange sun and its reflection, surrounded by a hazy atmosphere of cool blues and greys. Loose, gestural brushstrokes and indistinct forms emphasise the ephemeral nature of the scene.[26] The painting juxtaposes the natural beauty of the sunrise with industrial elements such as boats, cranes, and smokestacks, symbolising the changing landscape of 19th-century France.[27]

DALL·E interpretations

The three DALL·E generated images based on varying prompts inspired by Monet's painting offer intriguing interpretations of the work. Each image captures certain aspects of the original artwork, yet deviates in distinctive ways, demonstrating the nuances of AI image generation based on textual input.

A detailed prompt rich in evocative language effectively captures the interplay of light and atmosphere found in Monet's work (Figure 6.2, DALL·E-*i*). The limited colour palette evokes a sense of tranquillity and introspection, successfully mirroring the painting's thematic exploration of nature and human endeavour. However, industrial elements, symbolic of 19th-century France's changing landscape, are notably absent.

The image based on a less detailed prompt devoid of explicit art historical references captures the essence of a sunrise over a harbour with a more stylised and less impressionistic aesthetic (Figure 6.2, DALL·E-*ii*). The inclusion of 'industrial structures' prompted the model to integrate elements resonating with Monet's symbolic commentary. However, the brushwork lacks the loose, expressive quality characteristic of Impressionism.

The prompt focusing on the symbolism and tension between nature and human progress, produced an image (Figure 6.2, DALL·E-*iii*) incorporating industrial

[24] Kathryn Brown, Chapter 3 of this volume.

[25] M. Mathieu and D. Lobstein (eds), *Monet's Impression Sunrise, The Biography of a Painting* (Paris: Editions Hazan, 2015), p. 12.

[26] J. House, *Monet: Nature into Art* (New Haven, CT: Yale University Press, 1986), p. 15.

[27] S.Z. Levine, *Monet, Narcissus, and Self-Reflection: The Modernist Myth of the Self* (Chicago, IL: University of Chicago Press, 1994), p. 45.

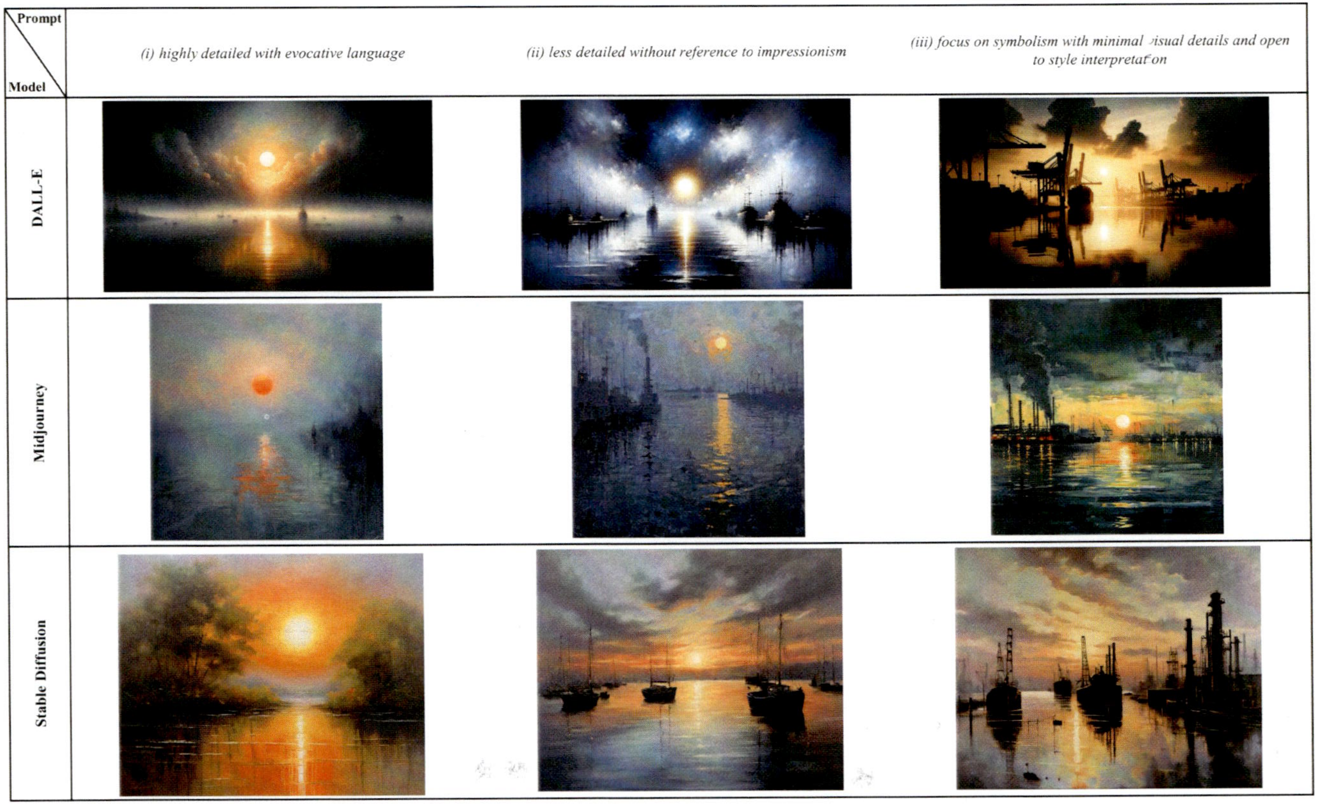

Figure 6.2 Interpretations of *Impression, Sunrise* by DALL·E, Midjourney, and Stable Diffusion, highlighting how different prompt phrasings influence each model's visual output and understanding. Rows show models; columns show three prompt types. Source: Author. © Amal a Foka

elements such as cranes and ships. The contrast between warm and cool tones effectively highlights the rising sun and its reflection on the water, reinforcing the painting's thematic concerns. However, it lacks the loose, expressive brushwork characteristic of Impressionism, opting for a more polished and detailed aesthetic.

Midjourney interpretations

Midjourney demonstrates a grasp of Impressionist techniques, successfully emulating loose brushwork, atmospheric light, and fleeting moments of light and colour typical of Monet's *Impression, Sunrise*.

The image generated (Figure 6.2, Midjourney-*i*) from the detailed and evocative prompt aligns closely with Impressionist principles. The loose, expressive brushwork, particularly in the depiction of the sky and water, creates a dynamic sense of movement and fluidity. The shimmering effect of light on the water is rendered effectively. However, like DALL·E, the generated image prioritises the natural beauty of the scene, omitting the industrial elements present in Monet's painting, which symbolise the changing landscape of 19th-century France.

The second image (Figure 6.2, Midjourney-*ii*), was generated from a minimally detailed prompt emphasising tranquillity. It succeeds in capturing a sense of peace through the depiction of calm water and atmospheric light. The brushstrokes, although visible and varied, lack the loose, expressive style that is a hallmark of Impressionism. While atmospherically similar to *Impression, Sunrise*, the image lacks the nuanced symbolism and detail that define the original.

The third image (Figure 6.2, Midjourney -*iii*), was produced by a prompt focused on symbolism including minimal visual details. It depicts a harbour scene with industrial elements such as cranes and ships, yet it falls short of fully conveying the intended symbolic tension between nature and human progress, as specified in the prompt. While thematically related and atmospheric, the image does not achieve the depth of meaning present in Monet's original.

Midjourney's strengths lie in its understanding of formal analysis, as demonstrated by its effective use of composition, colour, and brushwork to create visually appealing and harmonious images. However, its treatment of iconographical themes is less consistent. While the overall mood and atmosphere are often captured effectively, symbolic meaning, particularly in the third image, is less successfully rendered.

Stable Diffusion interpretations

Stable Diffusion's interpretations of *Impression, Sunrise* capture some Impressionist qualities, yet diverge significantly in composition, symbolism, and fidelity from Monet's original.

The first image (Figure 6.2, SD-*i*), generated from a detailed prompt, features loose, expressive brushstrokes that contribute to an Impressionistic quality.

However, it deviates significantly from Monet's composition. Notably, it includes trees that are absent in the original and omits the industrial elements central to the painting's commentary on the changing landscape of 19th-century France. The unexpected inclusion of trees may reflect an overrepresentation of traditional landscapes in Stable Diffusion's training data. The image prioritises natural beauty, overlooking the complex symbolism of industrialisation and the transient nature of light in Monet's work. Among the three models, this output diverges the most from the original.

The less detailed prompt results in a peaceful harbour scene with boats, echoing Monet's subject matter, yet leaning towards more traditional representations (Figure 6.2, SD-*ii*). This further suggests potential training gaps in recognising Impressionist aesthetics. The image evokes tranquillity through calm water and atmospheric light, employing a harmonious colour palette, but lacks the specific details and symbolic layers present in *Impression, Sunrise*.

The third prompt, emphasising symbolism and open to interpretation, yields an image (Figure 6.2, SD-*iii*) featuring industrial elements within a harbour scene. However, the composition places these elements centrally, creating a visual emphasis that diverges from Monet's more subtle treatment of the theme. The image tends towards realism with smooth brushwork, contrasting the loose, expressive quality typical of Impressionism. While it captures some atmospheric elements, it falls short in conveying the nuanced symbolism and compositional intent of the original painting.

Comparative analysis and discussion

In conclusion, DALL·E, Midjourney, and Stable Diffusion, each present distinct interpretations of Monet's *Impression, Sunrise*, based on varying textual prompts. DALL·E demonstrates a solid grasp of the painting's visual characteristics, particularly in capturing the interplay of light and atmosphere. However, it occasionally struggles to integrate the painting's industrial elements and underlying symbolism. Midjourney excels in replicating the loose brushwork, atmospheric lighting, and emphasis on fleeting moments of light and colour that define Impressionism. Stable Diffusion, while capturing some surface-level traits of Impressionist style, has more difficulty with composition, symbolism, and fidelity to the original work. Its outputs often lean towards traditional and realistic aesthetics, lacking the expressive brushwork essential to Impressionism. These tendencies may reflect limitations in its training data concerning artworks and Impressionist conventions.

***Autumn Rhythm (Number 30)* (1950) by Jackson Pollock**

Autumn Rhythm (Number 30) (1950) by Jackson Pollock, is a monumental Abstract Expressionist painting, created using poured and splattered enamel on unprimed canvas.[28] The all-over composition, lack of central focus, and dense network of lines create a rhythmic and dynamic visual experience, as noted by art critic Robert Goodnough.[29] The black, white, brown, and silver paint, with accents of teal blue, evoke a sense of depth and complexity.[30] The painting's title suggests a connection to the natural world and its cyclical changes, while also alluding to the musical inspiration behind the work, as explored by Matthew Rampley.[31] Pollock's drip technique and the use of unconventional tools result in a richly textured surface, embodying the energy and spontaneity of Abstract Expressionism.[32]

DALL·E interpretations

The first prompt, with its detailed description and evocative language, successfully guided the generation of an image (Figure 6.3, DALL·E-*i*) that echoes the essence of Pollock's *Autumn Rhythm*. The generated image mirrors the all-over composition, dynamic lines, and earthy colour palette of the original, creating a sense of rhythmic dance through bold lines, seemingly haphazard splatters of paint, and a lack of central focus. Its textured surface invites exploration, reinforcing the connection to Pollock's style.

In contrast, the second prompt, being less detailed and lacking references to Abstract Expressionism, resulted in an image (Figure 6.3, DALL·E-*ii*) that deviates significantly from Pollock's signature style. While its dynamic composition and energetic brushstrokes evoke the spirit of action painting, it incorporates more representational elements, a structured layout, and a broader colour spectrum, lacking the chaotic spontaneity of Pollock's drip technique. The image also appears more overtly artificial, highlighting the model's struggle with abstraction.

The third prompt, emphasising the feeling of autumn and specifically using the term 'rhythmic pulse', resulted in an image (Figure 6.3, DALL·E-*iii*) that successfully translates the season's vibrant energy. The depiction of trees, leaves, and dappled light effectively evokes the feeling of crisp air and rustling leaves. However, it falls short in conveying the prompt's other keywords, 'raw power' and 'cathartic release', lacking the intensity and emotional depth these suggest. Despite sharing a thematic celebration of autumn with the original, the image differs greatly in approach and emotional resonance. Additionally, it bears the clear signs of AI-generated aesthetics.

[28] S. Naifeh and G.W. Smith, *Jackson Pollock: An American Saga* (New York: Clarkson Potter, 1989), pp. 755–800.

[29] R. Goodnough, 'Pollock Paints a Picture', *Art News*, 50:3 (1951).

[30] Naifeh and Smith, *Jackson Pollock*, p. 881.

[31] M. Rampley, 'Identity and Difference: Jackson Pollock and the Ideology of the Drip', *Oxford Art Journal*, 19:2 (1996), pp. 83–94 (p. 87).

[32] Rampley, 'Identity and Difference', p. 88; Goodnough, 'Pollock Paints a Picture'.

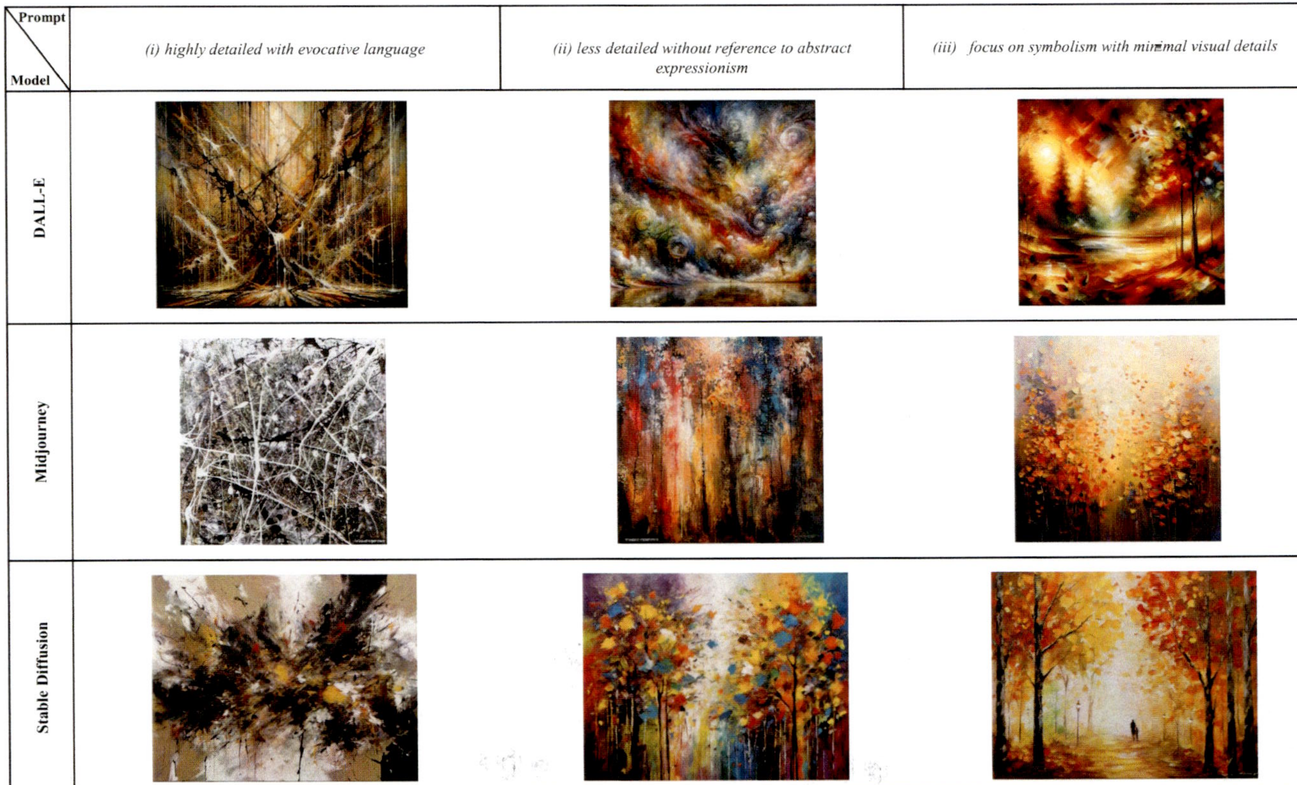

Figure 6.3 Interpretations of prompts inspired by Jackson Pollock's *Autumn Rhythm (Number 30)* using DALL·E, Midjourney, and Stable Diffusion, revealing a mix of abstraction and representation, with varying success in evoking the emotional depth and expressive energy of the original. Source: Author. © Amalia Foka

Midjourney interpretations

The first image (Figure 6.3, Midjourney-*i*), generated from a very detailed prompt, effectively translates the emphasis on unrestrained energy and raw emotion, particularly through the phrase 'raw, unfiltered energy'. Its chaotic composition and splattered paint application are reminiscent of Pollock's action painting, demonstrating Midjourney's superior training in artistic styles and movements compared to other models. The image captures the essence of Abstract Expressionism, evoking the movement's energy and emotional intensity while inviting viewers to engage with the work.

The second image (Figure 6.3, Midjourney-*ii*), derived from a less detailed prompt, deviates significantly from Pollock's abstraction. It employs a more vibrant and diverse colour palette, contrasting the original's predominantly earthy tones. Lines are more defined and organic, differing from the chaotic spontaneity of those in *Autumn Rhythm*. While evoking a connection to nature, the generated image presents a more discernible landscape, likely an autumnal scene, with explicit symbolism such as trees and a glowing light source. Nevertheless, Midjourney's output demonstrates a stronger grasp of abstraction than DALL·E.

The third image (Figure 6.3, Midjourney-*iii*) adopts a more representational approach than *Autumn Rhythm*. It captures the season's beauty through rustling leaves and a sense of movement, that connects viewers to the natural world. However, it falls short of conveying the 'raw power', 'cathartic release', and 'boundless possibilities of human expression' articulated in the prompt. Unlike Pollock's abstract and emotionally charged style, this image presents a literal depiction of an autumnal landscape, favouring traditional representation over the visceral dynamism that defines *Autumn Rhythm*.

Stable Diffusion interpretations

The first prompt (Figure 6.3, SD-*i*), emphasising 'unrestrained energy', 'raw emotion', and the 'rhythmic dance of colour and line', aligns conceptually with the core principles of Abstract Expressionism seen in *Autumn Rhythm*. The generated image shares with Pollock's work an all-over composition lacking a clear focal point. However, the visual activity is concentrated primarily in the centre of the canvas. Additionally, its colour palette diverges significantly from the original. Nevertheless, the output suggests that Stable Diffusion's training data likely include a range of Abstract Expressionist works.

The second prompt, which focused on emotional resonance and a connection to nature, produced an image (Figure 6.3, SD-*ii*) with a more structured layout and a broader colour palette. Although it successfully conveys the 'vibrant energy' and 'rhythmic pulse' of nature, it strays from the chaotic spontaneity characteristic of

Pollock's work, incorporating recognisable elements such as trees and leaves and moving away from a purely abstract visual language.

The third image (Figure 6.3, SD-*iii*), centred on the 'vibrant energy of autumn', yielded a clearly representational autumnal landscape, departing from the abstract nature and emotional intensity of Pollock's work. Rather than expressing energy through abstraction, the image conveys a subdued rhythmic pulse through repeated motifs such as tree trunks and a winding path, falling short of the 'raw power' and 'cathartic release' referenced in the prompt. This outcome suggests that Stable Diffusion's training data may be skewed towards natural scenes and realistic depictions, limiting its ability to convey abstract concepts or emotional depth unless explicitly prompted. As a result, the generated image falls short of capturing the expressive power and intensity that define Pollock's work.

Comparative analysis and discussion

In conclusion, Midjourney emerges as the most adept at capturing the essence of Pollock's style, while DALL·E and Stable Diffusion offer alternative interpretations with varying degrees of success. Midjourney consistently produced the most faithful responses to the prompts, showcasing a strong understanding of Abstract Expressionism and effectively conveying the essence of the original work. However, it still showed limitations in translating specific details and symbolism from the prompts into the generated images. DALL·E, unless explicitly directed, struggled to grasp the abstract nature of the prompts and defaulted to more representational imagery, diverging significantly from Pollock's signature drip technique and chaotic spontaneity. Similarly, Stable Diffusion tended to prioritise surface-level patterns and recognisable forms over the deeper emotional resonance and expressive power that define Abstract Expressionism. Its outputs were often more structured and simplified interpretations of landscapes, lacking the raw energy and unfiltered expression embodied in Pollock's work.

***Winged Victory of Samothrace* (c.190 BCE)**

The *Winged Victory of Samothrace* (*c.*190 BCE), a Hellenistic sculpture crafted from Parian marble, dynamically represents Nike, the Greek goddess of victory.[33] The dramatic pose, with outstretched wings and billowing drapery, conveys movement, power, and triumph.[34] The now missing head and arms add to its enigmatic allure. The statue symbolises a naval triumph, potentially over the Rhodians due to

[33] R.R.R. Smith, *Hellenistic Sculpture: A Handbook* (London: Thames and Hudson, 1991), pp. 77–86.

[34] Louvre Museum, 'A Stairway to Victory – The Daru Staircase', https://www.louvre.fr/en/explore/the-palace/a-stairway-to-victory [accessed 20 May 2024].

the use of Lartian marble in the ship's prow, and its original placement in a sanctuary suggests a votive function.[35]

DALL·E interpretations

The initial prompt, rich in descriptive detail, evocative language, and art historical terminology, yielded a sculpture that somewhat resembled the original *Winged Victory of Samothrace* in material, pose, dynamism, and symbolic representation of Nike as a triumphant figure (Figure 6.4, DALL·E-*i*). The sculpture accurately maintained the headless form and missing arms, as well as the intricate detailing of the wings and drapery. This demonstrates the model's overall understanding of Hellenistic sculpture's focus on realism, movement, and the symbolism of victory embodied by Nike. However, the ship's prow was rendered inaccurately, diverging significantly from the original.

The second prompt, though less detailed and omitting reference to the Hellenistic period, still captured the dynamism, intricate drapery, dramatic pose, and movement of the original sculpture (Figure 6.4, DALL·E-*ii*). It even approximated certain Hellenistic stylistic features, suggesting that DALL·E's training data may include numerous Hellenistic sculptures. The inclusion of 'marble' in the prompt produced a sculpture reminiscent of antiquity, indicating a learned association between the material with ancient art. Yet again, the ship's prow was misrepresented, this time replaced by sea waves, losing the specific historical and naval context. Additionally, the model failed to adhere to the prompt's instruction for a missing head and arms.

The third prompt, minimally descriptive but specifying 'marble sculpture', produced a dynamic pose with symbolic elements including wings and intricate drapery (Figure 6.4, DALL·E-*iii*). However, a lion figure was introduced, possibly reflecting the prompt's emphasis on triumph and power. The depiction of a male figure, despite the use of female pronouns, suggests a potential gender bias in associating 'triumphant pose' and 'powerful stance' with masculinity. As in previous outputs, the sculpture's form again invoked antiquity through material and stylistic choices.

The final prompt, requesting a 'modern sculpture', yielded a sculpture aligning with modernist aesthetics of sleek lines and minimalist drapery (Figure 6.4, DALL·E-*iv*). It conveyed the essence of victory, albeit associating it with an emphasis on form and motion. However, the downward-facing head conflicted the intended 'triumphant pose'. The recurring depiction of a male figure reinforces the earlier noted gender bias, likely stemming from the model's learned associations between power-related language and male representations.

[35] Smith, *Hellenistic Sculpture*, p. 78.

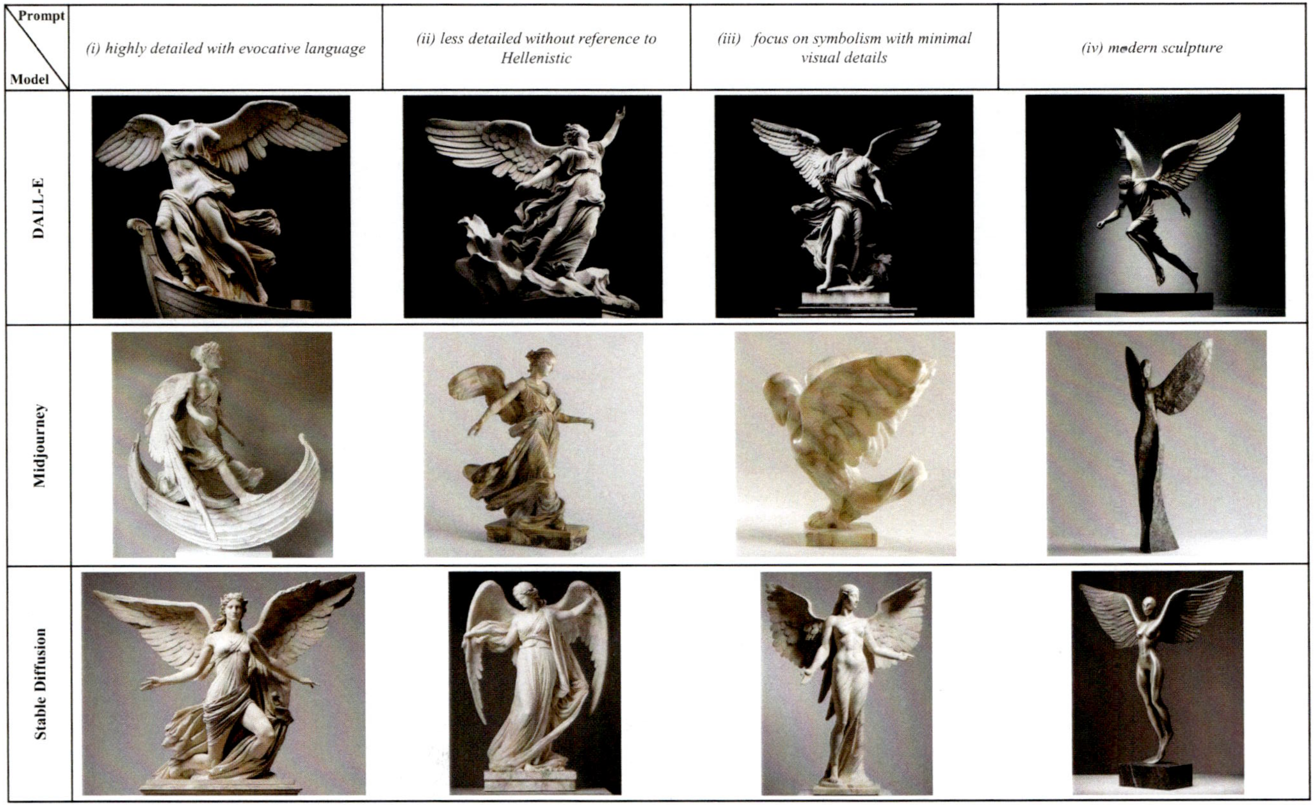

Figure 6.4 Interpretations of the *Winged Victory of Samothrace* from DALL·E, Midjourney, and Stable Diffusion generated from four different prompts, revealing stylistic range and varying success in conveying its power and symbolism. Source: Author. © Amalia Foka

Midjourney interpretations

The first prompt, though rich in art historical terms, yielded a sculpture that significantly diverged from the intended vision (Figure 6.4, Midjourney-*i*). While rendered in white marble with intricate detailed wings and drapery, the figure's pose lacks the dynamism and sense of flight described in the prompt. Furthermore, the wings are positioned downward, contradicting the directive for 'majestically outstretched' wings. The scale of both the figure and the ship fails to convey the grandeur and awe-inspiring quality specified. Compared to DALL·E, this interpretation was less successful.

The second prompt, devoid of specific Hellenistic references, nonetheless generated a sculpture evocative of ancient art (Figure 6.4, Midjourney-*ii*). As with the previous result, the output failed to fully convey the grandeur, awe-inspiring quality, and triumphant spirit of a goddess of victory. The absence of the ship's prow, explicitly requested, further emphasises the model's limitations in interpreting specific visual details.

The third prompt, prioritising symbolism and interpretation, unexpectedly resulted in a bird sculpture rather than a winged human figure (Figure 6.4, Midjourney-*iii*). This suggests challenges in handling abstract concepts and symbolic language. The bird, depicted mid-flight or landing, contradicts the prompt's direction for a triumphant pose embodying transcendence and ambition. This result highlights Midjourney's limitations in accurately translating deeper meaning into visual form, as it appears to favour literal interpretations over symbolic nuance.

The fourth prompt, aiming for a modern interpretation, generated a sculpture seemingly carved from a rough, stone-like material (Figure 6.4, Midjourney - *iv*). The outstretched wings suggest motion and power, while the overall form is abstract and stylised with broad, sweeping shapes. While the wings remain central, symbolising divine intervention and triumph, the sculpture falls short of conveying a truly 'powerful stance'. Instead, the stance felt more angelic than triumphant, lacking the intended expression of victory and power.

Stable Diffusion interpretations

The first, highly detailed prompt, rich in evocative language, art historical references, and symbolism, led to a sculpture reminiscent of the Hellenistic style (Figure 6.4, SD-*i*). The marble figure, with intricate detailing and a sense of movement, kneels with outstretched arms and flowing drapery that accentuates the form beneath. The prominent wings add a dramatic flair. While it shares features with the *Winged Victory of Samothrace*, such as outstretched wings and cascading drapery, Stable Diffusion's version presents a more grounded and intimate portrayal of Nike. However, it fails to incorporate key requested elements such as the ship's prow and the missing head and arms.

The second, less detailed prompt, devoid of Hellenistic references, produced a marble sculpture that captures fine details such as drapery folds and delicate features (Figure 6.4, SD-*ii*). The figure adopts a dynamic pose, with extended wings conveying movement and balance. While the expressive pose suggests grace and control, typical of deities, the sense of triumph, victory, and power remains understated, merely implied by the outward gesture. As with the first output, the ship's prow is absent, and the more intact figure appears less evocative of victory.

The third prompt, focused on symbolism and interpretation with minimal visual description, yielded a white marble sculpture of a figure with slightly extended arms and flowing drapery that suggests movement and grace (Figure 6.4, SD-*iii*). The figure evokes more an angelic rather than a victorious and powerful goddess. Despite the prompt's openness to stylistic interpretation, the model again gravitates towards classical aesthetics, likely influenced by the keyword 'marble'.

The final prompt, emphasising symbolism and interpretation in a modern or contemporary style, resulted in a sculpture seemingly crafted from bronze or a similar alloy, lending a sleek and contemporary appearance (Figure 6.4, SD-*iv*). The sculpture adopts a smooth, minimalist style that effectively conveys motion and dynamism. While the representation of power, victory, and triumph is more subtle than in the original, it is more clearly articulated here than in Midjourney's corresponding output.

Comparative analysis and discussion

While some models successfully convey the overall dynamism and symbolic elements of the original sculpture, others struggle with specific details, such as the missing head and arms, likely due to a learned preference for complete figures in their training data. Notably, all three models exhibit a strong association between marble and antiquity, consistently producing sculptures with classical aesthetics. This bias likely stems from the overrepresentation of marble sculptures in historical and art datasets, revealing a potential blind spot in the models' understanding of the material's broader artistic uses.

Furthermore, training data biases become evident, particularly in DALL·E's gendered interpretations, notably in its association of power and victory with male figures. While the other models did not explicitly reproduce this bias, they often struggled to faithfully convey the symbolism of power and triumph, particularly evident in the sculptures generated by Midjourney.

***The Dinner Party* (1974–9) by Judy Chicago**

Judy Chicago's *The Dinner Party* (1974–9) is a monumental feminist artwork, a triangular table set for 39 influential women from different historical periods.[36] Each place setting features a hand-painted porcelain plate with butterfly and vulvar

[36] J. Chicago, *The Dinner Party: Restoring Women to History* (New York: The Monacelli Press, 2014), pp. 9–13.

imagery, celebrating female identity and creativity.[37] Elaborate embroidered runners with personalised symbols and text accompany each plate.[38] The table rests on a porcelain tile floor inscribed with 999 names of other significant women. The artwork challenges patriarchal norms, celebrates female sexuality and power, showcases traditional women's crafts, and acknowledges marginalised women in history.[39]

DALL·E interpretations

The initial prompt, detailed and rich in evocative language, yielded an installation that accentuates the table's unique triangular end without fully realising a wholly triangular form (Figure 6.5, DALL·E-*i*). Each meticulously detailed place setting serves as a personalised homage to individual women, featuring porcelain plates adorned with floral and butterfly motifs, symbolising feminine creativity. The overall aesthetic celebrates the multifaceted nature of femininity. However, representations of female power and sexuality are entirely absent.

The second installation, generated from a less detailed prompt open to stylistic interpretation but specifying a 'triangular table' and focusing on symbolism, resulted in a large, pyramid-like triangular mural dominating the back wall (Figure 6.5, DALL·E-*ii*). The vibrant colours, diverse figures, and symbolic motifs contribute to a sense of celebration, unity, and reverence for the feminine principle. While spirituality was not directly hinted at in the prompt, the model may have been steered towards this interpretation by the language and themes of femininity, as well as the phrase 'the enduring spirit of the feminine'. This raises questions about the presence of gender bias in the training data, where feminine themes might be disproportionately associated with spirituality.

In both cases, while DALL·E incorporates elements of femininity, it omits representations of female power and sexuality. This may reflect limitations and biases within the model's training data. While the exclusion of explicit sexual content in text-to-image models is known, DALL·E also seems to lack understanding of symbolic references to female sexuality. It remains unclear whether the model is incapable of conveying sexuality through symbolism or whether it actively filters such content due to restrictive user policies. Regardless, this limits DALL·E's creative scope and hinders its ability to convey a full range of human experience. Sexuality, as a vital aspect of human identity and artistic expression, has historically held a central place in art with diverse and powerful explorations.

[37] J.F. Gerhard, *The Dinner Party: Judy Chicago and the Power of Popular Feminism, 1970–2007* (Athens, GA: University of Georgia Press, 2013), pp. 2–6.

[38] S.B. Deskins, 'Judy Chicago's "The Dinner Party": The Curatorial Context', *Woman's Art Journal*, 41:1 (2020), pp. 20–9 (p. 22).

[39] A. Jones, 'The "Sexual Politics" of *The Dinner Party*: A Critical Context', in *Sexual Politics: Judy Chicago's Dinner Party in Feminist Art History*, edited by Amelia Jones (Berkeley: University of California Press, 1996), pp. 84–118.

Prompt / Model	*(i) highly detailed with evocative language*	*(ii) focus on symbolism with less visual details and open to style interpretation*
DALL-E	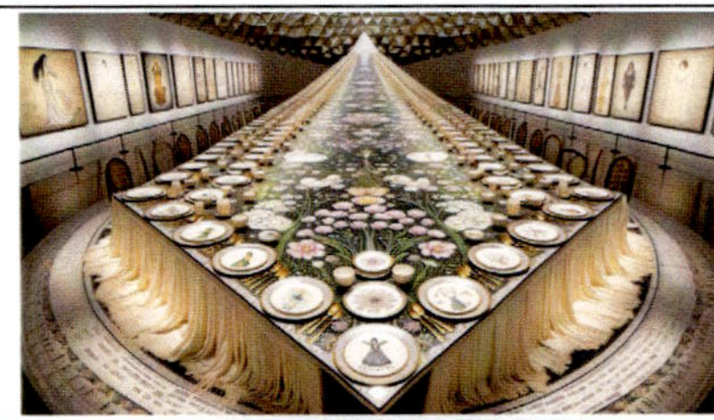	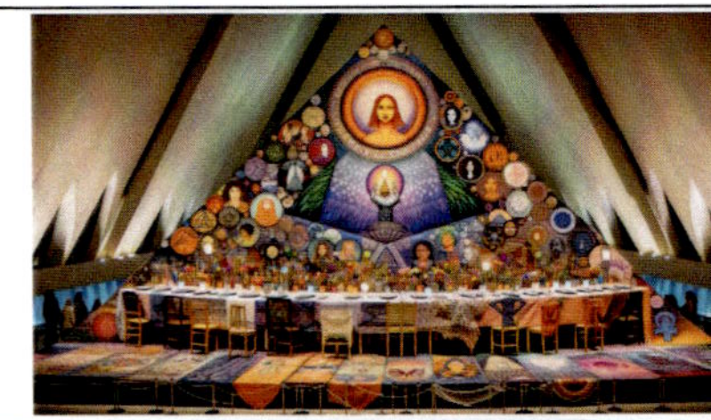
Midjourney	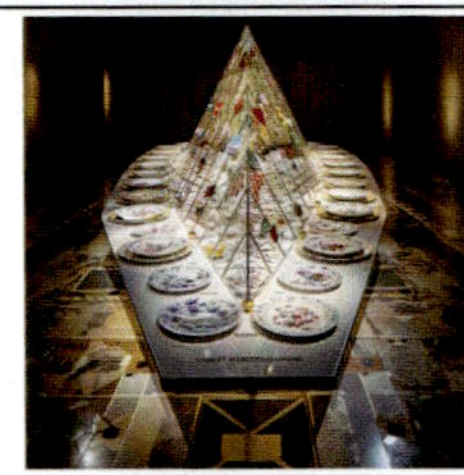	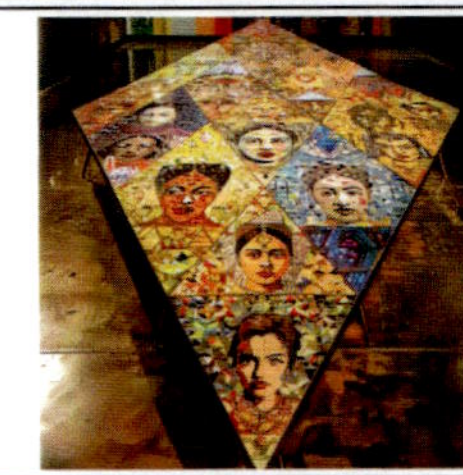
Stable Diffusion	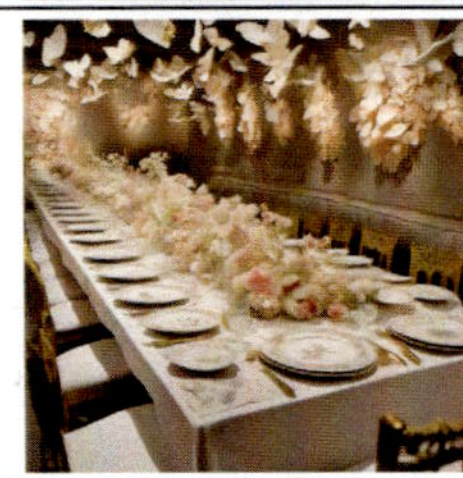	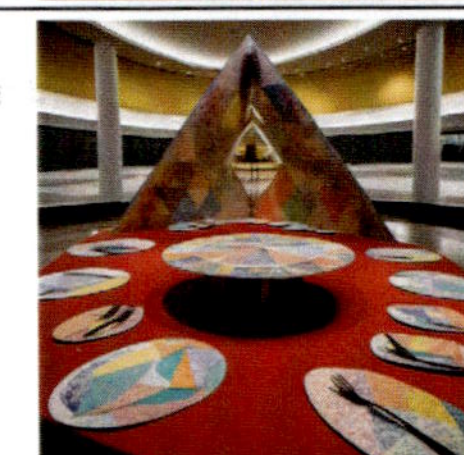

Figure 6.5 Interpretations of Judy Chicago's *The Dinner Party* using DALL·E, Midjourney, and Stable Diffusion, highlighting feminine aesthetics while omitting themes of female power and sexuality. Source: Author. © Amalia Foka

Midjourney interpretations

The first installation, prompted by detailed and evocative language, features a table with triangle-like sides but still does not fully realise the directed wholly triangular form (Figure 6.5, Midjourney-*i*). Each place setting, adorned with porcelain plate featuring floral and butterfly motifs, aligns with the concept of honouring individual women, echoing the prompt's description. The pyramid structure atop the table, not mentioned in the prompt, may stem from the mention of a 'triangular table' and the emphasis on 'monumental' scale. Although floral and butterfly motifs touch upon themes of femininity, explicit symbols of sexuality or power are once again absent.

The second installation, derived from a less detailed prompt open to stylistic interpretation but specifying a 'triangular table' and focusing on symbolism, resulted in a diamond-shaped mosaic table divided into triangular sections (Figure 6.5, Midjourney-*ii*). The central focus is a series of portraits of women from diverse cultures and ethnicities, conveying inclusivity and empowerment, though without the complex layers of meaning found in the original. Nevertheless, Midjourney appears somewhat less gender-biased than DALL·E, subtly portraying women in positions of power and leadership. However, both installations continue to omit any reference to sexuality.

Stable Diffusion interpretations

The detailed prompt led to an installation featuring a non-triangular table with meticulously arranged settings (Figure 6.5, SD-*i*). Like the other models, this interpretation fails to represent the themes of female power and sexuality central to *The Dinner Party*. The abundance of soft pink and white flower motifs celebrates female identity yet leans into conventional stereotypes of femininity. The overall aesthetic recalls a wedding banquet more than a radical feminist statement. This may reflect an overrepresentation of stereotypical imagery of femininity in Stable Diffusion's training data. The model seems to favour a sanitised view of female identity, at the expense of a more nuanced and complex exploration of female power and sexuality present in Chicago's work.

The second installation, based on the less detailed, symbolism-focused prompt, features a predominantly round table, again significantly deviating from the instructed triangular shape (Figure 6.5, SD-*ii*). A triangular or pyramid-like form at one end of the table might allude to the prompt's instruction. Each place setting is unique, adorned with vibrant colours and intricate patterns. This diversity could be seen as mirroring the unique stories, contributions, and experiences of women throughout history, as suggested in the prompt. However, the patterns lack a clear evocation of 'empowerment, unity, and the reclamation of feminine power', as stated in the prompt. Symbols representing 'transformation, liberation, and the enduring spirit of the feminine', outlined in the prompt and central to the original work, are missing.

Comparative analysis and discussion

Across all three models and both prompts, a consistent omission of key themes is evident. While stereotypical aspects of femininity are frequently rendered, the more complex themes of female power and sexuality, central to the original artwork, are notably absent. Midjourney subtly portrays women in positions of power, whereas Stable Diffusion presents the most stereotypical representation of femininity – particularly in the first installation, which evokes a wedding banquet aesthetic rather than conveying a feminist statement.

These patterns suggest underlying biases across all three models, which gravitate towards conventional beauty standards and avoid, or fail to understand, representations of female agency and sexual identity. As a result, the generated interpretations remain surface-level and reductive, unable to engage with the layered, subversive, and transformative feminist discourse embedded in the original artwork.

Conclusion

The analysis of DALL·E, Midjourney, and Stable Diffusion's interpretations of various artworks reveals a nuanced understanding of formal elements in art history, yet a more superficial grasp of iconography. All three models demonstrate the ability to replicate artistic styles, composition, colour palettes, and brushwork techniques. For instance, Midjourney's interpretations of Monet's *Impression, Sunrise* successfully emulate the loose brushwork and atmospheric lighting characteristic of Impressionism. However, challenges arise in replicating specific details, such as the triangular table in Chicago's *The Dinner Party*, suggesting a limitation in rendering precise geometric forms. Additionally, the models struggle with overly detailed prompts regarding composition, particularly in *The Arnolfini Portrait*, where numerous objects are often omitted or misplaced. Conversely, prompts written in evocative language or less prescriptive language tend to produce more coherent compositions, suggesting that allowing the model some creative freedom within the parameters of the prompt may be more effective.

In terms of iconographic analysis, the models consistently fail to interpret and represent deeper symbolic meanings embedded within the artworks. This is evident in their interpretations of Van Eyck's *The Arnolfini Portrait*, where crucial religious symbols are often omitted or distorted, and in their interpretations of Pollock's *Autumn Rhythm (Number 30)*, where visual aesthetics take precedence over emotional depth and expressive power. This suggests that while the models are adept at style replication, their comprehension of symbolic and cultural context remains shallow.

The misinterpretation of symbolic meaning reveals biases and limitations in the models' training data and underlying algorithms. All three models exhibit difficulty in transposing religious symbols into contemporary settings, indicating a gap in their understanding of symbolic transformation in contemporary art. Furthermore, DALL·E and Midjourney exhibit a potential bias towards Orientalism, revealing a tendency in their training data towards stereotypical representations of Eastern cultures.

Moreover, all three models consistently omit representations of female power and sexuality, even when prompted with detailed and evocative descriptions. This is evident in their interpretations of Chicago's *The Dinner Party*, where core themes of female sexuality and empowerment are not captured. This underscores a gender bias in the training data, where such representations might be underrepresented or filtered out. Stable Diffusion, in particular, defaults to stereotypical representations of femininity, emphasising stereotypical beauty standards, floral motifs, and soft colour palettes. DALL·E exhibits a stronger gender bias in its interpretations of power and victory, often associating these with male figures, evident in its outputs of the *Winged Victory of Samothrace*.

These findings reinforce ethical concerns raised by Kathryn Brown, who warns that AI-generated visual culture risks reproducing canonical biases and overlooking marginalised narratives.[40] As Leonardo Impett argues in the present volume, the training data behind such systems constitute not a neutral archive but a 'visual ideology' – a curatorial logic that encodes specific cultural imaginaries and patterns of exclusion.[41]

The analysis identifies distinct strengths and weaknesses among the models. Midjourney consistently produced the most creative interpretations of the prompts, likely due to its broader training on diverse artistic periods and styles. The only exception was Midjourney's performance in the *Winged Victory of Samothrace* experiment. In contrast, Stable Diffusion appears the least creative, frequently defaulting to more simplified, traditional representations, particularly evident in *Autumn Rhythm (Number 30)*, revealing limitations in its training data for modern and contemporary art.

One overarching conclusion is that the models' outputs are highly sensitive to prompt phrasing. This sensitivity highlights the importance of careful and precise prompt engineering, but also raises questions about the models' comprehension of symbolic terms and their ability to grasp overall contextual coherence. This difficulty in capturing symbolic meaning echoes concerns raised by Amanda Wasielewski, who interprets Joseph Beuys's 'How to Explain Pictures to a Dead Hare' as a metaphor for the performative opacity of AI systems – locked spaces in which meaning is enacted but not understood.[42]

Despite these limitations, the models exhibit a combination of remixing visual elements and exploratory creativity. While they can quite effectively

[40] Brown, Chapter 3 of this volume.

[41] Impett, Chapter 4 of this volume.

[42] Wasielewski, Chapter 1 of this volume.

replicate existing styles, they also demonstrate a capacity for generating novel interpretations and compositions. Future developments would benefit from training datasets that are more diverse, representative, and art historically informed. Including data curated and annotated by art historians could enhance the models' understanding of symbolic meaning, cultural context, and artistic complexity.

While this study offers valuable insights, it also has limitations. The small number of artworks and prompts does not reflect the vast and diverse landscape of art history. The qualitative nature of the analysis, while offering rich insights, may not generalise across all text-to-image models. Future research could address these limitations by expanding the corpus of artworks, incorporating a wider range of prompts, and using quantitative evaluation metrics. Importantly, collaboration with art historians during the model training process could improve the models' understanding of complex artistic concepts, symbolism, and cultural context, leading to more accurate and nuanced interpretations.

If developed responsibly, text-to-image models could offer art historians a valuable tool for analysis and interpretation. By generating images based on specific prompts and parameters, these models could help uncover hidden patterns, challenge existing interpretations, and present new visual hypotheses. The very process of selecting parameters for description and replication forces us to critically examine the core elements and meanings of an artwork, potentially leading to new insights and understandings.

However, if these models are not developed and used critically, they risk perpetuating biases, misrepresenting artistic intent, and fostering misunderstandings about art history. The limitations highlighted in this study, such as the difficulty in capturing nuanced symbolism and the tendency towards stereotypical representations, underscore the potential pitfalls of overreliance on automated visualisation tools for scholarly purposes.

In conclusion, text-to-image models hold immense potential for transforming the field of art history, but their effective and responsible use demands ongoing collaboration between computer scientists and art historians. Through critical engagement with these tools, confronting their limitations, and leveraging their capabilities, we can unlock new avenues for research, interpretation, and appreciation of art. Crucially, these models invite us to rethink traditional methods of visual analysis by reversing the process of ekphrasis, translating not image into text, as art historians have long done, but text back into image. As Nuria Rodríguez-Ortega argues, this inversion challenges the semiotic boundary between word and image, advancing a 'pansemiotic' model of interpretation grounded in latent space.[43] Text-to-image models, then, are not only tools for replication or illustration, but experimental frameworks through which the epistemological foundations of art historical practice can be reconsidered.

[43] Rodríguez-Ortega, Chapter 5 of this volume.

Table 6.1 Prompts for generating AI interpretations of artworks

	***The Arnolfini Portrait* (1434) by Jan van Eyck**
Highly detailed	Oil on oak panel depicting 15th-century wealthy man and woman in Bruges. The man is positioned slightly to the left, closer to the viewer. He wears a dark green fur-trimmed robe, a tall hat, and a silver ring. His left hand gently holds the woman's right hand (in a way that could signify a wedding portrait or a memorial to the woman who has died), while his right hand is raised, palm facing outwards (as if taking an oath). The woman is positioned slightly behind and to the right of the man. She wears a vibrant green gown with large folds, pleats, and dagging of fabric, a blue underdress, ermine fur trim, a gold necklace, ring, and bracelet, and a white headdress made of fine linen draped over her head and shoulders. Her left hand rests on her abdomen, slightly lifting her gown. The position of her left hand and her appearance may suggest that she is pregnant. The couple's clothing reflects their wealth and social status. The scene is the interior of a room with: brass chandelier with a single lit candle (above the man); convex mirror (glass with a wooden frame decorated with scenes from the Passion of Christ) on the back wall reflecting the scene and two additional figures; crystal rosary beads (next to the mirror); wooden bed with red velvet or silk covers (right side of the room) with a carved wooden figure of Saint Margaret on the bedpost; oranges (on the windowsill and the wooden table on the right); wooden sandals (discarded in the foreground, left of the man); small white dog (with fur) at the woman's feet; oriental rug (wool) on the floor under the bed. Light and shadow create depth and three-dimensionality; glazing technique for luminosity and texture; rich, saturated colours convey opulence; meticulous rendering of textures (fur, fabric, wood, etc.); use of linear perspective to create depth; mirror expands space and reflects hidden figures; precise, delicate lines define figures and objects.
Evocative language	An oil painting on oak panel, capturing a scene of quiet intimacy in a 15th-century Flemish interior. A wealthy merchant and his wife stand together, their hands clasped in a gesture that could signify both marital union and solemn remembrance. The man, clad in a rich, dark green fur-trimmed robe and tall hat, raises his right hand as if taking an oath. The woman, adorned in a luminous green gown with cascading folds and ermine trim, gently rests her hand on her abdomen, her figure hinting at the promise of new life. Bathed in soft, natural light streaming through a window, the room reveals a tapestry of textures and symbolism. A gleaming brass chandelier with a single lit candle hangs above, casting a warm glow upon the couple. A convex mirror adorned with religious motifs reflects the scene, revealing hidden figures in the doorway. A richly adorned bed draped in red velvet stands as a silent witness to the couple's union, while a small white dog symbolises fidelity at their feet. Oranges rest upon the windowsill and a nearby table, their vibrant colour a subtle reminder of life's fleeting pleasures. Utilise light and shadow to enhance the realism of the scene, highlighting the textures of fur, fabric, and wood. Employ linear perspective to create a sense of depth and spaciousness, allowing the viewer to be drawn into the intimate moment. Render each detail with meticulous precision, reflecting the mastery of early Netherlandish oil painting techniques.

Balanced without historical context	An oil painting on oak panel. A wealthy merchant and his wife, their hands clasped in a gesture that could signify both marital union and solemn remembrance in a bedroom with many symbolic objects that signify incredible wealth, and others with religious implications. The man has his right hand raised as if taking an oath. The woman's dress and hand gesture should raise questions about whether she is pregnant. Balanced composition with geometric and organic shapes; light and shadow create depth and three-dimensionality; glazing technique for luminosity and texture; rich, saturated colours convey opulence; meticulous rendering of textures (fur, fabric, wood, etc.); use of linear perspective to create depth; mirror expands space and reflects hidden figures; precise, delicate lines define figures and objects.
Modern time, emphasising modernity, 21st century	An image with balanced composition with geometric and organic shapes; light and shadow create depth and three-dimensionality; [glazing technique for luminosity and texture]; rich, saturated colours convey opulence; meticulous rendering of textures (fur, fabric, wood, etc.); use of linear perspective to create depth; mirror expands space and reflects hidden figures; precise, delicate lines define figures and objects. A wealthy merchant and his wife in [modern time/21st century] with their hands clasped in a gesture that could signify both marital union and solemn remembrance in a bedroom with many symbolic objects that signify incredible wealth, and others with religious implications. The man has his right hand raised as if taking an oath. The woman's dress and hand gesture should raise questions about whether she is pregnant.
	***Impression, Sunrise* (1872) by Claude Monet**
Highly detailed with evocative language	In the hushed stillness of dawn, a symphony of colour and light unfolds upon the canvas. The sun, a vibrant orange orb, emerges from the misty horizon, casting its radiant glow upon the tranquil waters below. Its reflection shimmers and dances, a mesmerising path of light that beckons the viewer's gaze into the heart of the scene. The sky, awash in a symphony of cool blues and greys, blends seamlessly with the water, creating a harmonious expanse that evokes a sense of tranquillity and mystery. Wispy strokes of paint suggest the gentle movement of the waves, while the thick, impasto brushwork of the sun's reflection adds a tactile dimension to the ethereal scene. In the foreground, dark silhouettes of boats emerge from the mist, their forms barely discernible in the diffused light. These humble vessels, symbols of industry and maritime life, stand in stark contrast to the ethereal beauty of the sunrise, hinting at the delicate balance between nature and human endeavour. The composition, asymmetrical and dynamic, draws the viewer's eye across the canvas, from the vibrant sun to its shimmering reflection, and finally to the shadowy figures in the foreground. The scene is one of fleeting beauty, a momentary impression of light and atmosphere captured with loose, expressive brushstrokes.

(*Continued*)

Table 6.1 (*Continued*)

	Impression, Sunrise **(1872) by Claude Monet**
Less detailed without reference to Impressionism	A harbour scene bathed in the ethereal glow of sunrise, where the sky and water merge in a symphony of blues and greys. The sun, a fiery orb, emerges from the horizon, casting its radiant light upon the tranquil waters. Its reflection shimmers and dances, a mesmerising path that draws the eye into the heart of the scene. Dark silhouettes of boats and industrial structures punctuate the composition, hinting at the bustling activity that lies beneath the serene façade. This is a fleeting moment, an impression of light and atmosphere, captured with loose, expressive brushstrokes that evoke a sense of wonder and awe.
Focus on symbolism with minimal visual details and open to style interpretation	Depict a sunrise over an industrial harbour, capturing the ephemeral beauty of light and atmosphere. Convey the tension between the natural world and human progress, showcasing the fleeting moments of transition and change. Emphasise the symbolic interplay between the rising sun, the reflective water, and the silhouettes of industry.
	Autumn Rhythm (Number 30) **(1950) by Jackson Pollock**
Highly detailed with evocative language	Step into a world of unrestrained energy and raw emotion as you encounter this monumental Abstract Expressionist canvas. The canvas, a vast expanse, becomes a stage for a rhythmic dance of colour and line, where poured and splattered enamel paint intertwine in a symphony of movement. Trace the intricate choreography of lines – a labyrinth of black, white, brown, and shimmering silver – that weave and intersect, inviting your eye to wander and explore. The absence of a traditional focal point encourages a personal journey through the artwork, where each drip, splatter, and gesture reveals the artist's emotional intensity and the power of spontaneous expression. Contemplate the painting's connection to the natural world in autumn. Does it evoke the vibrant colours of fall foliage, the rustling of leaves in the wind, or the melancholic beauty of a fading season? Perhaps it speaks to a deeper rhythm, the pulse of life and the cyclical nature of existence. As you delve deeper into the painting's textured surface, imagine the artist's bold movements as they danced around the canvas, dripping and flinging paint with abandon. Consider the emotional intensity embedded within each mark, a visual record of the artist's 'released experience'. Let your own emotions and interpretations intertwine with the artist's expression, as you connect with the raw, unfiltered energy of this painting.
Less detailed without reference to Abstract Expressionism	Embrace the untamed spirit of artistic expression as you stand before this monumental canvas. Let the symphony of colours and textures wash over you, evoking the raw energy and unfiltered emotions that fuelled its creation. Feel the rhythm of the artwork pulsate through you, a visual echo of the natural world's cycles and the ever-changing seasons. Allow your mind to wander through the intricate layers, discovering hidden depths and personal interpretations within the abstract forms. Experience the liberation of the artist's 'released experience', a cathartic outpouring of creativity captured on canvas. Connect with the intangible beauty and the emotional resonance that transcends the physical world, leaving you with a sense of awe and wonder. Let this artwork be a catalyst for your own introspection and exploration of the boundless possibilities of human expression.

Focus on symbolism with minimal visual details and open to style interpretation	Embrace the vibrant energy of autumn as you stand before this painting. Let the warm hues and earthy tones wash over you, evoking the feeling of crisp air and rustling leaves. Feel the rhythmic pulse of the artwork, a visual symphony echoing the natural world's cycles and the changing seasons. Allow yourself to be swept away by the energy and movement, as if dancing to the rhythm of nature itself. Experience the emotional intensity and raw power of the artist's expression, a cathartic release captured on canvas. Let the artwork ignite your own creative spirit and inspire a deeper connection to the world around you.
***Winged Victory of Samothrace* (*c.*190 BCE)**	
Highly detailed with evocative language	Depict a Hellenistic sculpture, a powerful female figure embodying Nike, the Greek goddess of victory. She stands atop a ship's prow, her wings majestically outstretched behind her, feathers meticulously detailed, capturing the essence of flight and triumph. Her garments, seemingly sculpted by the wind, cling to her form, revealing the strength and grace of her body beneath. The figure's pose is dynamic and theatrical, her body leaning forward as if alighting from the heavens, a testament to the Hellenistic emphasis on movement and emotion. The sculpture's missing head and arms only enhance her enigmatic allure, inviting contemplation and interpretation. The ship's prow, a symbol of naval power and victory, should be rendered with equal detail, its weathered surface hinting at the trials of battle. The contrast between the smooth, white marble of Nike's figure and the rough texture of the ship's prow should be emphasised, highlighting the juxtaposition of the divine and the earthly. The overall mood of the piece should be one of triumph and awe, capturing the spirit of the Hellenistic era and its celebration of human achievement and divine inspiration. The sculpture should evoke a sense of wonder and admiration, inviting viewers to contemplate the power of victory and the enduring legacy of ancient art.
Less detailed without reference to Hellenistic	A marble sculpture of a powerful female figure, her wings outstretched in a gesture of triumph. Her body is cloaked in swirling drapery, hinting at the form beneath. The sculpture's missing head and arms only add to her enigmatic presence, inviting contemplation and interpretation. This is a goddess of victory, a symbol of triumph and perseverance. Her presence atop a ship's prow suggests a naval victory of great significance. The statue's dramatic pose and powerful symbolism speak to the enduring power of the human spirit and the celebration of human achievement.
Focus on symbolism with minimal visual details and open to style interpretation	A marble sculpture of a winged figure, her body positioned in a triumphant pose, evokes a sense of victory and power. The figure's missing head and arms add to the mystery and invite contemplation of her identity and purpose. This sculpture symbolises triumph over adversity and the enduring spirit of the human will. The figure's powerful stance and the suggestion of flight speak to the transcendence of limitations and the pursuit of greatness.

(*Continued*)

Table 6.1 (*Continued*)

	Winged Victory of Samothrace **(*c*.190 BCE)**
Modern sculpture	A winged figure, her body positioned in a triumphant pose, evokes a sense of victory and power. The figure's missing head and arms add to the mystery and invite contemplation of her identity and purpose. This modern sculpture symbolises triumph over adversity and the enduring spirit of the human will. The figure's powerful stance and the suggestion of flight speak to the transcendence of limitations and the pursuit of greatness.
	The Dinner Party **(1974–9) by Judy Chicago**
Highly detailed with evocative language	A monumental installation, a sprawling triangular banquet table set for 39 honoured guests. Each place setting is a meticulously crafted tribute, a canvas for storytelling through artistry and symbolism. Delicate porcelain plates, each one adorned with intricate designs reminiscent of blossoming flowers and ethereal butterflies, speak to the boundless creativity and life-affirming power of the feminine. Luxurious embroidered runners cascade down the table's edges, adorned with personalised symbols and texts that whisper the tales of extraordinary women who have shaped the course of history. Beneath the table, a mosaic of names shimmers in gold on the porcelain tile floor, a testament to the countless women whose contributions have been obscured by the shadows of time. The triangular form of the table itself is a potent emblem, a geometric homage to the divine feminine and a defiant rejection of patriarchal norms. Every element, from the delicate stitchwork of the runners to the evocative imagery on the plates, is a celebration of female identity, sexuality, and power. The artwork stands as a monument to the marginalised and forgotten, a visual symphony that challenges conventional narratives and invites us to reimagine the historical tapestry. It is a testament to the enduring spirit of women, a tribute to their resilience, creativity, and unwavering strength.
Focus on symbolism with fewer visual details and open to style interpretation	Create a photo of a monumental art installation representation of a triangular table, a symbolic gathering place where the accomplishments and resilience of women throughout history are celebrated. Each place setting is a unique expression, a testament to the individual stories and contributions of these remarkable figures. Utilise vibrant colours, intricate patterns, and evocative imagery to evoke a sense of empowerment, unity, and the reclamation of feminine power. The artwork should challenge traditional notions of history and representation, highlighting the often overlooked achievements of women in various fields. Incorporate symbolic elements that speak to the universal themes of transformation, liberation, and the enduring spirit of the feminine. Consider the table itself as a powerful symbol of equality and community, a space where diverse voices converge and create a tapestry of shared experience.

7

Realism as Style? Art History, Artificial Intelligence, and the Search for the Styleme

MANAS MEHTA, ELIZABETH C. MANSFIELD, SHUHUA YANG, ZHUOMIN ZHANG, JIA LI, JOHN RUSSELL, AND JAMES Z. WANG

> The character of Mr. Constable's style is peculiarly English.
>
> Anonymous critic in *The London Magazine* (1824)

> Constable, in his peculiar and natural style, is gradually rising to the head of his department.
>
> Anonymous critic in *The European Magazine* (1825)

> Mr. Constable's style is rural.
>
> Anonymous critic in *The New Monthly Magazine* (1827)

Introduction

BY THE TIME John Constable (1776–1837) exhibited his famous painting *The Hay Wain* in 1821, he was an established figure in the London art scene (Figure 7.1). Critics had been reporting on his submissions to the annual exhibition at the Royal Academy – Britain's most prestigious public venue for contemporary art – since 1807.[1] Yet, as familiar as Constable's style had become by the 1820s, critics still found it difficult to describe. They deemed his style 'peculiar', 'original', and 'singular' throughout his career. What critics seemed to struggle with was how to account for the unusually lifelike character of Constable's scenes of the English

[1] Constable began exhibiting at the Royal Academy in 1802, though without prompting any published reviews of his work. See Judy Crosby Ivy, *Constable and the Critics: 1802–1837* (Woodbridge, UK: Boydell Press in association with the Suffolk Records Society, 1991), p. 63.

Proceedings of the British Academy, **285**, 149–180,

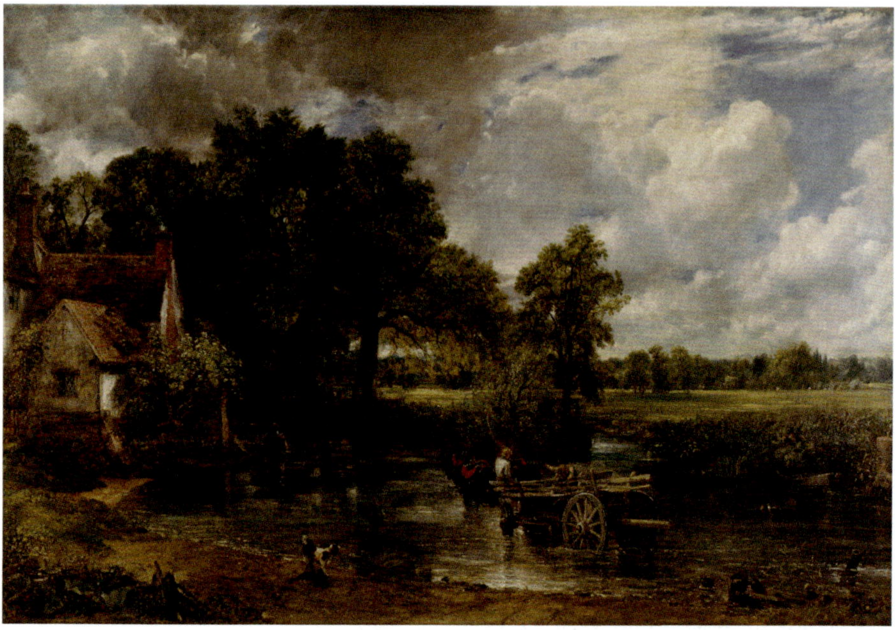

Figure 7.1 *The Hay Wain*, John Constable, 1821, oil on canvas, 130.2 cm × 185.4 cm, The National Gallery, London. Copyright: National Gallery, London/Art Resource, NY, N-1207-00-000052, AR6INV8343.

countryside.[2] The term most often used by commentators in relation to Constable's landscapes was 'truth'. One critic sidestepped the difficulty in describing *The Hay Wain* by simply stating that 'every part of this picture has the appearance of reality'.[3] Indeed, Constable became known to subsequent generations of artists and scholars as a progenitor of 19th-century Realism.

The term 'Realism' was not yet in use by art critics during Constable's lifetime, so they understandably fell back on words like 'singular' to describe the artist's style. Style mattered in the art world of 19th-century Britain.

Appraisals of style allowed contemporary works of art to be assessed in relation to familiar aesthetic standards and artistic precedents. This historical concern for style warrants consideration by researchers today. Scholarly attention to Constable's style – both as it manifests itself in his works and as it has been perceived historically – enhances our understanding of the cultural and social significance of his artistic practice. Art historians have taken various approaches to understanding what

[2] Perhaps related is the early modern antithesis between style and realism observed by Joost Keizer in discussions of Renaissance painting in Florence where Giotto's novel naturalism was seen as without a style. Joost Keizer, 'Style and Authorship in Early Italian Renaissance Art', *Zeitschrift für Kunstgeschichte* (2015), p. 371.

[3] Ivy, *Constable and the Critics*, p. 89.

made Constable's style seem so unusual to critics at the time. Analysis of published reviews, along with consultation of other documentary sources (much was written by and about Constable in his lifetime), provides useful insight, but it is the artist's works themselves that provide the clearest evidence of his style. This record, preserved in Constable's own works and occasionally evident in landscapes produced by his followers, offers visual testimony of the painter's style. Now, in addition to essential practices of close looking and technical analysis, the visual evidence of Constable's style can also be explored computationally via computer vision. Preliminary to such research, however, is the development of a computer vision model that can reliably recognise and then emulate algorithmically 'Constable's style'. This chapter describes the art historical and computational potential, as well as the limits, of this approach.

The style problem

The historiography of style is vexed. For many art historians, a mode of analysis that depends heavily – if not entirely – on an artwork's formal characteristics as evidence of cultural or historical meaning, is viewed as not just outmoded but reductivist, even essentialist.[4] This is understandable given some of the conclusions reached by art historians associated with the heyday of style-as-methodology.[5] The use of stylistic analysis as a means to identify, compare, and assess diverse expressions of visual culture is, of course, a technique as old as crafting itself; identifying formal patterns across examples of visual or material culture is not, in and of itself, culturally essentialising. Where reductivism becomes a problem is when particular formal patterns are assigned relative cultural value. The codification of stylistic analysis by 18th-century European art scholars as a means of identifying historic

[4] James Elkins provides an excellent summary of the historiography of this disciplinary scepticism towards the concept of style: James Elkins, 'Style', *Grove Art Online* (2003), https://doi.org/10.1093/gao/9781884446054.article.T082129 [accessed 10 May 2024]. For more in-depth consideration of the historiography of style, see Jas Elsner, 'Style', in *Critical Terms for Art History*, 2nd edn, edited by Robert S. Nelson and Richard Shiff (Chicago, IL: University of Chicago Press, 2003), pp. 98–109 and Whitney Davis, 'Style and History in Art History', in *The Uses of Style in Archaeology*, edited by Margaret W. Conkey and Christine Hastorf (Cambridge: Cambridge University Press, 1989), pp. 18–32.

[5] Perhaps the most pernicious outcomes of the early 20th-century reliance on style as a means of art historical analysis is the reliance on European visual practices as standards against which stylistic analysis is undertaken, and the tendency of stylistic analysis to circumscribe complex cultural phenomena into orderly, successive stages of artistic development. See Svetlana Alpers, *The Art of Describing: Dutch Art in the Seventeenth Century* (Chicago, IL: University of Chicago Press, 1983), esp. pp. xvii–xxvii. While such trenchant evaluations of some of the deleterious outcomes of art history's enduring reliance on style have encouraged much-needed critical reflection to disciplinary practice, they can also inadvertently condense the analytic sophistication and diversity of the style-based methodologies that emerged during what we refer to as style's turn-of-the-century heyday. Among the most significant theorists of style form are Heinrich Wölfflin, Alois Riegl, Erwin Panofsky, Meyer Shapiro, and Richard Wollheim. For useful sources on the historiography of style, see note 4.

patterns of cultural exchange, migration, and other social behaviours – as well as relative cultural 'maturity' or ethnic and racial 'tendencies' – integrated style into nationalist and colonialist discourse.[6] Reliance on style as a presumably objective gauge of a culture's relative value reached its apogee around the turn of the 20th century – concomitant with the height of European imperialism.

To advocate seriously for the usefulness of style as a category of art analysis, then, requires both close attention to its historiographic legacy and a compelling case for its scholarly rehabilitation. Recent advances in computer vision research provide a strong rationale for art historical re-engagement with style. As ubiquitous as it is undertheorised in computer vision literature, style – along with assumptions about its significance for art – has been pressed into service as a kind of touchstone for the field. The development of today's artificial intelligence (AI)-based image-generation models is an outcome of decades of computer vision research, with some key breakthroughs achieved thanks to experiments on images of artworks. There are many reasons that computer scientists have been drawn to images of art for their research: a genuine interest in cultural heritage, the availability of high-quality digital images and metadata, and an attraction to the cultural cachet of art, among them. The concept of artistic style also brings computational challenges, as Eva Cetinić notes in Chapter 2 of this volume, because it must be measured against 'a very fuzzy ground truth'. Of particular interest to computer vision researchers is the apparent capacity of artworks to comprise two fully integrated fields of information: *style* and *content*. Successfully designing a computer vision model that can discriminate between 'style' and 'content' in a single image – and further, extract style information and apply it to the content of a different image – remains a hallmark of a model's sophistication. This process, known as *style transfer*, has been applied across a range of research domains.[7] Demonstrating style transfer with images of artworks rather than, say, images of diseased livers or fog-obscured aerial photos of military installations offers obvious advantages.[8]

The term 'realism' presents disciplinary problems of its own. Art historians traditionally have shied away from using the term 'realistic' when describing visual representations, no matter how lifelike a work may appear. There are several reasons for this disciplinary reticence. One is simply the desire to avoid confusing images

[6] Considered foundational for the discipline of art history, the 18th-century writings of Johann Joachim Winckelmann relied on style as a means of classifying, comparing, and evaluating the visual culture of diverse societies around the world, especially those of antiquity. See, for example, Johann Joachim Winckelmann, *The History of Ancient Art*, translated by G. Henry Lodge (Boston, MA: J.R. Osgood, 1872 [orig. German 1764]). On the consequences of Winckelmann's theorisation of style for subsequent disciplinary engagement with the concept, see Eric Michaud, *The Barbarian Invasions: A Genealogy of the History of Art* (Cambridge, MA: MIT Press, 2019).

[7] Qiang Cai, Ma Mengzu, Chen Wang, and Haisheng Li, 'Image Neural Style Transfer: A Review', *Computers & Electrical Engineering*, 108 (2023), pp. 1–12.

[8] Rikiya Yamashita, Jin Long, Snikitha Banda, Jeanne Shen, and Daniel L. Rubin, 'Learning Domain-Agnostic Visual Representation for Computational Pathology Using Medically-Irrelevant Style Transfer Augmentation', *IEEE Transactions on Medical Imaging*, 40:12 (2021), pp. 3945–54.

with a high degree of verisimilitude with works produced during one of the several 'Realist' movements in European art and literature.[9] Reserving use of the term (often capitalised) for discussions of specifically Realist art – for instance, 19th-century Realism, Socialist Realism, or Magic Realism – is a well-established disciplinary convention.[10] When seeking merely to note that a picture has a lifelike quality, art historians tend to rely on standard descriptors intended to be devoid of historical specificity.[11] Most often, anglophone art historians apply the term *naturalistic*.[12]

Along with avoiding (or at least mitigating) unintended associations, the use of naturalistic as opposed to realistic is also meant to acknowledge that lifelikeness is a relative attribute. Pictorial lifelikeness is relative in at least two ways. First, by no means do all cultures at all moments even subscribe to such a concept. Phases of strong naturalism in the history of European art have accorded the quality of lifelikeness an exaggerated cultural importance. Second, as theorised by art historians, naturalism in visual imagery is understood as variable rather than absolute. No image can be perfectly lifelike. Because figural representations are, themselves, schema or proxies for observed reality, all representational art is, to some extent, abstract. Attending to the naturalism of a representation as opposed to its realism acknowledges that pictorial qualities associated with accuracy or truthfulness are culturally contingent.[13] That said, by keeping the term realism at bay, art historians may have inadvertently dampened disciplinary theorisations of lifelikeness in pictures.[14]

The rehabilitation of style and realism together – and in the context of our research on features of John Constable's landscapes – offers certain methodological advantages. As noted, style has played an important role historically for the reception of Constable's truthful-seeming landscape paintings. What is more, critical engagement with stylistic analysis offers a means of exploring how seemingly lifelike digital images produce meaning. Because our research is conducted using digital proxies of historical works of art, the effects of transmediation are always a

[9] On the 19th-century Realist movement, Linda Nochlin's book *Realism* (Cambridge: CUP Archive, 1971) remains the standard.

[10] Seymour Slive, 'Realism and Symbolism in Seventeenth-Century Dutch Painting', *Daedalus* (1962), pp. 469–500.

[11] It should be noted that 'lifelike' was used to describe artworks in English by the early 16th century. See 1522 attestation recorded in entry on 'lifelike, adj., sense 1' in the *Oxford English Dictionary* (2023), https://doi.org/10.1093/OED/1042266250 [accessed 2 July 2024].

[12] Admittedly, the term naturalism does not eliminate all confusion: there was also a 19th-century movement known as Naturalism. For a helpful discussion of naturalism and its relationship to realism in the 19th century, see Gerald Needham, 'Naturalism', *Grove Dictionary of Art* (2003), https://doi.org/10.1093/gao/9781884446054.article.T061451 [accessed 2 July 2024].

[13] Particularly relevant for the current discussion are 19th-century theories of naturalism and realism. See Joshua C. Taylor, *Nineteenth-Century Theories of Art* (Berkeley: University of California Press, 1987), Part III, pp. 246–350.

[14] This is a fairly recent retreat from sustained discussions of realism or verisimilitude in art, a retreat motivated in part by concerns about treating culturally specific concepts like realism as somehow universal. Exemplary of the discipline's earlier engagement with questions related to perception and pictorial lifelikeness is Ernst Hans Gombrich, *Art and Illusion: A Study in the Psychology of Pictorial Representation* (New York: Pantheon, 1960).

concern. Thus, the degree to which medium as well as style contribute to an image's lifelikeness needs to be acknowledged and, to the extent possible, accounted for. Testing the efficacy of style in relation to a class of images designated 'realist', therefore, is an opportunity to reconsider the usefulness of the concept of realism for art historical as well as computer vision research. At the very least, conceptualising lifelike images as just one expression of a complex of realisms further facilitates historical contextualisation of the cultural meaning and social function of images.[15] This is not to suggest that it is possible, or even advisable, to identify a generalisable or transhistorical 'realist style'. Instead, it is to propose that the concept of realism (or realisms) might be helpfully deployed when seeking to understand how visual images perceived as truthful, empirical representations of real-world phenomena achieve this effect. Determining whether or how this effect diminishes through time or across cultures can also provide useful information about the means by which strongly naturalistic imagery conveys truthful-seeming content.

Style, art history, and AI

Art historians and AI models recognise style by different means. For art historians, style is conventionally understood to comprise a constellation of formal features that occur together reliably across a particular group of artworks, with each cluster of features tethered to a particular, unifying identity. This identity might be one of place, period, culture, individual, or association of individuals. Understood this way, style refers to external features of an artwork. Such formal features, once recognised as a coherent style, have been interpreted by some theorists of artistic style as giving expression to the habits of thinking of the artist or culture that produced that style. Style, then, offers a means to historical interpretation. But what of the habits of thinking of the art historian or computer vision researcher? Certainly, their habits of mind are also bound up with a particular style or styles, and this affects their perception of historical styles.[16]

[15] It is perhaps not coincidental that art historians have relegated both realism and style to the disciplinary sidelines. As categories of historical analysis, both concepts have proved vulnerable to ideological exploitation. Realism's tricksy credibility, and style's susceptibility to positivism, make them difficult concepts to manage.

[16] This point is made in Richard Wollheim, 'Pictorial Style', in *The Concept of Style*, edited by Berel Lang (Ithaca, NY: Cornell University Press, 1979), p. 190. Our suggestion here of a 'stylistic lens' as a perceptual habit draws on Michael Baxandall's concept of a Period Eye, discussed by Kathryn Brown in Chapter 3 of this volume. Before Baxandall, literary scholar and early advocate of 'stylistics' Amado Alonso attributed a similar meaning to style itself: 'As regards "style", this is generally understood to mean an author's particular use of language, his idiomatic mastery and virtuosity, as representing an additional part of the literary construction; But the term "style" has another meaning which is more suitable to the purposes of stylistics: style is the expressive system of a work, of an author, of an epoch' (Amado Alonso, 'The Stylistic Interpretation of Literary Texts', *Modern Language Notes*, 57:7 (1942), pp. 489–96). See also Michael Baxandall, *Painting and Experience in Fifteenth Century Italy: A Primer in the Social History of Pictorial Style* (Oxford: Clarendon, 1972).

Along with peering through their own perceptual lenses, researchers today must also contend with distinct challenges due to transmediation. An often-cited example of the means by which transmediation can inflect stylistic analysis is the photographic reproduction of a work of art. As well documented as this phenomenon is, cultural historians – including those trained in art history – nevertheless succumb easily to the habit of looking through the photograph to assess the artwork it represents, as Tracy Stuber explains in Chapter 8 of this volume.[17] It is not just when looking at reproductions that art historians view works of art through an accretion of stylistic lenses; as noted, the art historian's own habits of perception have been tempered by the visual customs of their environment and experiences. In this way, style may be seen to inflect virtually all encounters with works of art, calling for a deliberate and self-aware approach to stylistic analysis. A critical stylistic analysis would need to account for – to the extent possible – all three layers of style content: local style of the artwork under consideration; mediating style inherent to the tools, reproductions, and other research materials used during analysis; and the perceptual style or modality of the art historian.[18] The mediating style of computer vision is especially significant for our research, because computational analysis is applied not to actual works of art or even to visual reproductions of artworks, but to representations of artworks made up of pixels (picture elements) transmitted as binary code via electrical signals.[19]

The landscape paintings of the British artist John Constable are exemplary of the historical contingency of both style and realism. Constable's contemporaries tended to attribute to his landscape paintings a striking faithfulness to observed reality. Indeed, it was Constable's perceived fidelity to nature that elicited critics' praise as well as censure. For instance, his 1821 painting *The Hay Wain* (Figure 7.1) prompted one commentator to declare that 'viewed from a proper distance, every part of this picture has the appearance of reality'.[20] Another stated that the painting 'approaches nearer to the actual look of rural nature than any modern landscape

[17] The conventions of art historical discourse permit representations of works to stand in as proxies without comment. This is evident in publications where discussions of specific works of art are illustrated by reproductions without comment; typically, not even technical metadata is included with reproductions, contributing to the equivalence of reproduction and work. It is also customary for art historians delivering 'slide lectures' to refer to projected images as if they were the works themselves. To be sure, some scholars routinely alert their audiences to the fact that they are seeing reproductions of works, but disciplinary protocols do not insist upon such disclosures. There is considerable literature on the mediating effect photography has on the practice of art history. See, for example, Costanza Caraffa (ed.), *Photo Archives and the Photographic Memory of Art History* (Berlin and Munich: Deutsche Kunstverlag, 2011).

[18] Zhuomin Zhang, Jia Li, David G. Stork, Elizabeth Mansfield, John Russell, Catherine Adams *et al.*, 'Reducing Bias in AI-based Analysis of Visual Artworks', *IEEE BITS the Information Theory Magazine*, 2:1 (2022), pp. 36–48.

[19] On the implications of computer vision for human visual perception (including the perception of art historians and other visual arts researchers, see Chapter 3 in this volume.

[20] Ivy, *Constable and the Critics*, p. 89.

whatever'.[21] At this time, however, strongly imitative scenes were considered by some viewers to be too clinical in their empiricism and, therefore, lacking in feeling or 'poetry'. This, ultimately, was the judgement of Victorian Britain's most influential art critic, John Ruskin (1819–1900), who frequently cast Constable as foil to his favourite painter, J.M.W. Turner (1775–1851). Writing in the decade after Turner's death in 1845, Ruskin contends that 'Constable perceives ... that the grass is wet, the meadows flat, and the boughs shady; that is to say, about as much as ... might in general be apprehended ... by an intelligent fawn and a skylark. Turner perceives at a glance the whole sum of visible truth open to human intelligence'.[22]

The invention of photography in 1839 undoubtedly contributed to viewers' ambivalence towards strongly naturalistic landscape scenes, as commentators on the new technology lamented its lack of artfulness in terms akin to those used by Ruskin to characterise Constable's paintings.[23] Setting up his comparison between Constable and Turner, Ruskin observes that 'there are some truths, easily obtained, which give a deceptive resemblance to Nature'.[24] Whereas Turner is cast as 'the good painter', Constable exemplifies 'the bad painter' who 'gives the cheap deceptive resemblance'.[25] Ruskin's harsh judgement dampened Constable's reputation in Britain for much of the 19th century. Yet, where Ruskin sees Constable's scenes as irredeemably banal, progressive artists in France, such as the Romantic painter Eugène Delacroix (1798–1863), and landscapists associated with the Barbizon School saw in Constable a singular model for aesthetic immediacy and truth. Today, viewers accustomed to the pictorial accuracy achieved by camera phones are hard-pressed to see a substantive difference in the 'truth' of Constable's *The Hay Wain* as opposed to a painting by Turner of a similar subject (Figure 7.2). But it was not just representational accuracy that informed contemporaries' divergent opinions of the relative truth of their paintings, it was also the two artists' perceived styles.

Constable's contemporaries understood the artist's frank naturalism as inherent to his style. That viewers observed in Constable's paintings a distinctive style is confirmed by Judy Crosby Ivy in her exhaustive review of the critical reception of Constable's paintings.[26] Ivy suggests that the assertiveness of Constable's style may have contributed to a tendency for critics to fault the painter for lapsing into a 'mannered' approach: so distinctive was Constable's style that it preceded whatever content or poetic message his paintings contained. The association between Constable's unique style – by which is generally meant his reliance on a dark palette punctuated by bright highlights; his use of thick impasto; his vigorous

[21] Robert Hunt, 'Review', in *The Examiner*, May 1821, pp. 331–2. Cited in Ivy, *Constable and the Critics*, p. 88.
[22] John Ruskin, *Modern Painters*, Vol. III (New York: Wiley & Sons, 1878), p. 126.
[23] See, for example, Elizabeth Eastlake, 'Photography', *Quarterly Review* (1857), pp. 442–68.
[24] Ruskin, *Modern Painters*, p. 126.
[25] Ruskin, *Modern Painters*.
[26] Ivy, *Constable and the Critics*. See note 1 above.

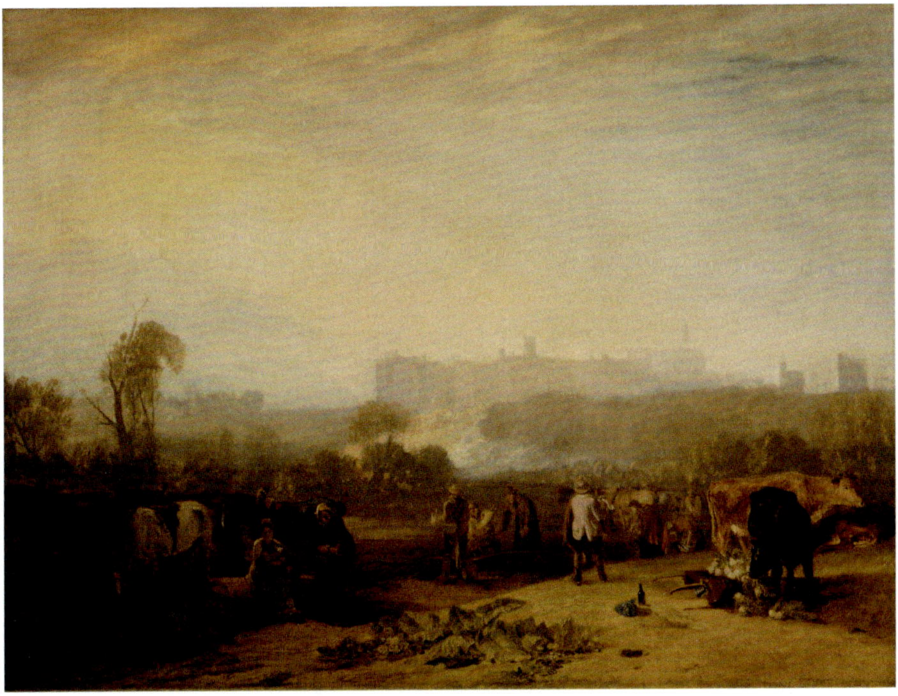

Figure 7.2 *Ploughing Up Turnips, Near Slough ('Windsor')*, J.M.W. Turner, exhibited 1809, oil on canvas, 101.9 cm × 130.2 cm, Tate Britain, London. Copyright: Tate, London/ Art Resource, NY, N00486, AR6INV8343.

or gestural brushstrokes and prominent dabs of local colour; and his organisation of the perspective of his fictive scene in relation to a picture plane that hovered a few feet in front of the canvas – and the truth of his depictions of nature is exemplified by this 1829 observation by a critic in response to two paintings, including *A Boat Passing a Lock* (1826, Figure 7.3): 'They have all the merit of his own peculiar style. The branches and leaves of his trees seem to tremble in the gentle breeze, while the colouring of his picture gives the spectator a truer idea of nature than almost any of the works of his contemporaries.'[27]

When complaints of a mannered technique or style arose, it was most often in relation to Constable's reliance on scattered points of white highlighting, intended to suggest dew or the play of light across grass or foliage. The 1821 review of *The Hay Wain* cited earlier addresses this concern:

[27] Ivy, *Constable and the Critics*, p. 132.

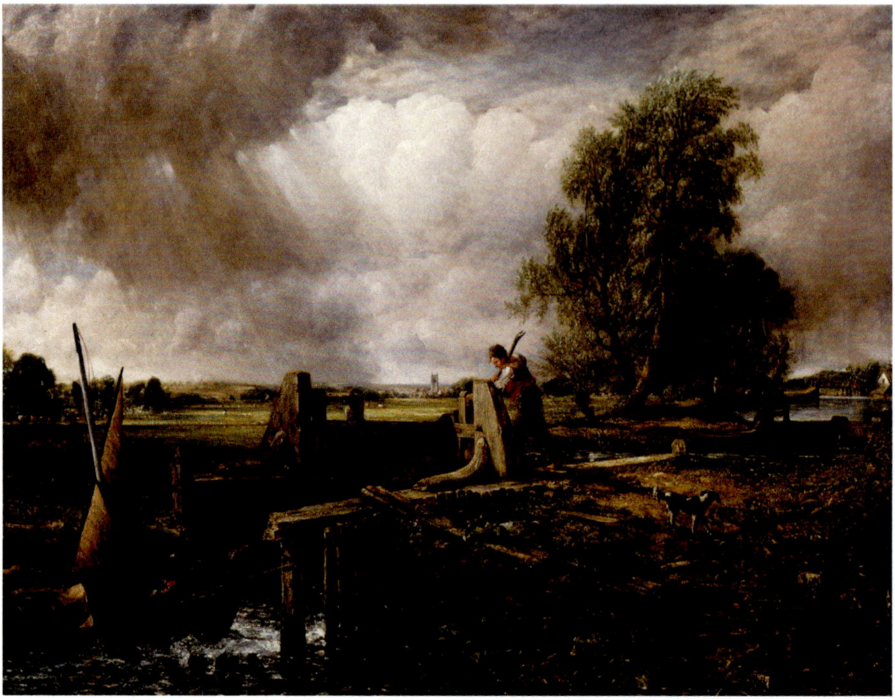

Figure 7.3 *A Boat Passing a Lock*, John Constable, 1826, oil on canvas, 101.6 cm × 127.0 cm, Royal Academy of Arts, London. © Photo: Royal Academy of Arts, London. Photographer: Prudence Cuming Associates Limited (RA ref. 03/923).

> Landscape—Night is a picture by Mr. CONSTABLE, which we think approaches nearer to the actual look of rural nature than any modern landscape whatever. An able judge of Art who saw and admired it with us, thought it a little mannered from a certain sparkle there is over it. We do not think so, but granting the objection to be just, it is a mere slight flaw in a diamond, for what an open air and fresh and leafy look it has with its cottage and foreground so brightly and yet so modestly contrasting their reddish hue with the green and blue and yellow tints of the trees, fields, and sky—a sky which for noble volume of cloud and clear light we have never at any time seen exceeded except by Nature.

Indeed, it was Constable's skies that served as the focus of much discussion of the truthfulness – the realism, even – of his landscapes. It was *The Hay Wain*'s sky that reportedly so impressed Delacroix that he resolved to repaint the background of his painting *Scenes from the Massacre at Chios* (1824, Figure 7.4). At first glance, however, the cloudy sky in the background of Delacroix's painting would seem to have little to do with Constable's *The Hay Wain*. Exploring anew the relationship

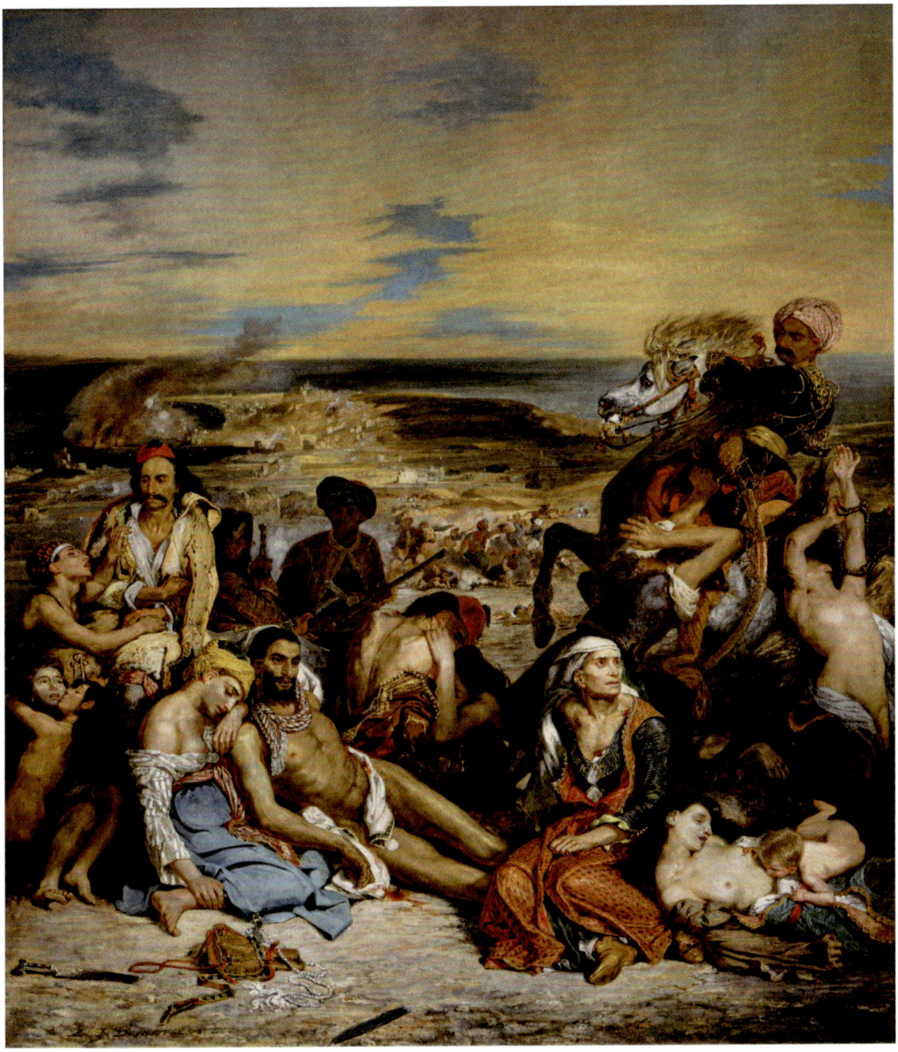

Figure 7.4 *Scenes from the Massacre at Chios*, Eugène Delacroix, 1824, oil on canvas, 419 cm × 354 cm, Louvre, Paris. Copyright: RMN-Grand Palais/Art Resource, NY, 20-504270, AR6INV8343.

between Constable and his emulators – including some of the Barbizon painters and their successors among the Realists and Impressionists – was the basis for our first experiments with computer vision. One question that computer vision seemed poised to address was whether Constable's style was somehow conveying visual truthfulness in a distinct – possibly measurable – way.

Style as signifier

Can style be quantified? Berel Lang explored this possibility in the 1970s by postulating the 'styleme'.[28] As the smallest unit of stylistic content still capable of conveying the distinctive formal character of a particular creator, culture, or period, the styleme would join the morpheme, phoneme, and mytheme as positive evidence in a context of structuralist analysis of cultural expression.[29] Lang first proposed the styleme in 1977, when structuralist (or, as Lang prefers, 'atomist') approaches still held a place at the vanguard of cultural research. According to Lang, identifying the styleme could render the concept of style itself more legible and provide measurable parameters. Without universally observable traits, style remains an elusive and impressionistic quality that can neither be described accurately nor accounted for historically.

> Is there not an atom of style that, writ small, impels or even mirrors the stylistic manner of artistic wholes? That could supply a least or common denominator to the later quite diverse expressions of style? That will enable us to say, as we appeal to style as a basis for interpreting and understanding works of art, precisely what that basis rests on?[30]

For Lang, the answer to all of these questions is, ultimately, no. Lang contends that isolating the styleme from the work is impossible, an effort he analogises to distilling an individual down to a single, unique, and essential quality. Style, according to Lang, is socially constituted and, therefore, is itself a form of expression.[31] Style, in this way, is irreducible.[32]

> The styleme, then, like all live fictions, is bound by its context—the entirety from which it is discriminated as a component. It requires a *decision*—on the part of the creator and then of the audience—to determine what the styleme in a particular work is; the styleme, applying itself to each moment of the stylistic whole, appears only as we trace it back from that whole.[33]

[28] Berel Lang, *The Concept of Style* (Ithaca, NY: Cornell University Press, 1987).

[29] An earlier – and much discussed – structuralist model of style was proposed by Arthur Danto. Danto ultimately rejected the utility of his 'style matrix' due to its ahistorical character. See Arthur Danto, 'The Artworld', *The Journal of Philosophy*, 61:19 (1964), pp. 571–84. On the reception of the style matrix, see Frank Boardman, 'Back in Style: A New Interpretation of Danto's Style Matrix', *The Journal of Aesthetics and Art Criticism*, 73:4 (2015), pp. 441–8.

[30] See Lang, *The Concept of Style*, p. 177.

[31] Lang's argument is by no means novel in its insistence that style is a response to social and cultural conditions. Heinrich Wolfflin's influential theory of style, described in his 1915 book *Principles of Art History*, characterised style as expressive of specific historical conditions. For a helpful discussion of style, especially as it pertains to computer vision research, see Kathryn Brown, 'Humanist-in-the-Loop: Machine Learning and the Analysis of Style in the Visual Arts', in *Modeling Visual Aesthetics, Emotion, and Artistic Style*, edited by James Z. Wang and Reginald B. Adams Jr. (Cham: Springer, 2024), pp. 219–28 and Alison Langmead, Christopher J. Nygren, Paul Rodriguez, and Alan Craig, 'Leonardo, Morelli, and the Computational Mirror', *DHQ: Digital Humanities Quarterly*, 15:1 (2021), np.

[32] Here, Nuria Rodríguez-Ortega's concept of intervectorality has clear advantages over traditional semiotic analyses. See Chapter 5 of this volume.

[33] Lang, *The Concept of Style*, p. 180.

Lang suggests that style be understood as 'a representation … of the process that produces it'.[34] Style, as Lang theorises it, is seen to signify not just the process of a work's creation but the process of its interpretation, refreshed and reframed with each encounter. Lang thus implicitly differentiates style from such representational systems as language and myth, which seem to yield to atomic description. Yet, even as Lang argues against the real-world existence of the styleme, he asserts that the *idea* of the styleme is revelatory in its own way. Occasionally, under certain social and cultural conditions, the styleme seems entirely logical, even essential. 'The styleme is thus fictional because … there quite simply is no such thing; but it is also fictional because for specific moments and contexts of art, the styleme brings comprehension and intelligibility'.[35] Presumably, given his reference to literary stylistics and Giovanni Morelli's morphological approach to art authentication as predicated on a notion of the styleme, Lang sees the turn of the 20th century as one of those moments. The early 21st century seems to be another.

The emergence of computer vision may account for renewed scholarly concern with style – and renewed efforts to make style legible. Certainly, style transfer experiments using digital images of works of art are, to some extent, reasserting the isolability of style for digital image analysis. Art historians, too, continue to rely on the concept of style in their research, despite widespread disciplinary scepticism towards its usefulness.[36] What accounts for the persistence, even resurgence, of style today? One answer may simply be the need for a generalisable means of negotiating today's visual environment. Thanks to the ease of image transmission – and image generation – via digital tools that are widely accessible via the internet, individuals with access to the web can easily encounter hundreds if not thousands of digital images each day. Style may provide one means of categorising or assessing this information. Long associated with individual taste as well as with commercial branding, style plays an especially important role in consumer culture – a role that has only been amplified with the advent of digital media. In other words, style facilitates visual communication in an image economy of hypercirculation.[37] Widespread use of style transfer apps and style filters further testifies to contemporary interest in pictorial style in the context of social media. These are all pragmatic reasons for style's currency today. There may be intellectual, even metaphysical interests behind the persistence of style in academic discourse.

[34] Lang, *The Concept of Style*, p. 180.
[35] Lang, *The Concept of Style*, p. 177.
[36] Even a cursory review of titles of papers presented at art history conferences, as well as recently published essays in art history journals, demonstrate that the term remains very much in play. For instance, a search of the ProQuest Dissertations and Theses Global database for theses completed in the last five years (2019–24) in the discipline of art history that include the word 'style' in their title or as a keyword yields over two dozen results, suggesting that the term remains current in scholarship.
[37] Daniel Palmer and Katrina Sluis, 'The Automation of Style: Seeing Photographically in Generative AI', *Media Theory*, 8:1 (2024), pp. 159–84 (pp. 173–4).

As stated earlier, for an image to contain style presupposes the presence of something else in addition to style, that is to say, content. This, of course, is the key premise of style transfer: that any image might be distilled into its two constituent parts, style and content. For an image to have style, therefore, means that an image must also have some essential, indissoluble referent. An image devoid of style would be pure content, the pictorial element closest to the actual thing represented. Photographic – or, rather, photo-like images – have come to stand for the style-less image.[38]

If photo-like images signify real-world content – regardless of whether the image is, in fact, a record of a thing or scene that existed at some point in the real world or not – it seemed to us to be not unreasonable to use photographic images as proxies for real-world phenomena when assessing the perceived accuracy of paintings created either subsequent to photography's popular dissemination or around the time of its invention.[39] In this way, we are attempting to leverage the phenomenon described by Tracy Stuber whereby 'in a CV [computer vision] training data set, an image is equivalent to its representation: an image of cat is a cat, and the image drops away'.[40] We also identified some historical rationalisation for this decision. That the same standards of pictorial accuracy that propelled the development of photography in the first decades of the 19th century might also have contributed to the emergence of so-called 'Realist' landscape painting around the same time is plausible. This conviction, in fact, helped to set the parameters for some of our first experiments using computer vision models to analyse digital images of works by John Constable.

Here, we set out to see whether computer vision might help us test the theory first put forward by art historian Kurt Badt in 1950 that Constable's ability to paint clouds naturalistically improved dramatically around 1821, and that this change was due to the artist's belated introduction to cloud taxonomy.[41] Over the years, Badt's theory has been alternately dismissed and accepted by art historians. His argument relies mostly on his own visual assessment of the relative naturalism of Constable's clouds before and after 1821. This, we felt, offered us precisely the kind of art historical conversation to which computer vision might helpfully contribute. According to our computer vision model (a CNN, or convolutional neural network), Constable's clouds performed well in terms of conforming to typological

[38] There is an enormous literature on this topic. For the current state of this discourse, see Vivian Mizrahi, 'Seeing through Photographs: Photography as a Transparent Visual Medium', *The Journal of Aesthetics and Art Criticism*, 79:1 (2021), pp. 52–63 and Kendall L Walton, 'Transparent Pictures: On the Nature of Photographic Realism', *Critical Inquiry*, 11:2 (1984), pp. 246–77.

[39] See, for instance, Beaumont Newhall, 'The First News Accounts of the Daguerreotype, January 6, 1839', in *Photography: Essays and Images. Illustrated Readings in the History of Photography*, edited by Beaumont Newhall (New York: Museum of Modern Art, 1980), pp. 17–21.

[40] Tracy Stuber, Chapter 8 of this volume.

[41] Zhuomin Zhang, Elizabeth C. Mansfield, Jia Li, John Russell, George S. Young, Catherine Adams *et al.*, 'A Machine Learning Paradigm for Studying Pictorial Realism: How Accurate Are Constable's Clouds?', *IEEE Transactions on Pattern Analysis and Machine Intelligence*, 46:1 (2024), pp. 33–42. The experiments are discussed at length in Elizabeth Mansfield with Zhuomin Zhang, Jia Li, John Russell, George S. Young, Catherine Adams, and James Z. Wang, 'Techniques of the Art Historical Observer', *Nineteenth-Century Art Worldwide*, 21:1 (2022), pp. 125–36.

characteristics, and the computer's assignment of cloud types largely matched the opinions of the expert meteorologists who separately labelled Constable's clouds in the images.[42] The results suggested that Constable recognised the distinctive features of cumulus, stratus, and cirrus clouds and noted those features in his paintings. While these results might weigh in favour of Badt's argument, our CNN did not register a change in Constable's performance in cloud accuracy around 1821. In other words, Constable's clouds could be classified by type before 1821, the year of his presumed technical breakthrough.

In a subsequent experiment, we expanded our dataset to include another 200 images of clouds painted by Constable's known emulators and other contemporaries noted for their naturalistic skies and their *plein air* paintings of clouds. The former included the artist's son Lionel Constable (1828–87), Frederick R. Lee (1798–1879), and Frederick W. Watts (1800–70); Pierre-Henri de Valenciennes (1750–1819), David Cox (1783–1859), and Eugène Boudin (1824–98) comprised the latter.[43] The results produced by our CNN again aligned with the meteorologists' ground truth: Constable's clouds could be classed by their features more consistently into Howard's typology than could clouds painted by his contemporaries or emulators.

Now confident in our CNN's ability to compare individual clouds – both photographic and painted – across our dataset, we next embarked on an experiment that engaged directly with Realism, a movement in European art and literature that was emerging in the 1820s and recognised by critics by the middle of the 1830s. Again, painted clouds by the artists listed above were assessed according to their similarities or differences from photographs of clouds made by NOAA, proceeding from the hypothesis that photographs of clouds are the most lifelike (or, more precisely, photo-like) images of clouds. In this experiment, Henri de Valenciennes' clouds were scored by the CNN as the most similar to photographic clouds. This result proved interesting, because the French academic painter Valenciennes is not typically associated with Realism. John Constable ranked quite closely behind Valenciennes, with Constable's emulators Lionel Constable, Frederick W. Watts, and Frederick R. Lee trailing them slightly. Historians of 19th-century art will perhaps not be surprised to learn that the computer deemed Eugène Boudin's clouds comparatively 'unrealistic' (that is to say, not as photo-like) and, in the first experiment, accorded lower probability to Boudin's clouds' classification as a specific type of cloud. Painting later in the century, Boudin is famous today as the teacher of Impressionist Claude Monet (1840–1926), and Boudin's looser technique can hardly be described as photographic.

[42] Meteorologists George Spencer Young and Kevin Bowley each assessed and labelled all the clouds created by Constable in our dataset.

[43] Although almost a generation older than John Constable, we included Pierre-Henri de Valenciennes in our study for the following reasons: (1) his career overlapped with Constable's; (2) his influence on subsequent French landscape painters is well-attested; (3) the naturalism of his many cloud studies is evident; (4) the art historical tendency to view Valenciennes as a fairly conservative painter offers an interesting historiographic counterpoint to the reception of Constable as the more progressive artist – a distinction not necessarily borne out by our experiments.

Style disentanglement and similarity

Our experiments on 19th-century cloud paintings led us to question whether something equivalent to a veristic or photo-like style could, in fact, be identified or even quantified. In other words, could we locate a 'styleme' that corresponded with lifelikeness, as perceived in paintings seen as highly naturalistic by some European viewers in the 19th century?[44] If we could compute a decoupled style for a painter, perhaps we could compare the stylistic similarity between digitised paintings and photographs as a step towards postulating a 'realist' painting style. To explore this hypothesis, we developed a method of style disentanglement and introduced two novel evaluation metrics to measure the similarity between the artistic styles of cloud paintings (or, more accurately, between their digital surrogates) – specifically those of John Constable, his contemporaries, and his emulators – and real-world cloud photographs.[45]

Style disentanglement is a computational technique that decomposes an image into two separate representations: content and style. In the case of our research, which focuses on images of clouds, content features capture the shared characteristics across all sets of images (characteristics constitutive of cloud content), while style features pinpoint the unique characteristics of each set. In our study, we treated the set of paintings by each artist as individual domains and the set of cloud photographs as the reference domain. In this way, cloud photographs served as a stand-in for ground truth.[46] By training style encoders for each artist's paintings and the cloud photographs, we were able to obtain disentangled style features for each collection of paintings, which correspond to an artist.

To evaluate the 'realism' (i.e., photo-likeness) of an artist's style, we introduced two novel metrics: 'Information Over Bias' (IOB) and 'Style Distance' (SD). The IOB metric measures the amount of information in a painting captured by its style features. A lower IOB value indicates that the style representation is less informative, implying higher similarity between the paintings and photographs and indicating this artist's painting style may be more realistic. The SD metric directly quantifies the dissimilarity between the disentangled style feature distributions of two sets of paintings. We computed the SD between pairs of artists to learn the style discrepancy among these artists, where the smaller the distance is, the more similar the painting styles of these two artists are.

Our analysis yielded some noteworthy findings. First, John Constable's digitalised paintings exhibited a style more akin to photographs than those of Boudin, Lee, and Cox, suggesting a higher degree of 'realism' in his cloud paintings (accepting photo-likeness as a measure of strong pictorial naturalism in the 19th century). Given Constable's popular reputation as a forerunner of the Realist movement, this was perhaps not surprising. Nor was the finding that the style of Lionel Constable

[44] To a certain extent, we are enlisting computer vision in the hope of gaining some insight into what formal features might have contributed to an experience of pictorial truth by a 19th-century European viewer, a research hypothesis informed by Michael Baxandall's theory of a 'period eye'. Our efforts are, of course, confounded in obvious and not-so-obvious ways. See Chapter 3 of this volume.

[45] Zhang *et al.*, 'A Machine Learning Paradigm for Studying Pictorial Realism'.

[46] On our rationale for this, see discussion above and Mizrahi, 'Seeing through Photographs', and Walton, 'Transparent Pictures'.

aligned most closely with that of John Constable, a result consistent with Lionel's known practice of emulating his father's techniques. However, our experiments also showed that the style of the digitalised paintings by Pierre-Henri de Valenciennes was the most photo-like among all the artists we evaluated, including John Constable. Valenciennes is not typically associated with the Realist movement, so the computer model's identification of Valenciennes as the most photo-like piqued our interest.

Style modelling

While earlier computer vision models focused on tasks such as image classification, segmentation, and object detection, the advent of image-generation models – namely, generative adversarial networks (GAN), autoregressive (AR) models, and variational autoencoders (VAEs) – have brought 'style' to the forefront through tasks such as image manipulation and style transfer.[47] As noted earlier, style transfer

[47] Ian Goodfellow, Jean Pouget-Abadie, Mehdi Mirza, Bing Xu, David Warde-Farley, Sherjil Ozair *et al.*, 'Generative Adversarial Nets', in *Advances in Neural Information Processing Systems*, edited by Z. Ghahramani, M. Welling, C. Cortes, N. Lawrence, and K.Q. Weinberger, Vol. 27 (Red Hook: Curran Associates, Inc., 2014), pp. 139–44; Tero Karras, Timo Aila, Samuli Laine, and Jaakko Lehtinen, 'Progressive Growing of GANs for Improved Quality, Stability, and Variation', in *Proceedings of the 6th International Conference on Learning Representations* (2018); Andrew Brock, Jeff Donahue, and Karen Simonyan, 'Large Scale GAN Training for High Fidelity Natural Image Synthesis', in *Proceedings of the 7th International Conference on Learning Representations* (2019); Tero Karras, Samuli Laine, and Timo Aila, 'A Style-Based Generator Architecture for Generative Adversarial Networks', in *Proceedings of the IEEE/CVF Conference on Computer Vision and Pattern Recognition* (June 2019); Tero Karras, Samuli Laine, Miika Aittala, Janne Hellsten, Jaakko Lehtinen, and Timo Aila, 'Analyzing and Improving the Image Quality of StyleGAN', in *Proceedings of the IEEE/CVF Conference on Computer Vision and Pattern Recognition* (June 2020), pp. 8110–19; Aäron Van Den Oord, Nal Kalchbrenner, and Koray Kavukcuoglu, 'Pixel Recurrent Neural Networks', in *Proceedings of the International Conference on Machine Learning* (2016), pp. 1747–56; Jacob Menick and Nal Kalchbrenner, 'Generating High Fidelity Images with Subscale Pixel Networks and Multidimensional Upscaling', in *Proceedings of the International Conference on Learning Representations* (2019); Nal Kalchbrenner, Aäron Oord, Karen Simonyan, Ivo Danihelka, Oriol Vinyals, Alex Graves *et al.*, 'Video Pixel Networks', in *Proceedings of the 34th International Conference on Machine Learning* (2017), pp. 1771–9; Aditya Ramesh, Mikhail Pavlov, Gabriel Goh, Scott Gray, Chelsea Voss, Alec Radford *et al.*, 'Zero-Shot Text-to-Image Generation', *Proceedings of the 38th International Conference on Machine Learning* (2021), pp. 8821–31; Mark Chen, Alec Radford, Rewon Child, Jeff Wu, Heewoo Jun, David Luan *et al.*, 'Generative Pretraining from Pixels', in *Proceedings of the 37th International Conference on Machine Learning* (2020), pp. 1691–703; Rewon Child, Scott Gray, Alec Radford, and Ilya Sutskever, 'Generating Long Sequences with Sparse Transformers', arXiv preprint, arXiv:1904.10509 (2019); Aäron van den Oord, Nal Kalchbrenner, Lasse Espeholt, Koray Kavukcuoglu, Oriol Vinyals, and Alex Graves, 'Conditional Image Generation with PixelCNN Decoders', in *Advances in Neural Information Processing Systems*, edited by D. Lee M. Sugiyama, U. Luxburg, I. Guyon, and R. Garnett, Vol. 29 (Red Hook: Curran Associates, Inc., 2016), pp. 4797–805; Diederik P. Kingma and Max Welling, 'Auto-Encoding Variational Bayes', arXiv preprint, arXiv:1312.6114 (2013); Ali Razavi, Aäron van den Oord, and Oriol Vinyals, 'Generating Diverse High-Fidelity Images with VQ-VAE-2', in *Advances in Neural Information Processing Systems*, edited by H. Wallach, H. Larochelle, A. Beygelzimer, F. d'Alché-Buc, E. Fox, and R. Garnett, Vol. 32 (Red Hook: Curran Associates, Inc., 2019), pp. 14866–76; Aäron van den Oord, Oriol Vinyals, and Koray Kavukcuoglu, 'Neural Discrete Representation Learning', in *Advances in Neural Information Processing Systems*, edited by I. Guyon, U. Von Luxburg, S. Bengio, H. Wallach, R. Fergus, S. Vishwanathan *et al.*, Vol. 30 (Red Hook: Curran Associates, Inc., 2017), pp. 6309–18.

is a computer vision task that involves altering the style of an image using another image as a reference. Image manipulation is similar to style transfer, but it can also involve modifying an image's content. Computer vision tasks such as style transfer and image manipulation have provided a framework for AI-based artistic applications including art generation, art design, and photograph editing.

Current computer vision algorithms and state-of-the-art models operate within the pixel space of an image. Researchers hypothesise that these models characterise 'style' as the local salient visual features observed in the artwork – such as the colour palette; the frequency, intensity, thickness, and shape of brushstrokes; and the relative shading between different content elements of the painting – while the 'content' is confined to the lines and shapes that define the structure of the content elements, i.e., these models characterise 'content' as 'what' a structural element is and the 'style' as 'how' it is depicted. In Chapter 6 of the present volume, Amalia Foka provides a useful overview of style in this context, focusing on formal elements such as line, shape, colour, texture, space, and composition, and argues that models should be evaluated based on their ability to capture these elements. As mentioned previously, quantifying something as subjective as 'art style' using computational AI models is a difficult task. This concern is shared by Cetinić, who, in Chapter 2 of this volume, highlights the complexity of style and how attempts to quantify it computationally in the past have been overly simplistic from an art historical perspective.

In Chapter 3 of the present volume, Brown argues that computational methods rely too much on formal and visual elements of artworks to capture style and thus underestimate the social context that contributes to their styleme as well. Stuber, in Chapter 8, furthers this argument by highlighting the difference in how computational algorithms perceive artists' photographs compared to humans, deeming it a battle between aesthetics and theory. Brown also provides a counterargument that focusing on visual elements and removing consideration of social concepts is not always an elimination of art historical analysis. In our experiments, we focus on the visual elements of paintings, while keeping in mind the aforementioned discourse.

It is important to note that these generative models function as 'black boxes' and it is a challenging task to determine which exact features the models deem to be the style or content of an image/painting. Consequently, as part of our research, we aim to develop strategies to explain how these models make such decisions.

Owing to their success in high-quality image generation, a majority of current state-of-the-art style transfer and image manipulation methods utilise GANs.[48]

[48] Wenju Xu, Chengjiang Long, Ruisheng Wang, and Guanghui Wang, 'DRB-GAN: A Dynamic ResBlock Generative Adversarial Network for Artistic Style Transfer', in *Proceedings of the IEEE/CVF International Conference on Computer Vision (ICCV)* (October 2021), pp. 6383–92. These approaches primarily utilise conditional GANs and GAN inversion methods. Jun-Yan Zhu, Taesung Park, Phillip Isola, and Alexei A. Efros, 'Unpaired Image-to-Image Translation Using Cycle-Consistent Adversarial Networks', in *Proceedings of the IEEE International Conference on Computer Vision* (2017), pp. 2223–32; Peihao Zhu, Rameen Abdal, Yipeng Qin, and Peter Wonka, 'SEAN: Image Synthesis with Semantic

However, GANs are hampered by performance drawbacks such as high computational requirements, training instability, and image quality issues such as reduced resolution and perceptual quality. In recent years, diffusion models have emerged as a robust and stable alternative, overcoming many of these limitations.[49] These models, which have become the de facto standard for high-quality image generation, leverage iterative guided generation processes to produce high-quality, diverse images.[50] Extensive research has gone into making diffusion models more robust, stable, and efficient.[51]

Inspired by non-equilibrium statistical physics, diffusion models were initially introduced as a flexible and controllable method for deep unsupervised generation.

Region-Adaptive Normalization', in *Proceedings of the IEEE/CVF Conference on Computer Vision and Pattern Recognition* (June 2020), pp. 5104–13; Tali Dekel, Chuang Gan, Dilip Krishnan, Ce Liu, and William T. Freeman, 'Sparse, Smart Contours to Represent and Edit Images', in *Proceedings of the IEEE Conference on Computer Vision and Pattern Recognition* (June 2018), pp. 3511–20; Phillip Isola, Jun-Yan Zhu, Tinghui Zhou, and Alexei A. Efros, 'Image-to-Image Translation with Conditional Adversarial Networks', in *Proceedings of the IEEE Conference on Computer Vision and Pattern Recognition* (July 2017), pp. 1125–34; Taesung Park, Ming-Yu Liu, Ting-Chun Wang, and Jun-Yan Zhu, 'Semantic Image Synthesis with Spatially-Adaptive Normalization', in *Proceedings of the IEEE/CVF Conference on Computer Vision and Pattern Recognition* (June 2019), pp. 2337–46; Elad Richardson, Yuval Alaluf, Or Patashnik, Yotam Nitzan, Yaniv Azar, Stav Shapiro *et al.*, 'Encoding in Style: A StyleGAN Encoder for Image-to-Image Translation', in *Proceedings of the IEEE/CVF Conference on Computer Vision and Pattern Recognition* (June 2021), pp. 2287–96; Rameen Abdal, Yipeng Qin, and Peter Wonka, 'Image2StyleGAN: How to Embed Images into the StyleGAN Latent Space?', in *Proceedings of the IEEE/CVF International Conference on Computer Vision (ICCV)* (October 2019), pp. 4432–41; David Bau, Hendrik Strobelt, William Peebles, Jonas Wulff, Bolei Zhou, Jun-Yan Zhu *et al.*, 'Semantic Photo Manipulation with a Generative Image Prior', *ACM Transactions on Graphics*, 38:4 (July 2019), pp. 1–11; Zongze Wu, Dani Lischinski, and Eli Shechtman, 'StyleSpace Analysis: Disentangled Controls for StyleGAN Image Generation', in *Proceedings of the IEEE/CVF Conference on Computer Vision and Pattern Recognition* (June 2021), pp. 12863–72; Jiapeng Zhu, Yujun Shen, Deli Zhao, and Bolei Zhou, 'In-domain GAN Inversion for Real Image Editing', in *Proceedings of the European Conference on Computer Vision* (Berlin and Heidelberg: Springer-Verlag, 2020), pp. 592–608.

[49] Robin Rombach, Andreas Blattmann, Dominik Lorenz, Patrick Esser, and Björn Ommer, 'High-Resolution Image Synthesis with Latent Diffusion Models', in *Proceedings of the IEEE/CVF Conference on Computer Vision and Pattern Recognition* (June 2022), pp. 10684–95.

[50] Prafulla Dhariwal and Alexander Nichol, 'Diffusion Models Beat GANs on Image Synthesis', *Advances in Neural Information Processing Systems*, 34 (2021), pp. 8780–94.

[51] Jascha Sohl-Dickstein, Eric Weiss, Niru Maheswaranathan, and Surya Ganguli, 'Deep Unsupervised Learning Using Nonequilibrium Thermodynamics', in *Proceedings of the International Conference on Machine Learning* (2015), pp. 2256–65; Jonathan Ho, Ajay Jain, and Pieter Abbeel, 'Denoising Diffusion Probabilistic Models', in *Advances in Neural Information Processing Systems*, edited by H. Larochelle *et al.*, Vol. 33 (Red Hook: Curran Associates, Inc., 2020), pp. 6840–51; Jiaming Song, Chenlin Meng, and Stefano Ermon, 'Denoising Diffusion Implicit Models', in *Proceedings of the International Conference on Learning Representations* (2021), n.p.; Alexander Quinn Nichol, Prafulla Dhariwal, Aditya Ramesh, Pranav Shyam, Pamela Mishkin, Bob McGrew *et al.*, 'GLIDE: Towards Photorealistic Image Generation and Editing with Text-Guided Diffusion Models', in *Proceedings of the International Conference on Machine Learning*, edited by Kamalika Chaudhuri, Stefanie Jegelka, Le Song, Csaba Szepesvari, Gang Niu, and Sivan Sabato, Vol. 162 (July 2022), pp. 16784–804; Rombach *et al.*, 'High-Resolution Image Synthesis with Latent Diffusion Models'; Song, Meng, and Ermon, 'Denoising Diffusion Implicit Models'.

Due to their iterative and controllable nature along with high generation quality, these models quickly found applications in image generation.[52] In simple terms, diffusion models are characterised by a forward diffusion process and a reverse generative diffusion process. During training, noise is gradually added to a clear image, e.g., a detailed photograph, per a schedule, making the picture less clear and more chaotic (noisy). Then, during the reverse process, a neural network is trained to estimate the noise that was added in the forward process and remove it to recreate the original clear picture. The denoising and image generation is done in an iterative manner as it is easier for the model to estimate and remove this noise in smaller increments. The output of the reverse process is the generated image. At the end of the training stage, a model is obtained that is able to generate an image from a random noisy input as it has learned how to denoise images. A 'conditioning' mechanism, often in the form of text descriptions, is also utilised during the training stage to make sure that the iterative denoising and generation is not completely random. The conditioning text guides how the generation happens and ensures that the generated image follows what is mentioned in the text condition. Through these mechanisms, diffusion models can create highly detailed and accurate images from just a few descriptive words. In Chapter 5 of this volume, Rodríguez-Ortega provides a detailed overview of the relationship between text and image in diffusion models.

For our experiments, we wanted to utilise a text description that captures the generic visual elements of all the digitised paintings used for fine-tuning the model to offer context without adding explicit text supervision highlighting the style of specific artists, as we want the model to learn that implicitly. Consequently, we used the description 'a 19th-century realist painting of clouds and the sky' for all digitalised paintings in fine-tuning our model.[53] Figure 7.5 is a visualisation of the reverse denoising process with a diffusion model utilising 20 timesteps.

Diffusion models have also been applied effectively to image style transfer and manipulation where the content of an image is preserved while its style is altered in accordance with an image or text prompt. These applications demonstrate that diffusion models can capture salient semantic and style features from images.[54]

[52] Ho, Jain, and Abbeel, 'Denoising Diffusion Probabilistic Models'; Sohl-Dickstein *et al.*, 'Deep Unsupervised Learning Using Nonequilibrium Thermodynamics'.

[53] While not all of the paintings in our dataset are by artists associated with Realism, we include the word 'realist' to steer the model to focus on a subset of data that was used to train it. Since the pretrained model was trained on a plethora of diverse images, the 'realist' tag helps the model focus on the subset of paintings that are more 'naturalistic'. This tag is particularly significant since publicly available painting data are dominated by artists like Van Gogh, whose works do not tend to be described as realist.

[54] Gwanghyun Kim, Taesung Kwon, and Jong Chul Ye, 'DiffusionCLIP: Text-Guided Diffusion Models for Robust Image Manipulation', in *Proceedings of the IEEE/CVF Conference on Computer Vision and Pattern Recognition* (June 2022), pp. 2426–35; Gihyun Kwon and Jong Chul Ye, 'Diffusion-based Image Translation Using Disentangled Style and Content Representation', in *Proceedings of the International Conference on Learning Representations* (2023); Chenlin Meng, Yutong He, Yang Song, Jiaming Song, Jiajun Wu, Jun-Yan Zhu *et al.*, 'SDEdit: Guided Image Synthesis and Editing with Stochastic Differential Equations', in *Proceedings of the International Conference on Learning Representations* (2022).

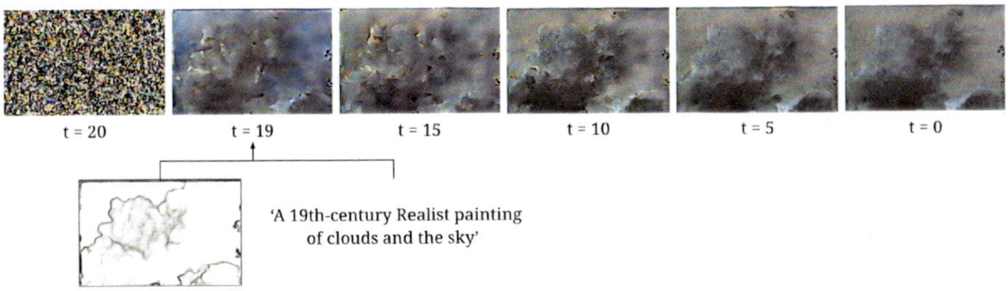

Figure 7.5 Visualisation of the reverse denoising process with a diffusion model utilising 20 timesteps. At timestep $t = 20$, the image is a random noised Gaussian. At $t = 19$, the first predicted denoised image is synthesised with the text prompt and the HED edge map as conditions. The predicted denoised image is iteratively synthesised and gradually becomes more stable in terms of colours, texture, and content with the final generated image obtained at timestep $t = 0$.

However, as mentioned earlier, 'style' is a subjective term and captures implicit aspects of a painting. Although substantial progress has been made in learning and transferring the style of images, efforts to quantify the style of paintings have been limited. This raises the question: is the quantification of artistic style even feasible?[55]

Our current experiments apply diffusion models to explore the possibility of quantifying the styles of John Constable and a selected group of contemporaries and emulators. Theoretically, at least, expressing style as a quantifiable characteristic of an image would allow for comparison of each artist's 'styleme'. To do this, we utilise ControlNet with a pretrained latent diffusion model as its backbone.[56] A learnable set of parameters deemed the 'style descriptor', are added as a condition to the diffusion model and are trained using digitalised surrogates of landscape paintings by the aforementioned artists. ControlNet allows us to control the content of the paintings and forces its parameters to focus on the stylistic features of the paintings, such as brushstrokes, colour palette, highlighting, and shading. ControlNet is then fine-tuned on these digitalised paintings with each set of style descriptors attributed to specific artists. With the content of the paintings controlled, the style descriptors learn the salient 'style' features of the paintings belonging to an artist as those features are recorded in the digitalised paintings. For instance, we can fine-tune ControlNet on digitalised paintings by John Constable, Valenciennes,

[55] For the moment, we hold at bay the further question: even if feasible, how might the quantification of style aid in art historical research?

[56] A backbone is a commonly used term in Computer Science for the main neural network that is tasked with feature extraction. The extracted features are utilised by other subnetworks for a variety of tasks. Lvmin Zhang, Anyi Rao, and Maneesh Agrawala, 'Adding Conditional Control to Text-to-Image Diffusion Models', in *Proceedings of the IEEE/CVF International Conference on Computer Vision* (2023), pp. 3836–47; Rombach *et al.*, 'High-Resolution Image Synthesis with Latent Diffusion Models'.

and Édouard Manet (1832–83). Style descriptors are added to each model and during training each set of descriptors is only trained on paintings belonging to the corresponding artist. Each ControlNet, and specifically each style descriptor, learns the salient stylistic features belonging to a specific artist, i.e., these descriptors are forced to learn what is not common in the styles of the artists. Style descriptors generated for different painters are compared using similarity measures such as cosine similarity and Euclidean distance to measure the degree of stylistic influence among painters and determine how 'far' the style of one artist is from the others. In the pursuit of explainability, we also generate counterfactual examples to highlight the stylistic features that determine the 'style' of an artist and how they differ from those of other artists.

Experimenting with diffusion models

To extract the style of paintings, we turn again to diffusion models. In this section, we provide an overview of the experimental setup, the results of the experiments, and modifications to the experimental conditions over time in response to the identified shortcomings. The goal of these experiments is to fine-tune and utilise a diffusion model to extract the style of various 19th-century landscape artists and to compare these extracted stylistic elements both quantitatively and qualitatively.

We first employ Latent Diffusion Models (LDMs) as the main network.[57] LDMs are a class of diffusion models that are more efficient and also produce higher-quality outputs. This is because, instead of operating directly on the image, they convert the image back and forth between the image space and a lower dimensional latent space. LDMs have been utilised extensively for style transfer and image manipulation, and have shown the capability to capture stylistic information from natural images. We utilise a pretrained LDM and modify it by adding a set of trainable parameters termed *style descriptors* to the conditioning mechanism.

Style descriptors are a set of learnable parameters added to the conditioning transformer utilised by the diffusion model during the reverse (generative) diffusion process. The pretrained LDM is kept frozen, meaning it is not further trained. Instead, we fine-tune these style descriptors on the images of paintings by each artist, i.e., the conditioning mechanism for the model is trained. A separate set of style descriptors is trained for each artist. The training process estimates the condition needed to guide the model to convergence for a given set of paintings and a noise estimation model.

The main motivation behind training these descriptors is that, when the rest of the LDM is frozen, they capture the common characteristics of the dataset that is being used to fine-tune them and guide the generation process. With the content fixed, this common property becomes the 'stylistic' visual components of the

[57] Rombach *et al.*, 'High-Resolution Image Synthesis with Latent Diffusion Models'.

paintings, such as the brushstrokes and colour palettes, i.e., the learnable style descriptors capture the salient aspects of the paintings in the dataset used to train them. To promote style disentanglement and ensure that the style descriptors preserve only the aforementioned visual elements, the dataset is refined to only contain images of clouds and skies. Thereby, each set of style descriptors captures what could be attributed as the cumulative style of a set of paintings.

To prevent the text conditioning prompt from influencing the style descriptors, the training is conducted with empty text prompts, adding another level of uniformity to the training procedure and allowing the similarity measurements to focus on the salient style differences between the artworks. We found that training eight style descriptors for each artist captures sufficient stylistic information while maintaining training efficiency.[58]

In Tables 7.1, 7.2, and 7.3 we detail the preliminary results from training the style descriptors for a set of artists. To illustrate our results, we provide the style descriptor comparisons to John Constable's style as captured by the model. All descriptors were trained for 100 epochs on 512 × 512 painting patches containing the skies and clouds of paintings from respective artists. We convert the paintings to greyscale to eliminate any noise introduced by colour changes and degradation due to exposure to the elements. The style descriptors trained for each artist are compared using cosine similarity in a pairwise manner. To further determine the significance of these similarity scores, we do statistical tests by bootstrapping the datasets for each artist and comparing the results over five runs using the t-test which helps determine whether the similarity scores are significantly different from each other and not simply the result of random variations in the dataset.

Table 7.1 contains the similarity scores comparing John Constable's style descriptors to other near-contemporary painters. These similarity scores suggest that Constable has a high degree of similarity with all of the artists in our study, with the closest being Valenciennes. Yet, because these similarity scores are so close, the statistical significance of the scores needed further confirmation. To determine the scores' significance, we conducted a t-test on bootstrapped datasets for these artists, generating two sets of 25 similarity scores. The results are shown in Table 7.2. For clarity, the results are shown for John Constable, Lionel Constable, and Valenciennes. The mean and standard deviation for the J. Constable–L. Constable and J. Constable–Valenciennes distributions are shown in Table 7.3.

The results are considered statistically significant at significance level 0.01, i.e., for p-values less than 0.01. Therefore, despite the closeness of the similarity scores, a t-test reveals that the scores are statistically significant for all pairs of artists. While the quantitative results are statistically significant and provide insight into the style similarity between different artists, the scores are very close. The

[58] The number of style descriptors was empirically ablated by visually comparing the outputs and quantitative analysis with no significant changes observed in the output.

Table 7.1 Quantitative results for the artist models.

Artist pair	Similarity score ↑
J. Constable–J. Constable	0.9999
J. Constable–L. Constable	0.9734
J. Constable–Valenciennes	0.9714
J. Constable–Boudin	0.9671
J. Constable–Watts	0.9732
J. Constable–Lee	0.9702

Note: Each pair of artist models is fine-tuned on digitalised paintings corresponding to the respective artist, utilising cosine similarity as the metric for evaluation. A higher score indicates greater similarity.

Table 7.2 t-test results for the bootstrapped datasets.

Distributions compared	p-value ↓
J. Constable–L. Constable and J. Constable–Valenciennes	0.0001
J. Constable–J. Constable and J. Constable–L. Constable	8.6922e-11
L. Constable–L. Constable and J. Constable–L. Constable	2.0615e-09
J. Constable–J. Constable and J. Constable–Valenciennes	2.5699e-07
Valenciennes–Valenciennes and J. Constable–Valenciennes	2.3171e-16

Note: Each pair of distributions compares the similarity scores for bootstrapped datasets belonging to the respective artists, with the p-value reported for each distribution pair (p-value < 0.01 indicates significance).

Table 7.3 Mean and standard deviation for the J. Constable–L. Constable and J. Constable–Valenciennes distributions.

Artist pair	Mean	Standard deviation
J. Constable–L. Constable	0.9690	0.0077
J. Constable–Valenciennes	0.9759	0.0059

reason for this is twofold: (1) Although content reliance is reduced by limiting the paintings to greyscale patches of clouds and the skies, it is not eliminated. This residue content information leaks into the style descriptor as noise, causing the style descriptors to inadvertently learn content information as they implicitly learn the common characteristics of the fine-tuning dataset, i.e., the fact that all paintings involve clouds and skies. (2) LDMs inherently lack an explicit mechanism to disentangle content and style features, which contributes to the suboptimal features learned by the style descriptors. To address these issues, we transitioned to a new architecture of diffusion models – ControlNet.

ControlNet is a convolutional network built on top of a stable diffusion model that allows greater control over the generation process by incorporating additional conditioning prompts in the form of holistically nested edge detection (HED) or Canny edge maps of the input image.[59] This approach allows the model parameters to better capture the stylistic features of the input images, as the edge maps divert the model's focus away from the structural elements and content of the images. Here, the model learns the HED edge map as the content of the digitalised painting and everything that is not the edge map, i.e., the brushstrokes and colour palette as the 'style' of the digitalised painting. In Chapter 6 of this volume, Foka's experiments show that stable diffusion produces some high-quality results owing to a greater emphasis on compositional elements and artistic principles in its training data, which further underscores our use of ControlNet with a pretrained stable diffusion backbone for our experiments.

As before, we freeze the pretrained LDM and fine-tune the ControlNet parameters along with the style descriptors. We utilise the HED maps of the input as another condition alongside the style descriptor. The HED map condition controls the content for the model, thereby forcing the style descriptors to focus on the stylistic elements of the paintings (Figure 7.6). Compared to the LDM, ControlNet provides explicit content control, which facilitates easier style disentanglement.

While conducting experiments on the digitalised paintings with ControlNet, we empirically observed that training on greyscale paintings produced style descriptors that had insufficient stylistic information. This finding can be attributed to the fact that, for ControlNet, the mechanism for controlling content with edge maps works against the style descriptors for greyscale images. With the edges removed, there are not enough stylistic features left for the descriptors to learn. Consequently, there

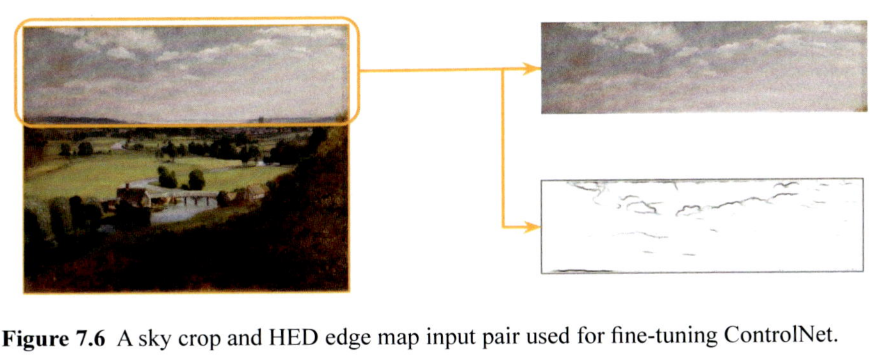

Figure 7.6 A sky crop and HED edge map input pair used for fine-tuning ControlNet.

[59] Zhang, Rao, and Agrawala, 'Adding Conditional Control to Text-to-Image Diffusion Models'.

are minimal observable stylistic differences between the samples generated from the style descriptors for different artists. Switching to coloured paintings resolved this issue, providing explicit stylistic differences between the painters, which are most apparent with counterfactual generation.

Our next phase of experimentation focused on images of paintings by John Constable, Eugène Boudin, Rosa Bonheur (1822–99), and Édouard Manet. Here, we present some qualitative examples from the artist models. Each artist model is a ControlNet model fine-tuned on digitalised paintings attributed to a specific artist. These artist models aim to capture the cumulative style of the respective artists. For instance, in Figure 7.7, Constable's style (Figure 7.7b) is represented by dense clouds, pronounced white highlights, and what might be interpreted as visible brushstrokes, while Bonheur's style as interpreted by the model (Figure 7.7a)

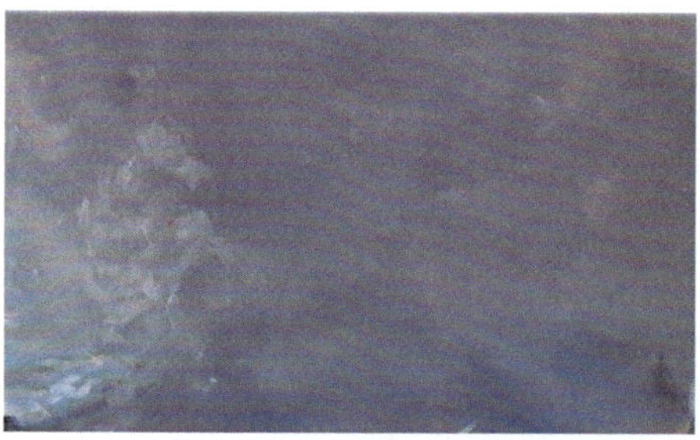

(a) Bonheur-style synthetic painting

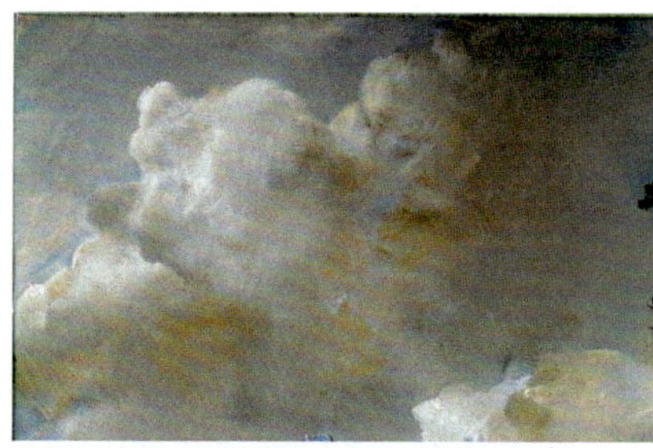

(b) J. Constable-style synthetic painting

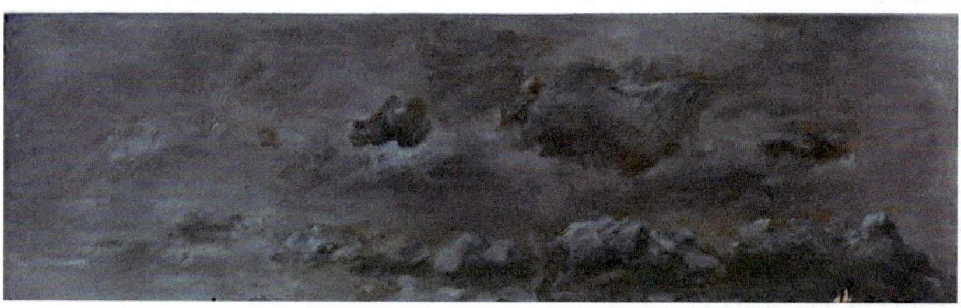

(c) Boudin-style synthetic painting

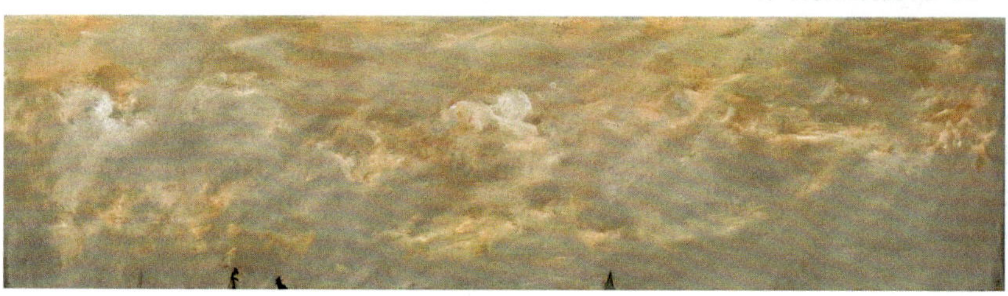

(d) Manet-style synthetic painting

Figure 7.7 Examples of ControlNet model outputs, i.e., synthetic painting images, showing stylistic differences among the artists' fine-tuned models.

lacks the emphasis on modelling with white highlights and may be perceived as less illusionistic in its suggestion of spatial depth.

As noted earlier, one way to assess the accuracy of an artist's synthetic style descriptor is to generate novel images that human viewers can compare to actual works by the artist. The creation of so-called counterfactual images or counterfactual visualisations is also a way of understanding how a given computer vision model solves a visual problem. Machine learning, particularly deep learning, often operates as a 'black box', because the internal decision-making processes have high complexity, and self-training by the model is generally expected. Owing to their black box nature, these AI models lack interpretability, a concern shared by Amanda Wasielewski, Foka, Stuber, and Cetinić in their chapters in the present volume. Wasielewski (Chapter 1), through the lens of Beuys's work, goes so far as to consider the training of contemporary AI models as 'disingenuous' owing to their lack of explanations, highlighting the importance of explainability in the widespread adoption of AI models. Stuber (Chapter 8) highlights how the lack of explainability further affects non-standard datasets such as our dataset of realist paintings. Foka (Chapter 6) provides a more analytical view of the black box nature of AI models and how they limit the understanding of whether AI models are simply remixing existing patterns to make decisions or actually exploring and generating new ones observed in the target dataset to make grounded decisions. Finally, Cetinić (Chapter 2) highlights the importance of making AI more accessible to people from varying backgrounds. To this end, we introduce the importance of bringing explainability into style analysis, followed by the creative generation of counterfactual examples.

Explainability is a broad concept that poses both technical and scholarly challenges. In the field of machine learning, explainability refers to the challenge of producing understandable explanations for model decisions and predictions; from a scholarly viewpoint, explainability serves as a broader and interdisciplinary concept that covers social, ethical, and philosophical aspects. Explainable AI (aka XAI) offers a promising solution to the challenges of adopting black box AI models by seeking to provide rational explanations for AI outcomes tailored to the needs of diverse stakeholders. Adopting XAI can also promote transparency and reliability in AI-driven analysis of artworks.

The application of diffusion models to the analysis of art brings both possibilities and challenges. Despite the widespread popular enthusiasm elicited by the performance of diffusion models in various image-generation and image-analysis tasks, scepticism persists among art historians and others involved in the study of cultural heritage regarding the opaque generation process of these models. Several studies have advocated the critical importance of understanding these models' inner workings in the context of art analysis.[60] These studies describe some of the

[60] Vicente Dominguez, Pablo Messina, Ivania Donoso-Guzmán, and Denis Parra, 'The Effect of Explanations and Algorithmic Accuracy on Visual Recommender Systems of Artistic Images', in *Proceedings of the International Conference on Intelligent User Interfaces* (2019), pp. 408–16; Natalia Díaz-Rodríguez and Galena Pisoni, 'Accessible Cultural Heritage through Explainable Artificial Intelligence', in *Adjunct Publication of the 28th ACM Conference on User Modeling, Adaptation and Personalization* (2020), pp. 317–24.

dilemmas faced by different research communities. For computer scientists, developing stronger black box AI models on paintings to distinguish artists and historical periods with better accuracy represents significant progress in AI advancements. However, for art historians, such improvements in statistical performance metrics may hold limited significance regarding visual aesthetics. The AI decision-making process is also susceptible to different biases due to the inherent subjectivity and lack of cultural grounding. Furthermore, using generative models in art analysis raises ethical and intellectual concerns.[61] For instance, diffusion models can repeat or even amplify harmful stereotypes and biased worldviews.[62] One step towards addressing these concerns is to utilise a more comprehensive approach to the development of generative models, an approach that combines the technical expertise of computer scientists with the aesthetic and cultural expertise of art historians. In the case of our research, we sought to enhance explainability in our approach by creating counterfactual examples for different artists, thereby providing convincing visualisation results using diffusion models.

To determine if the artist models captured the styles of their respective artists, we conducted counterfactual analysis by using edge maps of actual paintings by specific artists as inputs for different artist models. These edge maps serve as a template for semantic information, ensuring that the generated counterfactual images share consistent content. Figures 7.8 and 7.9 show the resulting counterfactual examples for artists John Constable and Rosa Bonheur, respectively. A template derived from a painting by one artist is first processed through their own artist model, with the generated output shown in Figures 7.8a and 7.9a. Then, it is fed through other artist models to observe how a cloud originally painted by one artist would appear in the 'style' of other artists as defined by the model. For instance, as shown in Figure 7.8, we see a digitalised painting from Constable in the synthetic 'style' extracted from the Constable artist model (Figure 7.8a) and then his painting in the synthetic 'styles' of Bonheur (Figure 7.8b), Boudin (Figure 7.8c), and Manet (Figure 7.8d), respectively. The counterfactual examples show distinct visual differences that could be suggestive of different artistic styles which are consistent for the same artist across paintings; for instance, the dark palette punctuated by bright highlights, gestural brushstrokes, and prominent dabs of local colour that tend to be characteristic of Constable.

To further explain what the model interprets as style and content, we consider additional counterfactual examples in Figure 7.10. We use the same John Constable surrogate utilised in Figure 7.8. As described before, the model learns the

[61] Christopher Nygren and Sonja Drimmer, 'Art History and AI: Ten Axioms', *International Journal for Digital Art History*, 10:9 (2023), pp. 5.02–5.13; Shawn Shan, Jenna Cryan, Emily Wenger, Haitao Zheng, Rana Hanocka, and Ben Y. Zhao, 'Glaze: Protecting Artists from Style Mimicry by Text-to-Image Models', in *32nd USENIX Security Symposium (USENIX Security 23)* (2023), pp. 2187–204.

[62] Delfina Sol Martinez Pandiani, Nicolas Lazzari, Marieke van Erp, and Valentina Presutti, 'Hypericons for Interpretability: Decoding Abstract Concepts in Visual Data', *International Journal of Digital Humanities*, 5:2 (2023), pp. 451–90.

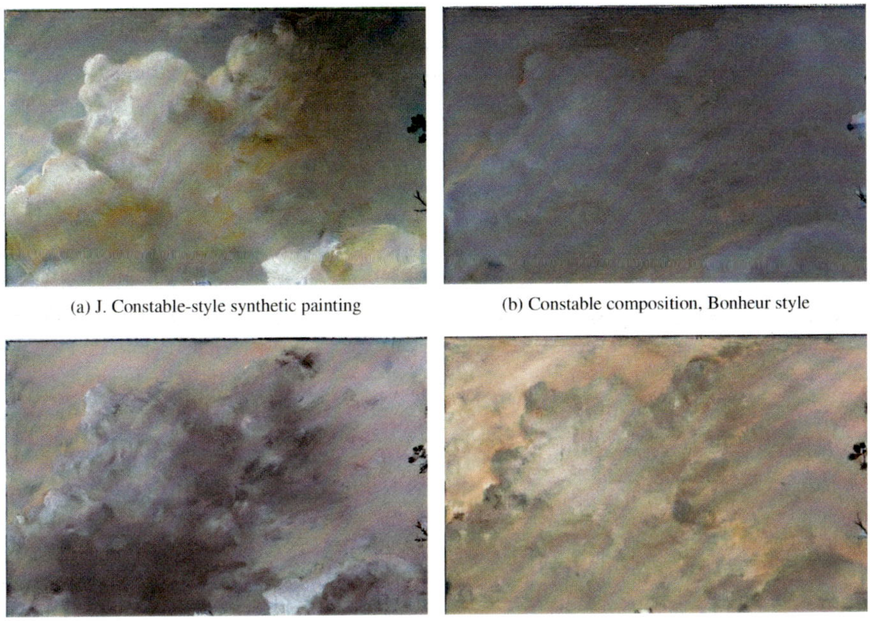

(a) J. Constable-style synthetic painting

(b) Constable composition, Bonheur style

(c) Constable composition, Boudin style

(d) Constable composition, Manet style

Figure 7.8 Generated counterfactual examples for John Constable. These examples illustrate the model's identification of salient features for each artist's style. (a) shows a synthetic image generated by the artist model fine-tuned on Constable's digitalised paintings with the edge map from a Constable digitalised painting as the input. (b), (c), and (d) show outputs for the artist models fine-tuned on Bonheur, Boudin, and Manet, respectively, with the same Constable edge map.

corresponding HED edge map of the digitalised painting (shown in Figure 7.10a) as the content of the painting. Using that edge map as the content, it learns the stylistic elements of the artist paintings used to fine-tune it to generate the artist models which are used to generate synthetic paintings in the 'style' of various artists as shown in Figures 7.8 and 7.9. Figure 7.10b highlights the learned 'style' of these artist models as it shows what ControlNet that is not fine-tuned on specific artist paintings determines to be the 'style' of a 19th-century 'realist' painting of clouds and the sky (our text description). It is termed as an 'unstylised' synthetic painting as it is not the result of artist models fine-tuned for specific artist 'styles'. However, it is important to note that the synthetic painting is not devoid of any 'style'. The 'style' observed in this synthetic painting is the amalgamation of billions of images and paintings used to train the base ControlNet model. Most importantly, even though the synthetic paintings generated in Figures 7.10b and 7.10d are naturalistic paintings of clouds and the sky, they show some visual differences, especially in terms of brushstrokes and colour palette, to the synthetics from the artist models in Figures 7.8 and 7.9, which may point to the capability of the artist

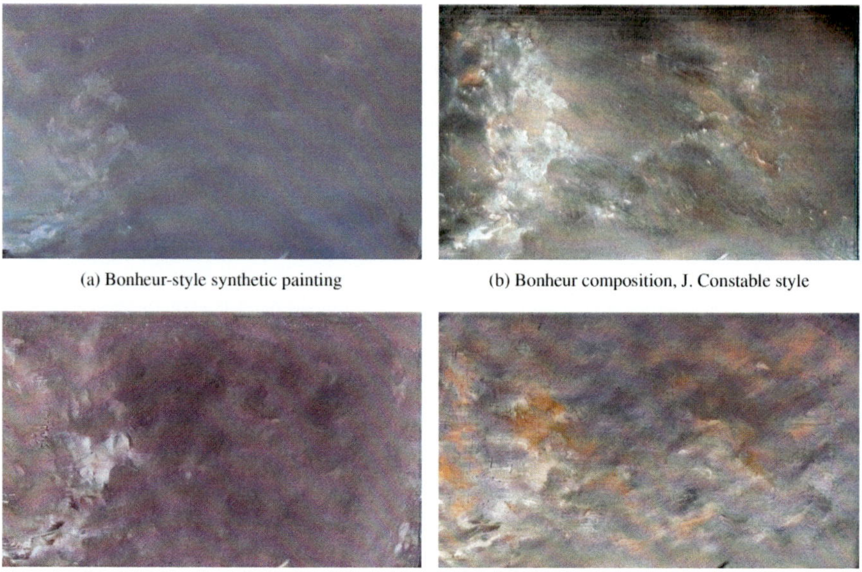

(a) Bonheur-style synthetic painting

(b) Bonheur composition, J. Constable style

(c) Bonheur composition, Boudin style

(d) Bonheur composition, Manet style

Figure 7.9 Generated counterfactual examples for Rosa Bonheur.

models in learning what they deem to be the ‘style’ of an artist. The counterfactual analysis provides insight into the salient aspects of the artists’ paintings identified by the model as their style and serves as evidence that the artist models sufficiently capture the differences in these salient visual elements. However, it is still up for debate whether these differences in salient visual elements captured by the artist models can be interpreted as stylistic differences.

The next phase of experiments will involve quantitative analysis of the artist models based on ControlNet and the comparison of the extracted style descriptors using similarity metrics to determine the degree of stylistic similarity between artists and infer stylistic influence. To ensure a true one-to-one comparison between the style descriptors, we are developing a joint model trained on all artists’ paintings, with separate style descriptors for each artist. This approach ensures that the base ControlNet parameters capture the common stylistic features of all artists, while the style descriptor captures the salient, distinct artistic features of their respective artists.

We are also developing modules to incorporate language prompts with rich descriptions of artist styles by art critics for these paintings as conditions to provide natural language supervision. Additionally, since ControlNet offers more explicit control over the content of the paintings, we are designing experiments with entire paintings instead of just sky/cloud patches, to utilise stylistic elements in the foreground and obtain a more complete understanding of the style of the artists. Finally, we aim to address a

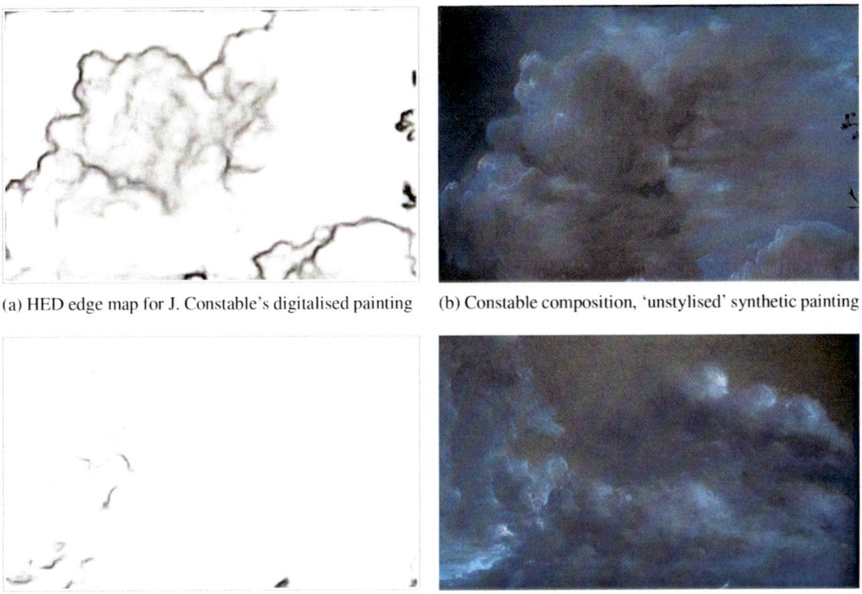

(a) HED edge map for J. Constable's digitalised painting (b) Constable composition, 'unstylised' synthetic painting

(c) HED edge map for Bonheur's digitalised painting (d) Bonheur composition, 'unstylised' synthetic painting

Figure 7.10 Further generated counterfactual examples for John Constable (a, b) and Rosa Bonheur (c, d). These examples illustrate the model's distinction between the style and content of a digitalised painting. (a) and (c) show the HED edge maps for Constable's and Bonheur's paintings that are learned by the model to be the content of the paintings. (b) and (d) show 'unstylised' synthetic paintings generated with the same textual description and corresponding edge maps using the base ControlNet that is not fine-tuned on specific artists' paintings.

major limitation of diffusion models – their categorisation as black boxes – by incorporating explainability into our approach to provide some insight into the decision-making process of these models.

Conclusion

AI is already exerting pressure on art history. Not necessarily on the fundamental work of art history, at least not yet: historical and aesthetic interpretation, visual analysis and formal description, authentication, and valuation remain very much within the domain of human expertise. Where AI is making itself felt most acutely is rather at the level of disciplinary identity, historiography, and purpose.[63] The

[63] Elizabeth Mansfield, Leonardo Impett, Emily Pugh, Mark Ledbury, John Russell, Kathryn Desplanque *et al.*, 'Special Collection: Art History after Computer Vision', *The Art Bulletin* (2024), pp. 6–38.

advent of computer vision – especially the emergence of easily accessible AI-based image-recognition and image-generation models – is leading art historians to reckon with certain disciplinary habits that tend to go unacknowledged. Among these is the central role that visual technologies have played in facilitating the practice of art history since its formation as an academic discipline. Rarely is the depth of mediation between the art historian and their object of study addressed explicitly, contributing to a fiction of empirical investigation that undergirds the validity of much art historical research. Another disciplinary habit is the persistence of formalist approaches, despite decades of disciplinary critique. Little art historical scholarship today foregoes entirely iconographical, formal, or stylistic analysis. No longer highlighted for their interpretative use, such formalist methods have simply been naturalised into art historical practice.

Direct engagement with AI-aided research thus benefits art historians in two ways. First, the potential for gaining new insights into visual culture – including historical artworks such as the landscape paintings of John Constable and Henri de Valenciennes – is already within reach. As demonstrated by our experiments, which led to a closer consideration of the relationship between the empiricism of *plein air* painting and the cultural conditions that fostered the invention of photography, judicious application of computer vision to the study of digital images of works of art can reorient the art historian's attention in productive ways. Second, AI-aided research can bring attention to those disciplinary habits that have been naturalised by longstanding practice. In other words, working with computer vision can help the art historian become more self-aware – and more self-critical – by heightening awareness of their own visual as well as methodological prejudices.

Acknowledgements

This research was primarily supported by the National Endowment for the Humanities (NEH) under Grant No. HAA-287938-22. This work used the Delta GPU cluster at The National Center for Supercomputing Applications through allocation #IRI180002 from the Advanced Cyberinfrastructure Coordination Ecosystem: Services & Support (ACCESS) programme, which is supported by National Science Foundation (NSF) grants #2138259, #2138286, #2138307, #2137603, and #2138296. J.Z. Wang and J. Li have been supported by the NSF under Grant No. CNS-2234195. J.Z. Wang has also been supported by generous gifts from the Amazon Research Awards programme. Z. Zhang is currently with Amazon. During 2023–24, J. Li was also affiliated with Umeå University, Sweden, and J.Z. Wang was also affiliated with Loughborough University, UK. J.Z. Wang is grateful to his host Kathryn Brown. The authors thank Catherine Adams for her assistance with the curation of painting image data. The authors also wish to thank the anonymous reviewer for their helpful comments.

8

Images of Photography: How Computer Vision Frames the Medium

TRACY STUBER

> From the first step, that of classification (we must surely classify, verify by samples, if we want to constitute a corpus). Photography evades us. ... We might say that Photography is unclassifiable.
>
> Roland Barthes, *Camera Lucida*[1]

FROM DAGUERREOTYPES TO 35 mm negatives, and from gelatin silver prints to Instagram posts, the technology of photography has changed dramatically and continually throughout its nearly two-century history. Despite these changes, and often because of them, the question of photography's identity repeatedly resurfaces. The appeal of Roland Barthes' *Camera Lucida* as a response to his 'ontological desire' to know 'what Photography was "in itself"' endures, in some part, because Barthes pursues the project even as he recognises its futility, seemingly unable to stop himself from examining this evasive, 'unclassifiable' medium.[2]

Developments in computer vision and artificial intelligence (AI) have once again raised questions about photography's identity. These concerns about photographic ontology respond in large part to the threat that AI-generated photorealistic images, lacking an indexical tie to reality, pose to photography's assumed evidentiary value: Barthes' 'that has been'.[3] Image-generation tools like Midjourney and DALL·E have already proven remarkably adept at producing images that look convincingly like photographs, sparking widespread concerns about cultural deception.[4]

[1] Roland Barthes, *Camera Lucida: Reflections on Photography*, translated by Richard Howard (New York: Hill and Wang, 1980), p. 4.
[2] Barthes, *Camera Lucida*, p. 3.
[3] Barthes, *Camera Lucida*, p. 115.
[4] Amanda Wasielewski, 'Unnatural Images: On AI-Generated Photographs', *Critical Inquiry*, 51:1 (Autumn 2024). https://doi.org/10.1086/731729

Proceedings of the British Academy, **285**, 181–204, © Authors 2025.

Less examined, however, are the contradictions between ways that photography operates across different types of AI. While generative AI threatens photography's truth value, analytic or 'traditional' AI – specifically computer vision – deeply depends on it. Photographs are the basic unit of computer vision: while the field refers to technology that enables computers to derive information from any sort of visual input, the majority of images analysed by contemporary computer vision algorithms are photographs. Overwhelmingly recent and entirely digital, these photographs represent but a slice of photography. Nonetheless, as mobilised in computer vision, they constitute an implicit theory of photography that activates and re-entrenches its longstanding status as a transparent window to the world.

In short, where image-generation algorithms are clearly trained to 'see' photographs in order to emulate their appearance, analytic computer vision algorithms are trained not to see photographs and, instead, to see *through* them to their content. These two distinct approaches to photography, one aesthetic and one theoretical, essentially mirror two camps within photographic discourse: those concerned with photography as an artistic medium, on the one hand, and those concerned with photography as a technology, on the other.[5] At the same time, image-generation algorithms also test the assumptions of both positions by creating 'photographs' that fall somewhere in the middle. Artificial but not necessarily art, mechanical but not necessarily factual, these photographs undermine both sides of the debate, and thereby the very nature of the debate itself.[6]

Does computer vision similarly trouble photographic ontology? Recent scholarship on the technology's use of photography suggests no, as the computer scientists behind recent computer vision developments have uncritically sided with photography's enduring tie to the real. As Joanna Zylinska writes, the image in computer vision 'is an emanation of "the thing in itself"; it is a direct line to, and a condition of, object recognition'.[7] Despite its reference to the image, the computer vision task of image classification similarly focuses on content: 'what is in an image'.[8] But what if what is in an image, is a photograph? Can computer vision respond to photography 'in itself', and if so, under what conditions and circumstances?

This chapter identifies art history, a field deeply familiar with and even arguably dependent on photographs of images, as an ideal context in which to pursue these questions. It begins by positioning current scholarship on photography in computer vision with regard to art historical debates on the medium. It then investigates how commercial image classification services developed by Google, Amazon, Clarifai, and Imagga describe digitised analogue photographs. These commercial services

[5] Diarmuid Costello, *On Photography: A Philosophical Inquiry* (Abingdon: Routledge, 2018), p. 2.

[6] While artists have arguably been doing something similar since the 'documentary turn' of the early 2000s, generative AI brings these possibilities into a wider public view.

[7] Joanna Zylinska, 'Diffused Seeing: The Epistemological Challenge of Generative AI', *Media Theory*, 8:1 (11 June 2024), pp. 229–58. https://doi.org/10.70064/mt.v8i1.1075

[8] 'Image Classification vs Detection vs Segmentation', *Clarifai* (2024), https://docs.clarifai.com/tutorials/image-classification-detection-segmentation/ [accessed 1 November 2024].

utilise general purpose models to categorise images according to predetermined vocabularies. The categories or labels typically describe the content of images and serve applications such as image tagging, visual search, and content moderation. While these services may seem poorly suited to art historical enquiry, it is precisely because of their general purpose that they offer insight into computer vision as a generalised technology.

Even though these commercial services are theoretically trained not to 'see' photographs, this chapter finds that they all include photographic terminology in the vocabularies they use to describe the visible world. Moreover, the services define photography differently, both in the specific terms they use and the images they associate with them. By reading the services' distinct concepts or framings of photography back through art historical discourses about the medium, this chapter demonstrates how computer vision absorbs and reflects photography's relentless contradictions. While in theory, computer vision aligns with traditional assumptions about photography's objectivity, in practice it illustrates the medium's continued resistance to classification.

Photography in computer vision

As the number of photographs taken each year has grown exponentially since the 1990s, the breadth of disciplines that have taken on photography and the problem of its identity – including art history, philosophy, media studies, history, anthropology, and of course art – has also expanded. The idea that there are many 'photographies', influentially advanced by art historians such as John Tagg and Geoffrey Batchen, is now compounded by ideas about those photographies that may be loosely networked, but not entirely contained by umbrella terms like 'history of photography' or 'photography studies'.[9] A key figure here is Ariella Azoulay, whose concept of a 'civil contract of photography' redefines photography as a set of political and social relations, rather than an image.[10] As expressed in a 2019 edited volume on photography and ontology, much of this more recent scholarship entails shifting focus from 'what photography is' to 'what photography does', enabling localised enquiries into photography's effects and affects in place of its overall essence.[11]

Prone to periods of reinvigoration, such as the disputes between modernist and postmodernist art historians in the 1970s and 1980s or the advent of digital photography in the 1990s, debates about photography's identity are currently responding

[9] John Tagg, *The Burden of Representation: Essays on Photographies and History* (New York: Palgrave Macmillan, 1988); Geoffrey Batchen, *Burning with Desire: The Conception of Photography* (Cambridge, MA: The MIT Press, 1997).

[10] Ariella Azoulay, *The Civil Contract of Photography*, translated by Rela Mazali and Ruvik Danieli (Princeton, NJ: Princeton University Press, 2008).

[11] Donna West Brett and Natalya Lusty (eds), *Photography and Ontology: Unsettling Images* (Abingdon: Routledge, 2019).

to the changes, both actual and potential, wrought by AI. In a moment of computational culture, operational images, and generative AI, communications scholar Paul Frosh argues that the 'cultural memory' of photography persists because it makes such new technologies culturally recognisable, essentially providing a stable anchor for a shifting assemblage.[12] Along similar lines, media studies scholar Andrew Dewdney proposes that it is time to 'forget photography' altogether because the term poses 'a barrier to understanding the altered state of the default visual image'.[13] Essentially, anthropologist Elizabeth Edwards' point that 'we all think we know what photographs are' is precisely the problem, because routines and habits obscure the realities of contemporary technology and culture.[14]

While Dewdney's argument is productively provocative, it is stymied by the central question the author raises, but does not address: if we are to forget photography, when did photography end? The repeated reanimation of photography to account for technological change, captured in the idea of 'post-photography' or what Dewdney calls 'zombie photography', discourages what might have been a relatively clean break at the juncture of analogue and digital. But this move, even if it could be recouped, is problematic. For one, it assumes a coherence of analogue photography that Tagg, Batchen, and others have argued against. For another, as Dewdney also recognises, it artificially isolates new technologies and cultural practices from the longstanding ideas about photography that are central to their formation.

Computer vision, a technology of contemporary computational culture, also manifests the key role of photography in that culture. The deep learning algorithms that, starting with the 2009 release of the ImageNet dataset, have revolutionised automated image processing, depend on training data in the form of billions of photographs, mostly scraped from the internet. Mobilised as supposedly transparent windows onto the world, these photographs provide a proxy for human vision by which computer vision algorithms learn to 'see'. In a computer vision training data set, an image is equivalent to its representation: an image of cat is a cat, and the image drops away. For Nicolas Malevé and Katrina Sluis, this deployment of photography amounts to a 'latent theory of photography' undergirding computer vision as a technology and a cultural practice.[15] This latent theory accepts and exploits existing beliefs about photography's mechanical objectivity and its unique tie to reality.

In essence, computer vision – along with the computer scientists who programme them and the users who apply them – subscribe to what Diarmuid Costello

[12] Paul Frosh, 'Seeing Photographically and the Memory of Photography', *Media Theory*, 8:1 (2024), pp. 53–78 (pp. 56–7).

[13] Andrew Dewdney, *Forget Photography* (Cambridge, MA: The MIT Press, 2021), p. 3.

[14] Elizabeth Edwards, 'Photography's Default History Is Told as Art – It Shouldn't Be', *The Conversation*, 23 February 2015.

[15] Nicolas Malevé and Katrina Sluis, 'The Photographic Pipeline of Machine Vision; Or, Machine Vision's Latent Photographic Theory', *Critical AI*, 1:1–2 (2023).

calls the 'folk theory' of photography.[16] Based on everyday wisdom, folk theory is at once a concept and a conception of photography that has remained more or less consistent since the medium's invention. Whether it describes photography as 'natural', 'causal', 'mechanical', or 'automatic', folk theory values the medium as a tool of non-human depiction. Throughout the 19th and 20th centuries, Paul Strand, André Bazin, Kendall Walton, and others formalised these ideas in statements and theories of photography; all share the same central trust in the medium's privileged relationship to reality.[17] Today, the same beliefs bubble up in technical and popular literature about AI, such as recent advice from the creators of the AI image generator Midjourney that equates 'more photographic' with 'less opinionated' and 'more literal'.[18]

Computer vision's particular version of folk theory subscribes into the automatic, mechanical qualities of snapshot photography.[19] With snapshots, the combination of camera design and corporatised chemical processing reduces the photographer's action to the push of a button. For computer scientists constructing training datasets, amateur photographs from photo-sharing sites such as Flickr offered unmediated 'real-world scenes'. But functional photographs like scientific images also exemplify folk theory, despite looking considered and uniform instead of spontaneous and artless. Formal consistency limits how the photographer can intervene so that images, and therefore their content, become comparable. In both scenarios, the design of the photographic process produces, as its end effect, the appearance that the photographer contributes as little as possible.

As is now well established, the discipline of art history is familiar with, and even dependent on, this latter way of ensuring and exploiting photographic transparency.[20] Indeed, Malevé has explicitly compared computer vision's use of photography to art history's, as most vividly demonstrated by André Malraux's *musée imaginaire*.[21] Drawing on Douglas Crimp's analysis of Malraux's photographic museum, Malevé argues that computer vision and art history face the same paradox in employing photography to 'homogenise the visual world', to level diverse objects and make them comparable: 'To resolve a photograph as data, all the

[16] Costello, *On Photography*, p. 9.

[17] Costello, *On Photography*, p. 10.

[18] Benj Edwards, 'How Much Detail Is Too Much? Midjourney v6 Attempts to Find Out', *ArsTechnica* (5 January 2024), https://arstechnica.com/information-technology/2024/01/a-crazy-update-midjourney-v6-upgrade-heaps-on-ai-generated-detail [accessed 4 July 2024].

[19] Katrina Sluis, 'The Networked Image after Web 2.0: Flickr and the "Real-World" Photography of the Dataset', in *The Networked Image in Post-Digital Culture*, edited by Katrina Sluis and Andrew Dewndey (London: Routledge, 2022), pp. 41–59.

[20] See, for example, Frederick N. Bohrer, 'Photographic Perspectives: Photography and the Institutional Formation of Art History', in *Art History and Its Institutions*, edited by Elizabeth Mansfield (London: Routledge, 2002), pp. 260–74. For art history's use of photography in relation to computer vision, see Emily Pugh and Tracy Stuber, 'Photography as Machine Vision: The Role of Imaging Technologies in Art History', *photographies* 16:2 (2023), pp. 211–33.

[21] Nicolas Malevé, 'On the Data Set's Ruins', *AI & Society*, 36 (2021), pp. 1117–31 (p. 1117).

heterogeneity that pertains to the medium, its apparatus and its circulation needs to be repressed.'[22] Photography must remain invisible.

Although this repression remains more or less active in contemporary computer vision, its status is more complicated in art history. While Malevé's text 'is not an essay on art history', attending to the art history of photography offers a valuable perspective on this paradox.[23] Published in 1947, Malraux's famous account of the *musée imaginaire* dates from the gradual process of photography's acceptance into the fold of fine art and art history. This process, under way at least since the 1940 appointment of Beaumont Newhall as the first curator of the Department of Photography at the Museum of Modern Art (New York), hastened in the 1960s during John Szarkowski's tenure as director of the same department.[24] The rise of photography as a contemporary art form accompanied the flourishing of photography's *history* in fine art's cultural, educational, and commercial institutions, endowing historical photographs with new aesthetic, intellectual, and market value.

Writing at the time of photography's artistic ascendence in the 1970s and 1980s, postmodern critics such as Crimp perceived the phenomenon, at least initially, to be a coup within art's institutions and discourses. By entering the museum, photography reinstates the heterogeneity it was previously thought to mask, challenging the institution's claims to universal knowledge.[25] For this reason, Crimp took issue with the efforts of art institutions, above all the Museum of Modern Art, to tame photography into the established categories of art. Relocating photographs from the contexts of their creation into the encompassing category of 'photography' diffused the medium's threat by consolidating its multiplicity and bounding it into a singular box.[26] Although Crimp saw this consolidation as part of a larger reorganisation of culture associated with postmodernism, he also recognised it as a problem of classification. The physical relocation of photographs into departments of art and photography changed the terms on which photographs were studied and understood.

The role of photography in computer vision poses a similar problem of singularity versus multiplicity. On the basis of Malevé and Sluis's account, computer vision algorithms should be blind to photographs. At the very least, they should be blind to a small selection of photographs, specifically the digital colour photographs made by internet users that comprise some of computer vision's key datasets, since these photographs serve as real-world scenes.[27] Yet as soon as we entertain this latter hypothesis, we end up at a familiar impasse. When does photography end? What do

[22] Malevé, 'On the Data Set's Ruins', p. 1128.

[23] Malevé, 'On the Data Set's Ruins', p. 1118.

[24] Christopher Phillips, 'The Judgment Seat of Photography', *October*, 22 (1982), pp. 27–63.

[25] Douglas Crimp, 'On the Museum's Ruins', in *On the Museum's Ruins* (Cambridge, MA: 1993), pp. 44–65 (p. 56).

[26] Douglas Crimp, 'The Museum's Old/Library's New Subject', in *On the Museum's Ruins*, pp. 66–83 (p. 76).

[27] Malevé and Sluis, 'The Photographic Pipeline'.

photographs look like? These are not matters for computer vision to settle definitively, but they are questions that it implicitly must answer.

Classifying photography

When enquiring into photography, philosopher Diarmuid Costello suggests, 'A good way to flush out one's own intuitions … is to ask oneself two seemingly simple questions at the outset. What is a photograph? What is photography?'[28] This section asks these questions of computer vision by following Barthes' suggestion to start with classification. Classification, a task to which computer vision is well suited. Image classification is a fundamental computer vision task designed to label images according to a predefined vocabulary. This vocabulary can be very small (for example, deciding only between dogs and cats) or it can draw on a large, multipurpose vocabulary. Imagenet, once the gold standard for this vocabulary, has been the subject of multiple critiques that reveal its cultural and social biases.[29] This research is part of a broader interest in how studying training data and images can give insight into algorithms' different ways of 'seeing' and into the visual culture that sustains AI.[30]

Companies like Google, Amazon, Microsoft, and others offer image classification as a service that uses proprietary algorithms, training sets, and vocabularies. Most of these services perform multi-label classification, meaning they can assign an image input more than one term from their vocabularies. Each term also receives a confidence score, indicating the calculated probability that the term correctly applies. Often called 'off-the-shelf' systems, these commercial services are designed to serve a broad constituency and are not specifically oriented to the realm of art. Some studies have, therefore, explored how relevant these classifications are for works of art. In a 2021 article, Elena Villaespesa and Seth Crider compare the responses of Google's Cloud Vision, Amazon's Rekognition, and IBM's Watson to public-domain digital surrogates of objects from across the collection of the Metropolitan Museum of Art.[31] They frame their study primarily as an evaluation of these services that can help museums interested in machine-generated metadata make informed technological choices. Meanwhile, Gabriel Pereira and Bruno Moreschi use their 2019 experiments with commercial services to frame computer

[28] Costello, *On Photography*, p. 7.

[29] Trevor Paglen and Kate Crawford, 'Excavating AI: The Politics of Images in Machine Learning Training Sets' (2019). http://www.excavating.ai [accessed 3 July 2024].

[30] Mitra Azar, Geoff Cox, and Leonardo Impett, 'Introduction: Ways of Machine Seeing', *AI & Society*, 36:4 (2021), pp. 1093–104.

[31] Elena Villaespesa and Sean Crider, 'Computer Vision Tagging the Metropolitan Museum of Art's Collection: A Comparison of Three Systems', *Journal on Computing and Cultural Heritage*, 14:3 (2021), pp. 1–17. https://doi.org/10.1145/3446621

vision as a tool of institutional critique.[32] Precisely because these services are oriented towards commercial applications and not the art world, they produce irrelevant and sometimes erroneous output that denaturalises the terms of conventional art discourses.

Like these studies, this chapter analyses the output of commercial computer vision services, but it also differs from these precedents in some important respects. Most significantly, it focuses on a single medium, photography, and specific concepts expressed in each service's output. This approach recognises that analysing photographs with computer vision only *seems* more straightforward than other artistic mediums. Most research on computer vision and art tackles what is sometimes called the 'cross-depiction' problem: because image-recognition algorithms are trained on photographic images, they often do not achieve the same levels of success when applied to paintings, drawings, and other non-photographic types of images.[33] By contrast, even analogue photographs, which differ materially from the digital images used to train computer vision algorithms, operate within the same representational paradigm, thereby reducing this barrier. But once again, this perspective assumes an essential unity of photography that is at odds with its multiplicity and, moreover, its history.

The primary dataset consists of digitised pre-1925 photographs that the Harvard Art Museums explicitly classify as 'Photographs'. Out of approximately 60,000 objects in the collections, this dataset includes around 12,000 objects and 13,500 images, since some objects have more than one digital image. It also includes classifications generated by four services: Google's Vision API, AWS Rekogniton, Clarifai, and Imagga. These classifications refer intentionally to the digital image, rather than the depicted artwork or object, and total just under 1.5 million. This dataset was selected primarily due to availability. As part of a project called *AI Explorer*, the Harvard Art Museums' department of Digital Infrastructure and Emerging Technology generated the image classifications between 2016 and 2023 and made them available through an API.[34]

Certainly, the Harvard Art Museums' photography collection is not fully representative of the history of photography, and this chapter does not conceive of it that way. The collection is typical of photography collections in art museums in how it contains both canonical art photography and an idiosyncratic breadth of vernacular photographs. At the image level, however, the collection is unique to

[32] Gabriel Pereira and Bruno Moreschi, 'Artificial Intelligence and Institutional Critique 2.0: Unexpected Ways of Seeing with Computer Vision', *AI & Society*, 36:4 (2021), pp. 1201–23.

[33] Amalia Foka, Lina Eklund, Anders Sundnes Løvlie, and Gabriele Griffin, 'Critically Assessing AI/ML for Cultural Heritage: Potentials and Challenges', in *Handbook of Critical Studies of Artificial Intelligence*, edited by Simon Lindgren (Cheltenham: Edward Elgar Publishing, 2023), pp. 815–25 (p. 816).

[34] Harvard Art Museums, 'AI Explorer', Harvard Art Museums (2024), https://ai.harvardartmuseums.org/ [accessed 1 November 2024]. The museum's API is available at https://harvardartmuseums.org/collections/api

the Harvard Art Museums' acquisition history. Like all museum collections, it is selective, uneven, and biased. Furthermore, this study is additionally selective in focusing on 19th-century photographs, adopted here as a rough designation for photographs made before 1925. This selection is by reason of early photography's distance, temporally as well as materially, from the contemporary digital photographs that comprise computer vision training datasets. This distance suggests that early photographs might be most likely to be classified as 'photography' because they look the most different from the photographs that algorithms are trained not to see.[35] In addition to raising obvious problems of anachronism, working with historical photographs also poses questions about how computer vision algorithms respond to images made with different spectral sensitivity and tonal values, among other aspects of analogue materiality.

A related but distinct issue pertains to how historical photographs are digitised. The material turn in photography studies since the early 2000s has coincided with a shift in digitisation practices that contextualises, rather than isolates, photographic images. In the case of the Harvard Art Museums, many (but not all) of the digital surrogates for pre-1925 photographs extend beyond the edges of the reproduced photograph. How far they extend varies widely. Sometimes it is just a small border, while other times the entire sheet of paper on which a photograph is mounted is included, along with a small border indicating the edges of the mount. Since these visual cues are meant to convey a photograph's physical materiality to the human user, we might hypothesise that they also signal an image's status as photographic.

While these potential explanations shaped my choice of dataset, my primary interest in this chapter is more conceptual. Unlike other studies of computer vision output and art, accuracy is not my main concern. After all, a truly accurate 'photography' classifier would positively label every image it processed, at least according to current terminology, because every image is a digital photograph (or a composite of many). Anything less than total comprehensiveness constitutes a statement, however weak or unintentional, about what photography is not, and therefore what photography is. Working with the limited dataset of pre-1925 photographs facilitates my close examination of the images and data that constitute these statements. At times, I attempt to complicate this purview by comparing the results from the pre-1925 dataset to the photographic classifications from across the Harvard Art Museums' collections. Since these collections also include images of art objects that are not photographs, they offer another angle on how the services conceive of photography.

Adding to these caveats about the dataset, I will also emphasise that the following observations and analyses are necessarily speculative. Because we do not have access to the training data for these commercial services or the inner workings of

[35] Although not explored in depth here, this hypothesis raises interesting questions in relation to historical monochrome photography, since converting colour images to greyscale is a common pre-processing step in many computer vision pipelines.

their algorithms, it is impossible to determine how they were taught to recognise photographs. Even with this information, the 'black box' nature of deep learning makes it impossible to determine if the algorithm is *learning* according to the same logic by which it was taught. This is especially relevant in non-standardised datasets, such as this one, where seemingly random features with no correlation to the question being pursued influence an algorithm's decision-making. For example, in a 2018 dermatological study applying image classification to images of skin lesions, scientists found that because of the unintentional presence of rulers in images of malignant lesions, 'the algorithm inadvertently "learned" that rulers are malignant'.[36]

As an experiment in close reading, this chapter seeks to face the challenges of interpreting computer vision output head-on. In drawing connections between each service's output and art historical discourse, I do not mean to suggest that the computer scientists who designed and developed these algorithms consciously adopted and implemented art historical concepts of photography. For several reasons, including computer vision's 'latent theory' of photography and the general audience for these services, this is unlikely to be the case. Instead, this analysis aims to highlight the challenges of bridging theory and practice, of linking photography and photographs, that computer vision introduces.

Overall observations

At the outset of this study, I hypothesised based on anecdotal experience that 'photography' or 'photograph' terms would be tied to visual cues that differentiate 19th-century photographs from 21st-century digital photographs. These might include visual evidence of photographic surface or materiality, such as paper edges, frames, and monochromaticity, all of which are prevalent in the pre-1925 dataset. According to this logic, most images in the dataset would then be classified as photographs. In actuality, photography-related terms were much scarcer than expected. The service most likely to classify images as photographic was Google's Vision API, which labelled 33 per cent of images as 'photograph' and assigned 60 per cent of images at least one of several related terms with the word 'photo' in them. The next highest number of classifications came from AWS Rekognition, which labelled 9 per cent of images as 'photography', followed by Imagga's 'photograph' (2 per cent). Clarifai labelled the lowest number of images as 'photograph': only four, or about 0.0003 per cent.

This relative sparsity of photography-related terms in the dataset indicates that none of the services define photography based *solely* on visible indications of

[36] Akhila Narla, Brett Kuprel, Kavita Sarin, Roberto Novoa, and Justin Ko, 'Automated Classification of Skin Lesions: From Pixels to Practice', *Journal of Investigative Dermatology*, 138:10 (2018), pp. 2108–10.

photographic surface or materiality. For every image of a black-and-white photograph mounted on creamy paper and framed by a dark backdrop that gets classified as somewhat photographic, there is at least another, if not two, that slides by. This is not to say that visible context, such as margins, borders, and frames, does not impact image classification at all. While a full investigation of this impact is outside the scope of this chapter, my analyses of each service will point to examples where the visual context of the photograph comes into play.

The distribution of photographic classifications across services roughly aligns with the number of photography-related terms in each service's vocabulary. The classification vocabulary for Google's Vision API includes 11 explicitly photography-related terms: 'photograph', 'photography', 'stock photography', 'monochrome photography', 'photographic paper', 'still life photography', 'photograph album', 'flash photography', 'portrait photography', 'photo caption', and 'aerial photography'. Of these terms, 'stock photography' was the most commonly applied (35 per cent), followed closely by 'photograph' (33 per cent) and 'photography' (27 per cent). The other services were comparably limited. AWS offers 'photo' and 'photography'; Imagga uses 'photograph', 'photography', and 'photographic'; and Clarifai provides 'photograph' and 'photojournalism'.[37]

More significantly, the four services do not have a shared concept of what a photograph is, either visually or semantically. In fact, within the pre-1925 dataset, there are no photographs that all four services classify as 'photographic', by which I mean via a photography-related term. Among the three services with the most photography labels (Google, Amazon, and Imagga), only 69 photographs (0.005 per cent) fit the bill, and only 18 are labelled as explicitly 'photograph' or 'photo' by all three services.

Within each service, however, there are discernible patterns. Remembering again that these services are black boxes, they nonetheless demonstrate concepts of photography that are legible in relation to art historical and theoretical understandings of the medium. Coherent but not always consistent, at least by human interpretation, the output is provocative as an illustration of the fraught nature of classification as an enterprise, not least where photography is concerned.

Google

In the pre-1925 dataset, Google's Vision API assigns the label 'photograph' to approximately one third of the images, and only with high confidence (>94 per cent). Of the four services, Google's 'photograph' group is the most diverse, though most might be broadly described as vernacular, including snapshots, documentary

[37] There are other photography-related terms in these vocabularies, such as 'photo booth', 'photographer', 'photographic paper', and 'photo frame', but for the purposes of this study, I excluded them as primary terms of analysis because they are tied more directly to the content of the image.

images, and popular formats such as stereoviews and tintype portraits.[38] The service is most confident (97.7 per cent) about a *c.*1900 picture of two young women sitting together in a yard (Figure 8.1). In the overall collection, the top-scoring image (98 per cent) is a similarly casual-looking shot, made *c.*1935–40, of four men playfully piled together; the negative receives a similarly high score of 97.3 per cent (Figure 8.2). Although both depict people posing informally for the camera, it is worth noting that these photographs were made for distinct purposes. Judging by the men's visible camaraderie, the latter image was almost certainly made for fun. The former picture, meanwhile, was intended to document 'crime, children, [and] reform schools' for Harvard's Social Museum Collection, a turn-of-the-century initiative aimed at investigating and ameliorating modern social conditions.[39]

In addition to pictures of people, the Google 'photograph' results cover a fairly wide swathe of the vernacular, including architectural views and other ostensibly functional photographs, and both anonymous images and those identified with

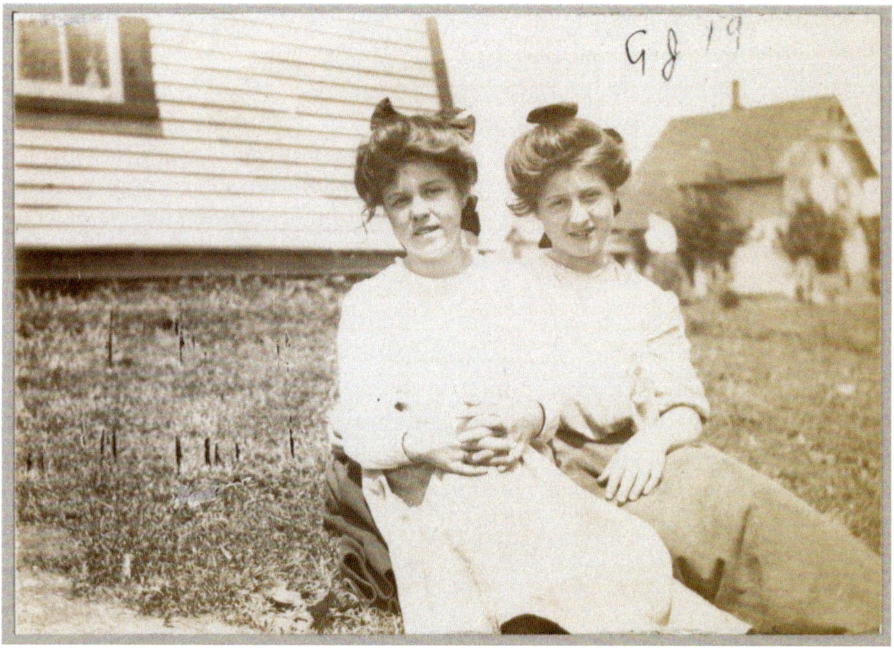

Figure 8.1 Unidentified artist, *Crime, Children, Reform Schools: United States. New York. Freeville. George Junior Republic: George Junior Republic, Freeville, N.Y.*, gelatin silver print, *c.*1900, Harvard Art Museums, Cambridge, MA. https://hvrd.art/o/19390.

[38] Clément Chéroux (ed.), *Walker Evans* (Paris: Prestel, 2017).

[39] Deborah Martin Kao and Michelle Lamunière, *Instituting Reform: The Social Museum of Harvard University, 1903–1931* (Cambridge, MA: Yale University Press, 2012).

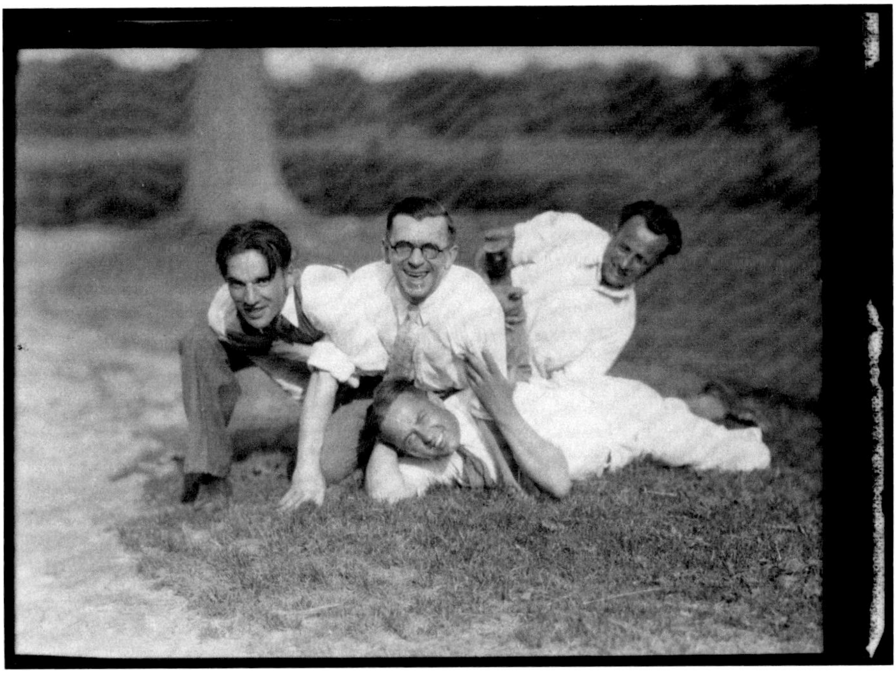

Figure 8.2 Durette Studio, *Untitled (men posing in pile on ground outdoors)*, gelatin silver negative, *c.*1935–1940, Harvard Art Museums, Cambridge, MA. https://hvrd.art/o/137805.

specific photographers and studios. Accepting that 'vernacular photography' is a very broad classification, we might simply see Google's results as reflecting the statistical prevalence of everyday photographs as compared to more rarefied subcategories such as art. Commonplace images are the most common, and therefore they are the most representative. At the same time, the abundance of snapshots and 'straight' documentary photographs in Google's results resembles a tendency within photography theory to take the snapshot as the medium's quintessential form.[40] Well-known 20th-century theorists including Siegfried Kracauer and André Bazin, and philosophers such as Roger Scruton and Kendall Walton base their theories on folk theory's intuitions about photography as automatic and immediate. In Costello's view, these theories risk 'unwittingly distorting the data by mistaking a subsection of the field for the whole'.[41] This selectivity leaves these theories poorly equipped to understand photography as an artistic medium.

Where photography theory has tended to overemphasise the snapshot, art history has traditionally been less welcoming. Geoffrey Batchen argues that ordinary

[40] Costello, *On Photography*, p. 121.
[41] Costello, *On Photography*, p. 8.

photographs have 'always been excluded from photography's history' because they resist and ever contradict the medium's artistic pretensions.[42] At best, curators like Szarkowski admitted vernacular photographs by favouring their aesthetic properties over their cultural functions. Anonymous family snapshots could – and often did – hang on the museum's walls beside images made by revered art photographers, as long as they demonstrated the medium's fundamental characteristics.[43] Returning to the example mentioned earlier, Google's equation of visually similar but functionally distinct photographs is a useful reminder that computer vision image classification is also formally driven, although the service also takes metadata and search results into account. To the extent that Google's 'photograph' category highlights the medium's everyday forms, it facilitates Batchen's suggestion to 'closely attend to that which history has chosen to repress'.[44]

The variety of photographic terms in Google's vocabulary provokes observations about contemporary photographic culture and the place of historical photographs within it. While we may approach 'stock photography' as a visual genre, the application of this term may also reflect the absorption of historical photographs into the catalogues of digital image companies such as Getty Images and Alamy. Since the late 1990s, these companies have adopted the dubious practice of selling rights to photographs in the public domain.[45] Meanwhile, 'monochrome photography', a distinct tag from 'monochrome' and 'black and white', raises the question of whether it is the digital image or the reproduced photograph being described. While the majority of the photographs in the dataset would be considered monochrome, the majority of the digital images in the dataset are colour. This difference is especially apparent in digital images that capture the photograph's material context, such as a paper mount.

In some sense, Google's take on photography is similar to that of computer vision: both rely on the snapshot. But where computer vision makes the snapshot invisible, Google's 'photograph' category makes it visible. This contrast stresses the distinction between the historical, material phenomenon of the snapshot and the theoretical concept of photography it has spawned. It also raises the snapshot's dual status as an image of the past and as a present, material object.

Amazon

Compared to Google's Vision API and its relatively sprawling vision of the vernacular, Amazon's AWS Rekognition service presents a finer idea of photography that, moreover, positions it most closely in relation to art. In the pre-1925 dataset, every image assigned the 'photo' classification is also assigned 'photography', and the confidence

[42] Geoffrey Batchen, *Each Wild Idea: Writing, Photography, History* (Cambridge, MA: The MIT Press, 2022), p. 57.

[43] John Szarkowkski, *The Photographer's Eye* (New York: Museum of Modern Art, 1966).

[44] Batchen, *Each Wild Idea*, p. 59.

[45] Paul Frosh, 'Beyond the Image Bank: Digital Commercial Photography', in *The Photographic Image in Digital Culture*, edited by Martin Lister (Abingdon: Routledge, 2013), pp. 131–48.

scores for both terms are the same. This suggests a substantial overlap between 'photo' and 'photography', although there are some 'photography' images that are not classified as 'photo' to which I will return. For now, what stands out is that the vast majority of the almost 2,000 images labelled with both terms are pictures of people. Most could reasonably be described as portraits, defined as images where posed people are the primary subject. Amazon's other classifications bear out this observation: 91 per cent of the 'photo' images are also labelled with 'person', 'portrait', or 'face'. The service assigns the highest confidence to dramatic, close-up portraits: of the ten 'photos' about which Amazon's service is most confident in the pre-1925 dataset, eight are portraits from Edward Curtis's *The North American Indian* portfolios (Figure 8.3). As in these images, the highest-confidence 'photo' labels apply to pictures where the human subject takes up most of the space and/or is surrounded by the negative space of a studio background, a frame or vignette, or less often, a simple landscape.

While the pre-1925 'photograph' results signal a straightforward alignment of 'photography' with 'photographic portrait', the results from across the Harvard Art Museum's collections complicate the story. While these results also consist almost entirely of portraits, they are not all photographs. Of the top 2,000 most-confident 'photograph' results, 17 per cent of the images document works of art from other areas of the Museum's collections, mainly paintings, drawings, prints, and sculpture, compared to just 1 per cent in Google's results. These results situate the photographic portrait in its art historical heritage. Daguerreotypes and tintypes appear as successors to oil painting, illustrating their inheritance of its conventions and their democratisation of its privilege, and occasional chromogenic prints carry the lineage at least into the late 20th century.[46] Looking back at the pre-1925 'photograph' results, this association of photography with art, and especially with painting, helps make sense of some of the non-portrait results, such as picturesque scenes of mountains and ruins, that also appear. These results echo Joel Snyder and Neil Walsh Allen's assertion that 'even in the realm of serious and inventive photography there is no clear-cut break with older traditions of representation'.[47]

Amazon's apparent association of photography with traditional art and genres raises the question of how the service's 'photography' classification compares to its 'art' classification. Sixty-four per cent of the pre-1925 'photography' images are also labelled 'art', but there are no strong patterns that distinguish them from those that escape the tag. Meanwhile, 'art' as applied across the Harvard Art Museums' collections returns a much wider array of results that, at the highest levels of confidence, includes plenty of portraits and landscapes, but also vases, graphic ornaments, and abstract paintings, among other types of artistic production. Of course, 'art', like 'photography', is not a self-evident term, and further research is necessary to pursue this question in depth.

[46] Sally Miller, *Contemporary Photography and Theory: Concepts and Debates* (New York: Bloomsbury Publishing USA, 2019), pp. 9–10.

[47] Joel Snyder and Neil Walsh Allen, 'Photography, Vision, and Representation', *Critical Inquiry*, 2:1 (Autumn, 1975), pp. 143–69 (p. 164).

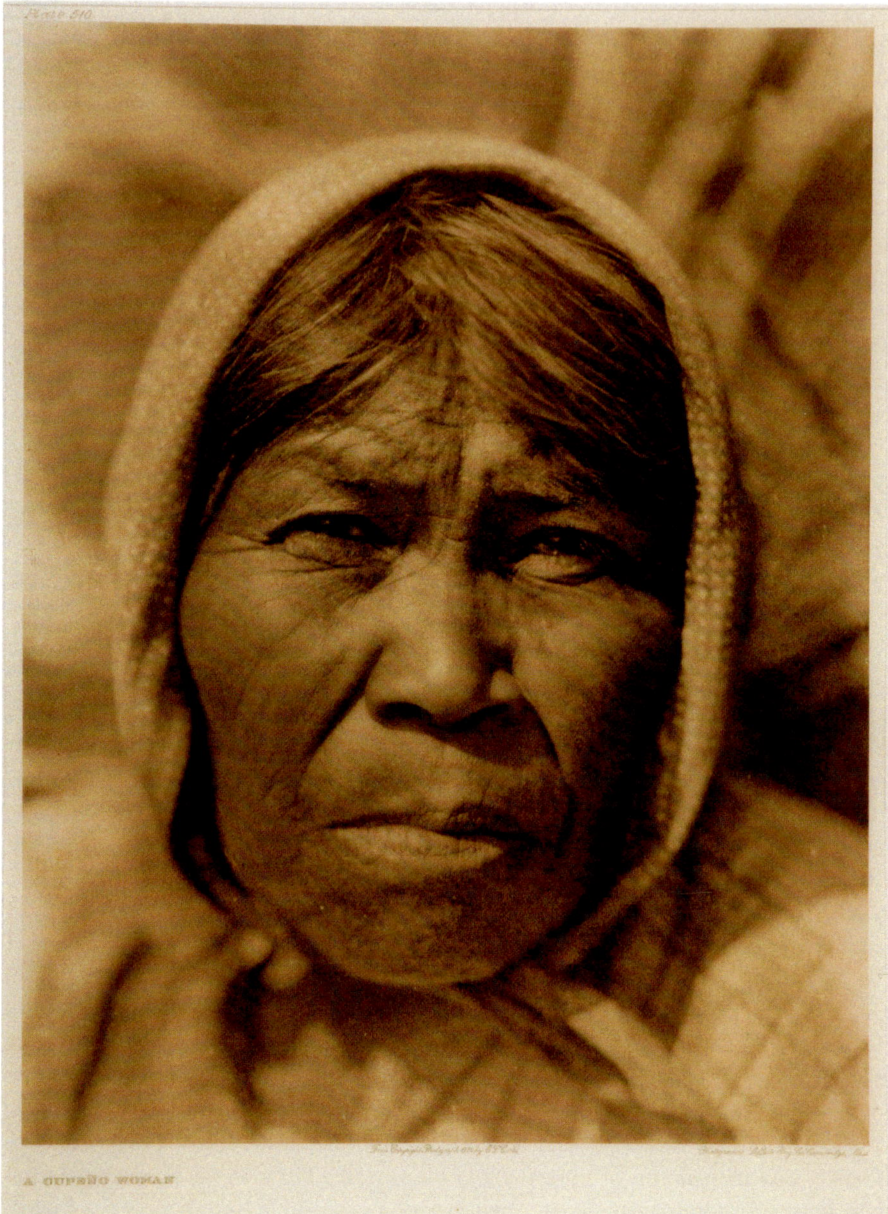

Figure 8.3 Edward Sheriff Curtis, *A Cupeño Woman*, photogravure, 1924, Harvard Art Museums, Cambridge, MA. https://hvrd.art/o/285600.

For now, the question may direct our attention back to the 95 pre-1925 images Amazon classifies as 'photography', but not 'photo'. Within this group, there are a number of early photographs that depict other works of art, such as a daguerreotype of an engraving of George Washington and John Wood's salted paper prints of sculptures and painting decorating the U.S. Capitol (Figure 8.4). These images signal yet another relationship between art and photography – the art reproduction – that has

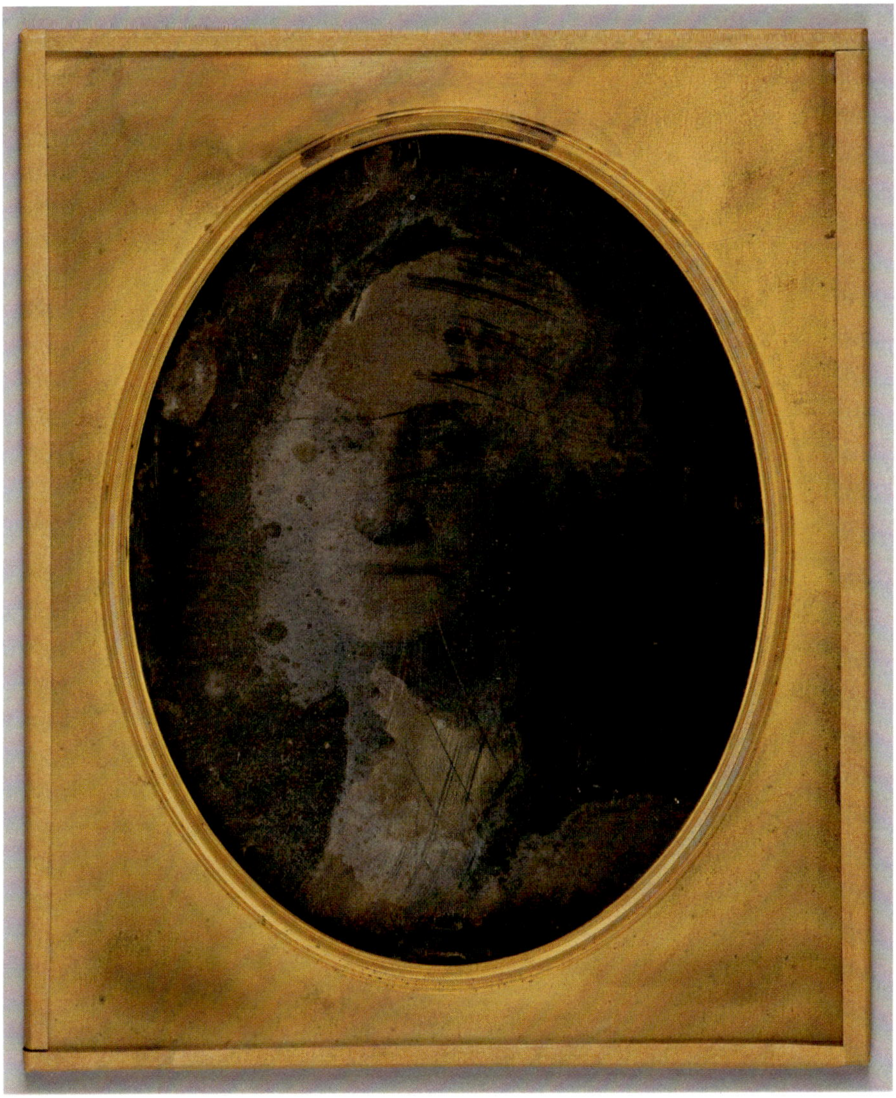

Figure 8.4 Unidentified artist, *Untitled (reproduction of engraving of George Washington)*, daguerreotype, *c.*1840–*c.*1860, Harvard Art Museums, Cambridge, MA. https://hvrd.art/o/160474.

been present since the medium's inception. Looking at Amazon's image of photography, we see the complicated relationships between photography and art and, moreover, photography and art history.

Clarifai

Clarifai's image-recognition service presents the narrowest definition of photography and is most attuned to the visual and material characteristics of images. The service has only one photographic term, 'photograph', and applies it to only four images in the pre-1925 dataset. The service is most confident about a Hans Richter collage of contact-printed 35 mm negatives. The other three images are photographs of waterfalls from around the 1890s: one albumen silver print by the explorer Teobert Maler, and two gelatin silver prints by an unknown photographer (Figure 8.5).

Across all of the Harvard Art Museums' collections, Clarifai assigns the label 'photograph' to a mere 1.8 per cent of digital images processed by the service. Nonetheless, these classifications add valuable context to the even smaller number of pre-1925 results. Seventy-eight per cent of the Clarifai 'photograph' images are 35 mm gelatin silver negatives. Some negatives appear as scanned (inverted), some are digital positives, and many have visible sprocket holes. Among these negatives, the small number of positive prints that slip through are mostly high in contrast. The only exceptions to these overall trends are a few studio photographs of camera equipment, including a lens and case that once belonged to Barnett Newman.

Clarifai's concept of photography is compelling foremost because it does *not* align with many theories of photography. Indeed, theories of photography that emphasise its indexicality are notable for how they actively ignore the negative as an intermediate step in the photographic process. If any part of photography constitutes a 'trace' of reality, it is the negative, not the final print, that is touched by the light reflecting off a photograph's subject. The irony of this elision is that negatives have figured in defining moments of photography's history. Although daguerreotypes could reproduce the world, William Henry Fox Talbot's negative-positive method made it possible to capture that reproduction, changing photography from a medium of mere documentation into a medium of visual circulation. When Kodak packaged together its roll film, camera, and processing services, photography became more accessible and popular than ever before.[48] Finally, digital photography's elimination of the negative sparked ongoing debates about photography's identity.

Then again, we can read Clarifai's emphasis on 35 mm negatives as linking photography to cinema, another common tendency in photography theory. Some of the most commonly cited theorists – for example, Water Benjamin, André Bazin,

[48] Brian Cole, 'The Rollfilm Revolution', in *The Story of Popular Photography*, edited by Colin Ford (North Pomfret, VT: Trafalgar Square Publishing, 1989), pp. 60–89 (p. 62).

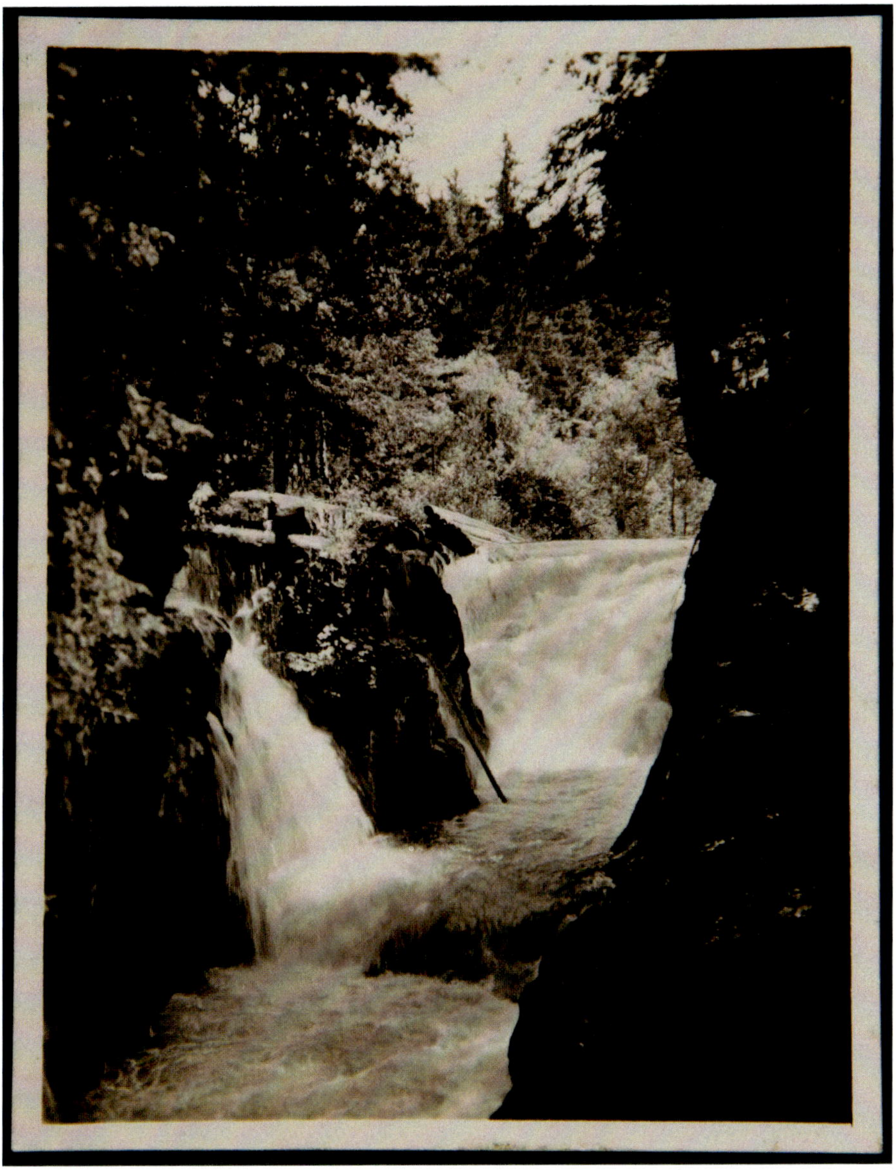

Figure 8.5 Unidentified artist, *Untitled (waterfall near Gössl, Austria)*, gelatin silver print, *c.*1890–*c.*1915, Harvard Art Museums, Cambridge, MA. https://hvrd.art/o/149363.

and Siegfried Kracauer– introduce their ideas about photography in service of theories about film. Furthermore, the 35 mm negative places Clarifai's concept of photography firmly in the 20th century, which may explain the results of the pre-1925 dataset. Even though the service processed 172 single-image negatives in the pre-1925 dataset, the lack of visual evidence of a very specific material form of photography excluded those images from the 'photograph' tag. As for the waterfalls that were labelled, we might speculatively align their high contrast levels and blurs of white with the inverted shapes of negative images.

Although Clarifai's 'photograph' tag is materially and temporally specific, the other classifications the service provides for the pre-1925 dataset confirm the service's sensitivity to the visual characteristics of the digitised image. Clarifai classifies 48 per cent of the images as 'old', an admittedly ambiguous term that could describe the age of depicted people or objects, in addition to describing the image. Accordingly, while these images include photographs of older people and ancient ruins, they also include photographs of babies and more timeless landscape formations such as mountains. In fact, the two 'old' images with the highest confidence are two daguerreotypes: one of Martin van Buren in the last decade of his life, and one of a woman with her deceased infant. Still, the possibility that 'old' can also describe the analogue photographic image gains support from Clarifai's labelling of 96 per cent of these images as 'vintage' and 69 per cent as 'retro'.

Placing photography firmly in the past, Clarifai's image classification output poses the question of 'what photography is' as a question of 'what photographs look like'. While terms such as 'vintage' and 'retro' may describe clothing or objects, they can also be interpreted as potential stylistic terms that recall the early filters of Instagram or, more recently, the prompts that control the output of large language model (LLM)-based image-generation tools. In this way, Clarifai taps into the 'cultural memory' of photography through purely visual means, drawing attention to the role of digital photography in preserving (or perverting) analogue photography's identity.

Imagga

At first glance, the images Imagga classifies as 'photograph' seem to cut across the tendencies of the previous three services. Fifty of the 241 images are Google 'photographs', 47 are Amazon 'photography', and 67 are photographs for all three services. There are many portraits and snapshots, sometimes on album pages, as well as a few negatives. There are photographs by Talbot, Curtis, and Muybridge; there are daguerreotypes, salted paper prints, and cyanotypes; and the photographs' dates range from 1840 to 1925. The overall effect might be described as a short history of photography.

Of the 79 Imagga-only 'photograph' images, one stands out. It looks like little more than a black rectangle, and Imagga is very confident (0.9) it is a photograph (Figure 8.6). In fact, it is a digital image of a *c.*1911 Duburnet Diascope, a type of autochrome viewer. Patented by the Lumière brothers, the autochrome was an early form of colour photography made with glass plates coated with dyed potato starch.[49] The starch grains filtered the light, but they also made the image very

[49] Bertrand Lavedrine and Jean-Paul Gandolfo, *The Lumiere Autochrome: History, Technology, and Preservation* (Los Angeles: The Getty Conservation Institute, 2013).

Figure 8.6 Unidentified artist, *Untitled (portrait of Betty Amory Bartlett, later Mrs. John McAndrew, as a young girl)*, autochrome, *c.*1911, Harvard Art Museums, Cambridge, MA. https://hvrd.art/o/330647.

dark. With a Diascope viewer, the transparent autochrome – in this case a portrait of a young girl – is loaded into one of two connected leatherette frames. The other frame contains a mirror, and when the autochrome side is hinged upward, it is lit from the back and reflected in the mirror. The Harvard image shows the top of the Diascope; what is unclear is whether the black rectangle in the centre represents the autochrome or its absence. Because the case is closed, there is no light to illuminate the autochrome, but it is also possible that museum photographers have used strategies to reduce reflection, like those employed with daguerreotypes and other reflective media.[50]

On the one hand, this image could be a literal demonstration of the algorithm responding to pixel patterns the human viewer cannot see. On the other hand, this image can also be read as the algorithm detecting what should be there: a photograph inside a frame. The 'photograph' results from across the Harvard Art Museums' collection suggest that, in any event, the algorithm appears to be responding to the frame. Like the results from other services, Imagga's 'photograph' category returns many images with some sort of frame, border, or edges. Unlike the other services, Imagga's category includes a number of images that are *only* the frame, such as blank negatives, empty pages, and of course, ornate gold picture frames.

The overall Imagga 'photograph' results indicate that the frame does matter after all. They even suggest that, according to Imagga, the frame might be constitutive of photography, perhaps along the lines of Szarkowksi's claim that 'the central act of photography, the act of choosing and eliminating, forces a concentration on the picture edge—the line that separates in from out'.[51] In *The Photographer's Eye*, Szarkowski describes how the difficulty of enlarging photographs motivated early photographers to use the full plate as a matter of economy. But it is also the case that photographers did not always abide by the boundaries of the negative. Szarkowski's 1970 exhibition of turn-of-the-century American photographer E.J. Bellocq offers a case in point. After discovering Bellocq's 8 × 10 glass plate negatives, art photographer Lee Friedlander created prints that extended to the negatives' edges, showing how Bellocq posed his sitters in front of hanging backdrops such as blankets. As Nicolette Bromberg has shown, it was unlikely that Bellocq printed his images this way in the early 20th century. Instead, like most studio photographers, Bellocq would have focused on his sitter by using an oval mat or even printing the photograph with a vignette.[52]

Oval frames and vignettes appear repeatedly in the pre-1925 dataset, providing two examples where the edge of the photograph, 'the line that separates in from out', is not so easy to determine. This point has practical and conceptual implications for computer vision applications that seek to influence image classification output by removing visual context and isolating the image. This act of cropping is also a way of defining the boundaries of the photograph, and with it, the boundaries of photography, especially if that act is meant to include or exclude terms or term types for metadata generation. Trying to remove frames and borders to make

[50] Amy McCrory, 'Rare Items, Precious Time: Devising an Efficient Workflow to Digitize Nineteenth Century Cased Photographs', *Archiving 2018 Final Program and Proceedings* (2018), pp. 77–82. https://doi.org/10.2352/issn.2168-3204.2018.1.0.18

[51] Szarkowski, *The Photographer's Eye*, p. 4.

[52] Nicolette Bromberg, 'Loss of Vision: How Early 20th Century Photography Was Misjudged by Critics and How Archives Obscure the Image', *exposure* (June 2018). https://medium.com/exposure-magazine/loss-of-vision-ebf2339713c2

historical photographs less material and 'more transparent' once again applies a limited conception of photography to a multifaceted medium.

Framing photography with computer vision

Comparing different commercial image classification services demonstrates that computer vision, understood as a generalised technology, is not necessarily blind to photography. The computer vision algorithms studied here all classify images as photographs, if erratically and likely unintentionally. Furthermore, the services 'see' photographs in different ways – as images, objects, and content – at the same time.[53] Studying photographs with computer vision is, therefore, not as straightforward as often assumed.

To be sure, content predominates: across the board, the services generated fewer photography-related labels than expected. Like Barthes, we might say, the services struggle 'to focus on Photography' because 'the referent adheres'.[54] When they do focus on photography, the output is inconsistent. This inconsistency is relevant to archives and other cultural heritage institutions looking to use computer vision to generate metadata for their digitised collections. In this study, photography-related labels did not clearly align with visual evidence of a photograph's materiality, intimating that the services do not explicitly distinguish between analogue and digital photography. Crucially, many of the patterns observed in the positive output of the services also weaken when compared to the negative output. That is to say, the shared characteristics of images labelled 'photograph' are not unique to those images and can easily apply to images not labelled 'photograph'. This is most clear in the case of Imagga, as the variance within the 'photograph' output invites the question of why the service tags so few images in the pre-1925 dataset. Even if we account for all images deemed somehow photographic – including 'photograph', 'photography', 'photographic paper', and 'photographic equipment' – it amounts to about 550 images, or four per cent of the total processed by the service. Such mercurial classifications, both of photography and more generally, make out-of-the-box commercial services inadequate for labelling heterogeneous photographic materials at scale.

Internally inconsistent, the services' images of photography are nonetheless remarkably distinct and relevant to art historical discourse on the medium. This chapter has read the services' output as giving visual form to different aspects of photography that complicate essentialising definitions. Google's vernacular vision distinguishes between the snapshot in theory and the snapshot in practice, recognising the visual conventions that make certain photographs look amateurish or

[53] Joanna Zylinska, 'Diffused Seeing: The Epistemological Challenge of Generative AI', *Media Theory*, 8:1 (2024), p. 2348. https://doi.org/10.70064/mt.v8i1.1075

[54] Barthes, *Camera Lucida*, p. 6.

artless. At the other end of the spectrum, Amazon's output highlights the artistic potential of photography and its place in an historical lineage of image-making. Clarifai zeroes in on the negative as a significant but often overlooked aspect of photographic reproduction. Finally, Imagga's output illustrates how photography does not passively reproduce the world but, instead, actively frames it.

Claiming to classify images, computer vision ends up attesting to photography's essential diversity and multiplicity. While 'an explicit understanding of photography as a versatile technology' may be absent from computer vision discourse, as Malevé and Sluis argue, this chapter shows that this versatility manifests in computer vision practice.[55] Each service analysed offers a single image of photography; none of them provide, in themselves, the whole picture. Even together, the services do not comprehensively define photography, leaving out the political, sociological, and cultural dimesions. Computer vision instead shows photography to be a multi-label medium, reinforcing the difficulty, if not impossibility, of capturing this ever-evolving technology.

By emphasising a difference between the theory and practice of photography, this chapter also points to a gap between the theory and practice of computer vision that bears on the broader issues regarding AI and its role in art history addressed throughout this volume. Leonardo Impett argues it is important to study the 'iconology of AI' by examining the visual, social, and ideological values of reference datasets.[56] But how algorithms are trained in theory does not necessarily equate with how they perform in practice, especially with complex, multivalent, and not entirely visual concepts like photography. This multiplicity of AI is easy to lose sight of amid the development of LLMs and diffusion models. With this more recent technology, specific, narrow tasks like image classification are pushed out by general purpose tools such as chatbots. Furthermore, as Nuria Rodríguez-Ortega argues, specific media forms are ontologically flattened into a shared vectorial space.[57] These generalisations feed the sense of AI's pervasiveness and even inescapability at the core of AI hype.

In this moment, photography's history and historiography might model an approach to the necessary task, called for throughout this volume, of critically analysing AI. Studying not just AI but 'artificial intelligences' would mean attending to AI's own diversity and multiplicity. This is not simply a matter of trying out different models or tools, just as photographies are not merely products of different processes or cameras. Instead, like studying photographies, focusing on artificial intelligences entails shifting focus from potential to power, and from 'what AI is' to 'what AI does'.

[55] Malevé and Katrina Sluis, 'The Photographic Pipeline'.

[56] Leonardo Impett, Chapter 4 of this volume.

[57] Nuria Rodríguez-Ortega, Chapter 5 of this volume.

Conclusion: Art and Intelligence

KATHRYN BROWN

CHAPTERS IN THIS volume have sought to delineate the parameters of art history in an era that is increasingly dominated by debates about the potential, risks, and values associated with a range of technologies commonly referred to as 'artificial intelligence' (AI). As contributors have demonstrated, it is easy for two disciplines rooted in differing traditions of the humanities and the sciences to talk past each other, either denying the contributions that each discipline can make to the other or allowing one set of analytical goals and problem-solving methods to be subsumed by another. The challenge is to determine how each discipline might productively expand the other while preserving the distinctive intellectual achievements, ambitions, and values of both.

The agenda for this volume has been shaped not just by a desire to bring art history and computer science into a closer discursive relationship, but also to debate the exercise of art history in fast-paced technological environments of the 21st century. In 2000, Robert S. Nelson reflected on a century of art historical practice through one of its core methods of communication, namely, the slide lecture.[1] In Nelson's analysis, the introduction of technology – the photographic slide – into the illustrated lecture profoundly impacted both the 'performance' and discourse of art history. The image in the slide lecture became part of a 'performative triangle consisting of speaker, audience, and image' that, together, created the social bonds that underpinned a distinctive epistemological network.[2] In Nelson's account, it was also the advent of the slide lecture that encouraged inductive as opposed to deductive reasoning in art history. Artworks were now present by visual proxy in a new discursive space, and historians were free to develop arguments based on 'observed particulars' rather than on a priori categories and concepts.[3] Nelson concluded that

[1] Robert S. Nelson, 'The Slide Lecture, or The Work of Art "History" in the Age of Mechanical Reproduction', *Critical Inquiry*, 26:3 (Spring 2000), pp. 414–34.
[2] Nelson, 'The Slide Lecture', p. 415.
[3] Nelson, 'The Slide Lecture', p. 432.

Proceedings of the British Academy, **285**, 205–209, © Authors 2025.

the language and reference of art lectures – and, indeed, art history as a whole – would continue to adapt to new technologies, but wondered where this would lead the discipline and impact those who practise it.

Today, we might argue that the performative triangle to which Nelson referred has been squared to include a new party: the computer. As chapters in this volume have shown, the presence of this new party also introduces a new set of visual proxies for analysis – digital objects that effect a further shift in both the 'observed particulars' of artefacts and the agent who undertakes the act of observation. For some scholars, this newly constituted technological space connects to debates about existence in a post-humanist age where computational methods and machinery seamlessly extend, and in the process change, human capacities, ethics, and epistemologies.[4] An alternative view is that sharing an intellectual space with computers throws human thinking and values into sharper relief, allowing us better to appreciate the distinctive intellectual resources and social bonds that bring art worlds into being and sustain their relevance.

While the study of digital objects, use of PowerPoint in lectures, digitisation of archival documents, and examination of online images have become commonplace in the everyday work of art historians, the practice of art history now incorporates autonomous computational technologies that are capable of reshaping the intellectual parameters of the discipline itself. Unlike conservation techniques that remain within the purview of a researcher's execution and agency, the incorporation of AI into art history implies training, and hence delegating, elements of visual analysis to a non-human agent – a machine. Does this mean that the art historian is no longer an independent researcher? While the impact of mechanical reproduction (in analogue and digital forms) has long been debated in art history, the use of AI necessitates investigation into the implications of accepting a place for computational autonomy in the analysis of artworks.[5]

On the one hand, humans remain central to the use of computational methods in art history. The 'learning' process of the machine might remain a black box, but art historians and computer scientists must collaborate to create research questions, determine the framework of machine learning (i.e., the range and quality of data selected and employed to train an AI), develop new code, and connect outputs to questions. To endorse the view that machines might replace, surpass, or diminish the role of art historians in the writing of art history is to subscribe either to a

[4] Rajakishore Nath and Riya Manna, 'From Posthumanism to Ethics of Artificial Intelligence', *AI & Society*, 38 (2023), pp. 185–96, https://doi.org/10.1007/s00146-021-01274-1; M. Prabhu and J.A. Premraj, 'Artificial Consciousness in AI: A Posthuman Fallacy', *AI & Society*, 40 (2025), pp. 2995–3008, https://doi.org/10.1007/s00146-024-02061-4; Jill Walker Rettberg, *Machine Vision: How Algorithms Are Changing the Way We See the World* (Cambridge: Polity Press, 2023), p. 59.

[5] Walter Benjamin, 'The Work of Art in the Age of Mechanical Reproduction', in Walter Benjamin, *Illuminations: Essays and Reflections*, edited by Hannah Arendt; translated by Harry Zorn (London: Pimlico, 1999); Douglas Davis, 'The Work of Art in the Age of Digital Reproduction (An Evolving Thesis: 1991–1995)', *Leonardo*, 28:5 (1995), pp. 381–6, https://doi.org/10.2307/1576221.

science fiction view of AI (e.g., the advent of an Artificial Art Historian) or to an overinflated view of algorithmically guaranteed objectivity in scientific analysis.[6]

In 2007, Lorraine Daston and Peter Galison offered a compelling historical account of the lure of objectivity and its associated virtues in scientific practices in Europe and North America.[7] They demonstrated, in particular, the role of imagery in propelling the search for a 'form of unprejudiced, unthinking, blind sight we call scientific objectivity'.[8] Daston and Galison equate objectivity with 'blind sight' because it suggests that knowledge is capable of eliminating traces of the knower. Objectivity is, they argue, a form of 'seeing without inference, interpretation, or intelligence'.[9] Although not intended by the authors, this stripped-down model of vision is an apt description of computational analyses of artworks. Indeed, as Amanda Wasielewski has argued, computer vision is capable of promoting the ideal of 'a resurgent mechanical objectivity', but it is one that adds a promise 'that machines can also exercise trained judgment'.[10] Challenging the promise of scientific objectivity, chapters in the present volume show that human concepts and biases impact all manner of computational approaches to the study of objects, images, and people. This means that understanding and acknowledging the situatedness of knowledge (and the data that underpin it) has become even more important when practising art history in an era of AI. It also necessitates close attention to the kinds of question that might now be posed about both art works and their networks of production and circulation.

David Stork has suggested that '[t]he pinnacle – and very distant goal – is to have a computer generate a novel interpretation [of an artwork], one that revises and expands our understanding of such a work and its relation to other works and culture more generally'.[11] Yet, is this the goal? Is how a machine 'interprets' art even relevant to an art world that is designed to express and respond to human needs and ideas? While methods for expanding approaches to the interpretation of art are undoubtedly welcome, it is worth considering what we want computers to achieve and the kind of epistemic community we want to inhabit. To give just one example: the co-creation of ideas by humans about art (however imprecise) may be intrinsically more important for social or ethical reasons than the creation of new facts about – or more speculatively, 'interpretations' of – art by machines. The use of computer vision to debunk David Hockney's ideas about the use of optical

[6] See also Mercedes Bunz's discussion of AI as a collaborator rather than a replacement of human input and knowledge in 'The Role of Culture in the Intelligence of AI', in *AI in Museums: Reflections, Perspectives and Applications*, edited by Sonja Thiel and Johannes C. Bernhardt (Bielefeldt: Transcript Verlag, 2024), pp. 23–9.

[7] Lorraine Daston and Peter Galison, *Objectivity* (Brooklyn: Zone Books, 2007).

[8] Daston and Galison, *Objectivity*, p. 16.

[9] Daston and Galison, *Objectivity*, p. 17.

[10] Amanda Wasielewski, *Computational Formalism: Art History and Machine Learning* (Cambridge, MA: The MIT Press, 2023), p. 29.

[11] David G. Stork, *Pixels & Paintings: Foundations of Computer-Assisted Connoisseurship* (Hoboken, NJ: Wiley Blackwell, 2024), p. lviii.

devices in Renaissance painting might be an important corrective to a misguided theory, but understanding why a contemporary artist holds such a view and considering how that view connects to the artist's own creative preoccupations has a different kind of intellectual value and art historical relevance.[12]

This line of enquiry prompts reflection on intelligence itself. One of the issues debated by Emily M. Bender and Alex Hanna in *The AI Con* concerns preconceptions about 'intelligence' that inform the concept of 'artificial intelligence'.[13] Aside from general concerns about attempts to replace human labour with technology and the exacerbation of economic inequality that this entails, Bender and Hanna highlight that the concept of 'intelligence' is difficult to define and that attempts to do so lapse quickly into gendered and racialised hierarchies that have historically been used to classify, measure, and rank human beings.[14]

In the context of the present volume, questions about intelligence raise two issues about art and art history. Art is – among other things – a form of advanced thinking that is difficult to categorise in conventional academic terms. Historically, it sat outside traditional academic research disciplines until the rise of the practice-based Ph.D. in the 1990s. The idea that the communicative, intellectual, and affective content of art can be captured quantitively necessitates a refocusing or even narrowing of its content to facilitate the object's representation and interpretation as data.

Further complications arise from the fact that artworks communicate complex ideas by appealing to a range of senses either literally or metaphorically. To the extent that we ask a computer to offer a novel 'interpretation' of art, we would do well to remember that such an enterprise is inherently limited by the absence of the machine's synthetic sensory experience and ability to connect visual perception to a wider range of connotations that aid interpretation. With its emphasis on the recognition and classification of visual features – particularly of images – computer vision risks giving priority to normative ways of experiencing art that omit the value of non-visual experience even of artworks that are typically thought of as 'visual'.[15]

More important for the purposes of the present volume, however, is the kind of expertise that art historians bring not just to the study of artworks, but to the critical evaluation of computational technologies in wider cultural landscapes. Put another way: What is the role of visual intelligence in an algorithmic culture? Following the advent of digital art history over the past two decades, *critical* digital art history has now emerged as a distinct subject area. For Amanda Waseliewski and Anna

[12] David G. Stork, 'Computer Vision, ML, and AI in the Study of Fine Art', *Communications of the ACM*, 67:5 (May 2024), pp. 68–75 (pp. 71–2). DOI: 10.1145/3633454

[13] Emily Bender and Alex Hanna, *The AI Con: How to Fight Big Tech's Hype and Create the Future We Want* (London: The Bodley Head, 2025).

[14] Bender and Hanna, *The AI Con*, pp. 35–6.

[15] See Georgina Kleege, *More Than Meets the Eye: What Blindness Brings to Art* (Oxford: Oxford University Press, 2018).

Näslund, this new field offers opportunities to interrogate digital art history as a form of critical enquiry and to position research in this area 'as historically and theoretically situated'.[16]

Moving beyond such disciplinary critique within an expanded field of art history, scholars are also drawing attention to the various ways in which art history can pose new challenges for computer science or offer a broader commentary on AI and its uses.[17] Art historical approaches to contextualising and analysing the uses, misuses, and social functions of images, for example, equip humanities researchers with skills to debate the content of datasets that provide the fodder for machine learning. Equally, art historians have the expertise to offer theoretical insight into the use of AI surveillance technologies to delimit social 'types' (a throwback to histories of physiognomy) and – as chapters in the present volume show – can shed light on the changing relationship between word and image in the use of generative AI. A critical understanding of museum history, curation, and creativity is now essential in evaluating the ways in which cultural institutions are absorbing and communicating ideas about AI to publics through exhibitions, artificial conversational agents, and robot 'creators'.[18] In all of these cases, art historians now have (at least) two objects of analysis: the art work and the computational methods and models being used to assist in the presentation and interpretation of that artefact and/or its digital surrogate.

Far from threatening the importance of art historical research methods and human visual literacy, AI is, therefore, creating new opportunities for art historians to apply their skills and curiosity to the impact of computational technologies on a wide range of social practices, cultural projects, and public policies. Research at the intersection of art history and AI is still at an early stage, but it is both intellectually exciting and culturally important to map the emerging terrain of a new cross-disciplinary field. The parameters of the discussion will continue to shift quickly, and this volume hopes to set the stage for an emerging discourse that demonstrates the importance of history for an understanding of the present.

[16] Amanda Wasielewski and Anna Näslund, 'Critical Digital Art History: An Introduction', in *Critical Digital Art History: Interface and Data Politics in the Post-Digital Age*, edited by Amanda Wasielewski and Anna Näslund (Bristol: Intellect, 2024), pp. 1–19 (p. 3). See also Amir Baradaran, 'Towards a Decolonial I in AI: Mapping the Pervasive Effects of Artificial Intelligence on the Art Ecosystem', *AI & Society*, 39 (2024), pp. 7–19, https://doi.org/10.1007/s00146-023-01771-5

[17] Leonardo Impett, 'Digital Art History as Critical AI', *The Art Bulletin*, 106:2 (2024), pp. 11–14.

[18] See, for example, Alisa Maksimova, 'Negotiation of Dominant AI Narratives in Museum Exhibitions', *AI & Society*, 40 (2025), pp. 3813–26, https://doi.org/10.1007/s00146-024-02140-6; Kathryn Brown, 'Artificial Exchange: Chatbots and the Ethics of Museum Experience Design', in *Museum Experience Design at a Time of Transformation*, edited by L. Calvi, A. Vermeeren, and A. Sabiescu (Cham: Springer, 2025); Eleonora Lima, 'AI Art and Public Literacy: The Miseducation of Ai-Da the Robot', *AI Ethics*, 4 (2024), pp. 841–54, https://doi.org/10.1007/s43681-024-00488-5

Index